MALCOLM BRADBURY

POSSIBILITIES

Essays on the
State of the Novel

OXFORD UNIVERSITY PRESS
LONDON   OXFORD   NEW YORK
1973

Oxford University Press

LONDON OXFORD NEW YORK

GLASGOW TORONTO MELBOURNE WELLINGTON

CAPE TOWN IBADAN NAIROBI DAR ES SALAAM LUSAKA ADDIS ABABA

DELHI BOMBAY CALCUTTA MADRAS KARACHI LAHORE DACCA

KUALA LUMPUR SINGAPORE HONG KONG TOKYO

Paperback edition ISBN 0 19 281126 6
Clothbound edition ISBN 0 19 212189 8

© Malcolm Bradbury 1973

First published as an Oxford University Press paperback,
and simultaneously in a clothbound edition, by
Oxford University Press, London, 1973

*Printed in Great Britain
by Hazell Watson & Viney Ltd,
Aylesbury, Bucks*

To the late
RONALD S. CRANE
and
to my friend
DAVID LODGE

CONTENTS

Preface   ix

PART ONE: THE NOVEL AND REALITY

✓ I   The Open Form: The Novel and Reality   3

PART TWO: THE NOVEL AND THE COMIC MODE

  II   Fielding, Sterne, and the Comic Modes of Fiction   31
  III 'The Most Interesting Moving Picture': *Fanny Hill* and
       Comedy   41
  IV   Persuasions: Moral Comedy in *Emma* and *Persuasion*   55

PART THREE: MODERNISMS

  V   Phases of Modernism: The Novel and the 1920s   81
  VI   E. M. Forster as Victorian and Modern: *Howards End*
       and *A Passage to India*   91
  VII Virginia Woolf and Ford Madox Ford: Two Styles of
       Modernity   121
  VIII The Modern Comic Novel in the 1920s: Lewis, Huxley,
       and Waugh   140

PART FOUR: THE NOVEL TODAY

✓ IX   The Postwar English Novel   167
  X   Malcolm Lowry as Modernist   181
  XI   William Cooper and the 1950s: *Scenes from Provincial
       Life*   192
  XII C. P. Snow's Bleak Landscape   201
  XIII The Fiction of Pastiche: The Comic Mode of Angus
       Wilson   211
  XIV 'A House Fit for Free Characters': Iris Murdoch and
       Under the Net   231

viii   *Contents*

✓ XV   Muriel Spark's Fingernails   247
  XVI   The Novelist as Impresario: John Fowles and His Magus   256

PART FIVE: TOWARDS A POETICS OF THE NOVEL

✓ XVII The Novel and Its Poetics   275

        Index   293

PREFACE

The essays here are all about the novel, and especially the English novel from its 'rise' in the eighteenth century to its present-day situation: they are about the novel's formal nature, its historical exposure, about our ways of thinking about the genre and criticizing it, about the possibilities open to it. The novel has long been a central form of literary action in our culture and—because of its open, referential, empirical nature—in our history; in its structures and styles are rooted some of our deepest forms of individual and social experience. Over recent years such matters have become of great interest to critics, and the result is a decided rise in the level of critical speculation about the novel, past, present, and to come. One presumption that has become commonplace is that the novel has a telling history and a compelling contemporary situation; a form always historically very naked, it is now under the time's stresses, and today is dying or groping, collapsing under new knowledge and new need. We live in a time very disposed to discover necessity, inevitability; this stretches into our considerations of style and form. When criticism is written pre-eminently by critics rather than creators, this disposition is all the more apt to occur; critics, after all, have their own plots to complete. The title of this book is intended to embody a somewhat different critical attitude; criticism is, I presume, a *post facto* activity, and its task to produce a working discourse which does not—by terminological limitation, or through historicist or other deterministic theories of form or literary action—foreclose options, or suppose the art we are concerned with complete and over.

These essays, then, are about the novel as a form and the novel as a history. The two essays that frame this collection—one on 'The Novel and Reality' and the other on 'The Novel and Its Poetics'—perhaps best suggest the thrust of the argument. By a poetics I mean the exercise of an activity which I take as essential to criticism, and have tried to exemplify: a steady moving back and forth between the reading of individual texts and the consideration of larger questions of structure and style, out of which might arise a basis, a terminology, for comparing and considering the works we read, those we have yet to read, and those we have yet to write. But structures and styles arise in a culture, and culture changes historically; the problem is to keep our terminology, our ways of thinking and talking, eclectic and extensive, so that, for example, we can see the novel as both realism *and* modernism, a record of knowable experience and a free-standing construct. Hence the group of preoccupations in these essays: with the relation between individual authors and works and phases of style, the question of the novel's realism and its fictiveness, its humanism and its formalism. My interest in these matters has been active for some long time (and one end of the concern I have explored in my book *The Social Context of Modern English Literature*). Not all these essays are, therefore, new, though almost all have been either written or rewritten for the present occasion.

For those that first appeared elsewhere, I should like to express my gratitude to a number of editors and publishers, for their original help as well as their permission to reprint. The essay on 'The Novel and Reality' first saw life in *Encounter*; that on Sterne and Fielding in *The Winged Skull: Papers from the Laurence Sterne Bicentenary Conference*, ed. A. H. Cash and John Stedmond (Kent, Ohio: Kent State University Press; London: Methuen, 1971). The essays on *Fanny Hill* and on Muriel Spark's fiction, as well as parts of those on Jane Austen, E. M. Forster, and Iris Murdoch, appeared in *The Critical Quarterly*. Another part of the Jane Austen essay appeared in *Essays in Criticism*; another part of the Forster essay in *Aspects of E. M. Forster*, ed. Oliver Stallybrass (London: Arnold, 1969). Various sections of Part Three of this book draw on my essay 'The Novel in the 1920s' in *The Sphere History of Literature in the English Language*, vol. VII: *The Twentieth Century*, ed. Bernard Bergonzi (London: Sphere Books and Barrie and Rockliff, 1970); the essay on the postwar English novel likewise draws from my chapter 'The Novel' in *The Twentieth-Century Mind*, vol. III: *1945–1965*, ed. C. B. Cox and A. E. Dyson (London: Oxford University Press, 1972). The essay on C. P. Snow draws on a *New Statesman* review; that on William Cooper was the introduction to the reissue of his *Scenes from Provincial Life* (London: Macmillan, 1969); that on John Fowles appeared in *Sense and Sensibility in Twentieth-*

Century Writing, ed. Brom Weber (Carbondale, Ill.: Southern Illinois University Press; London: Feffer and Simons, 1970). Finally 'The Novel and Its Poetics' revises my essay 'Towards a Poetics of Fiction: (1) An Approach Through Structure' which appeared in the first issue of the magazine *Novel: A Forum on Fiction* (Fall, 1967).

Anthony Thwaite, Tony Dyson, Brian Cox, Bernard Bergonzi, Sybil Greatbach, Park Honan, and Mark Spilka all helped prompt this writing, and I am most grateful to them. To Catharine Carver, who helped bring it to its present form, I owe a deeper debt still. And lastly I am grateful to Professor Henri Petter and the faculty and students of the Englisches Seminar, University of Zürich, where the re-thinking and revising were done in the happiest possible circumstances.

MALCOLM BRADBURY

Zürich, 1972

Man rejoices in an incomparable faculty for presently mutilating and disfiguring any plaything that has helped create for him the illusion of leisure; nevertheless, so long as life retains its power of projecting itself upon his imagination, he will find the novel work off the impression better than anything he knows. Anything better for the purpose has assuredly yet to be discovered. He will give it up only when life itself too thoroughly disagrees with him. Even then, indeed, may fiction not find a second wind, or a fiftieth, in the very portrayal of that collapse? Till the world is an unpeopled void there will be an image in the mirror. What need more immediately concern us, therefore, is the care of seeing that the image shall continue various and vivid.

Henry James, 'The Future of the Novel' (1899)

PART ONE

THE NOVEL AND
REALITY

I

The Open Form:
The Novel and Reality

> The tradition of nineteenth-century realism, which underlies
> most contemporary fiction, depended on a degree of relative
> stability in three separate areas: the idea of reality; the nature
> of the fictional form; and the kind of relationship that might
> predictably exist between them. . . . It goes without saying
> that for many twentieth-century novelists and critics this
> assumption is no longer credible. . . .
>
> Bernard Bergonzi, *The Situation of the Novel*

I

At different points in its evolution, literary criticism seems to take up
different prototypical forms, genres, or groups of works, as the central
object of its attention, awarding them exemplary status and asking of
them that they show us just what it is that literary art most typically is.
Such works then come to serve as a touchstone for the literary in
prevailing aesthetic debate, so that most of the contemporary efforts
at distilling literary critical presumption and theory have to tackle
them in order to prove themselves effective. A few years ago it seemed
fairly clear that the prime object of critical attention was the lyric
poem, the economical and central poem-like poem that was left once
the dross of narrative, or metrics, had withered away. Before that, of
course, the narrative or discursive poem had had *its* period of essen-
tiality; such changes of emphasis are also changes of basic theory or
critical method, and the dross of one phase is the essential matter of
another. Today, there are very strong signs that the novel is becoming
the prototypical form, and that, once again, the change is part of a

general change in critical aesthetics. For the novel, systematically considered as a form, is many things that the lyric poem is not; and if we look with increasing attention at the novel and its propensities, look at it for itself and to elicit *itself*, then we are compelled to consider many matters which once constituted an implied insufficiency in the form, and gave grounds for *not* taking it as compellingly central.

From the very early days of the novel, one notion has deeply inhabited discussion of the species: that there is something inherent in it which is at odds with the needs of form or art. This dross is contingency or reality, the over-bulk of reality: the unformed looseness of event, the shapelessness of life and of persons, the disposition of the slack prose instrument to set its own pace, catch up what it wishes, maintain endless options upon itself until the work is done. In part it is this very contingency, this openness of the narrative weave, that is coming back to interest the critics. It is not entirely clear that this new emphasis is good for fiction, an area of writing which is becoming decidedly more active and speculative and yet less and less assured, as some of the popular audience dies away and the publishing economics grow bleaker. Nor, indeed, is it clear that this new set of interests is good for criticism, for the obsession with the 'realism' of fiction—a realism that is, I want to suggest, being both given and taken away—is much of a piece with a number of current theories about literature's historical exposure, and its equivalence with all forms of language and expression prevalent in a culture. But such shifts do normally involve the generation of a fresh literary energy, both creative and critical; they redesign possibilities, and they bring alive—or should—in new ways our sense of how certain types and forms of art, not only now but in the past as well, have served as speculative instruments, creative centres of verbal innovation. What is, I think, clear is that there is growing in literary practice and literary criticism alike a new sort of discussion of prose language, that the discussion reaches over a very long span of fictional modes, from the highly symbolistic to the reportorial or documentary, and that it has implicit significance for all our discussion of writing, be it poetry or drama, autobiography or reportage, and for our views of the status of any fiction.

The force of the change I have in mind is not easy to illustrate; it is best to begin by thinking back to the 1930s and 1940s, and the climate of the New Criticism, which has, of course, by no means ceased to prompt us. In this climate, if you wanted to understand what literary language was, and how it differed from other language-use in the culture, the languages of common speech or science, how it was more intense, more generative, had its own radical value, then the primary instance you turned to was the poem—especially the short poem of wit, tension, and ambiguity, the distilled, self-subsistent, grammatically ordered lyric. The ideal poem to read was the ideal kind of poem for the poets of the modern movement of 1908 to 1922 to write—imagistic, neo-symbolist, a thought–feeling complex, an impersonal, energetic, and free-standing construct. This was the 'inner' poem that the modern revolution in poetry, and the working aesthetics of Valéry, Hulme, Yeats, Pound, Eliot, and others, had rescued from the decline of romantic and narrative verse. Around this time, or rather a little before it, a not dissimilar revolution is visible in the novel too; one might wonder why it was that this shift, which produced a distinctive set of new forms in fiction and a major body of working poetics from novelists like Henry James, Joseph Conrad, Ford Madox Ford, D. H. Lawrence, James Joyce, Virginia Woolf, and E. M. Forster, did not have a similar impact on the New Criticism. Certainly the lore about fiction penetrated a good deal more slowly; and when it did, it was largely through emphasizing those aspects of it that were consistent with modern theory about poetry. The inclination was to justify the new novel by analogy with the poem, to stress fiction's poem-like as opposed to its narrative character. Indeed both modern writers and later modern critics showed themselves ready to assume that the narrative activity which generates, in fiction, both 'story' and 'realism' was the lowest part of novels, redeemed only by other kinds of action. 'Yes, yes—but is this *all?*' James has us asking. 'These are the circumstances of the interest— we see, we see; but where is the interest itself, where and what is its centre, and how are we to measure it in relation to *that?*'[1] The correct answer is some variant of the word 'form', which is to say an intensity of authorial consciousness or control so sharp that story and character lose some of their compelling dominance, and more abstract entities or weavings, which we call 'pattern' or 'design' or 'consciousness', take their place. In other words, a part of the subject of the novel becomes the process of its own making, which is what very articulately happens in much modernism, in which the making of the work becomes a theme shared between writer and reader, and a transcendent

[1] Henry James, 'The New Novel'; reprinted in *Henry James: Selected Literary Criticism*, ed. Morris Shapira (London, 1963).

basis of the work's authority. In some ways—as readers who find the
modern novel difficult know very well—this situation increases the
contingency of fiction, or at any rate breaks up a familiar kind of
completeness and elegance that we know *as* a story—which we might
define as a human matter whole and entire which is told and, in being
told, worked to the ultimate point of its own elucidation. But it
typically validates that contingency by finding alternative bases for
order in the written matter, through symbols and hidden figures,
linguistic recurrences and elegancies of form; thus it poetizes the novel.
This was the lore the New Criticism understood, and it made it easy
for it to move in critical analysis from poems to novels, which in
many cases it ably did.

Hence the novel was like a poem. It was not the orders drawn, say,
from sociology, history, or journalism, or the telling of a story, that
made for its significance or structure; it was design or strategy or form,
form not simply as an enabling but as the one vitalistic element in the
making of the fiction. Leonard Woolf, after reading his wife's *To the
Lighthouse*, called it a 'psychological poem'—an apt response to a work
which attempts to redeem itself from all the risks of gross materialism
by celebrating the bright atoms of contingency, not as they appear to
some unreflective level of consciousness, but to consciousness alive
and actively aesthetic or poetic. The novelist was like the poet. 'Mr.
Bennett recording his possession or, to put it more completely, his
saturation' (this sounds like Virginia Woolf, but is actually James again)
is hence a man aiming too low in fictional art, misusing his instrument,
producing an unredeemed materialism of content which lacks the
'higher' form which is, simultaneously, the basic strategic constituent
or means, and the finalized and balanced achievement which holds
up the entire work in permanence, livingness, and wholeness. The
analogue could be expressed, in fact, in many different ways, and so
it was; but there is no mistaking its symbolist implication, and the
problem—very explicitly explored in the novels of Thomas Mann,
Forster, and Ford Madox Ford—of relating the formal novel to history,
to the plots of reality and the low registers of documentation and
record which engage with life in time. And what the New Critics
came to stress was the nature of novels as 'dramatic poems', or complex
verbal structures, constructs of images and symbols, metaphors and
linguistic recurrences, epiphanies and archetypes, Freudian or Jungian,
strategies of irony and narrative distance and point of view—in other

words, large-scale instrumentalities or motifs through which, amid which, at some lower and unredeemed level, the old and atavistic tasks of story-telling and documentation webbed their way.[1]

This was obviously a major development in the criticism of the novel, very much in the Jamesian spirit of things; it gave an extraordinary sense of dignity to the form, it cut deeper, and it brought forward to notice a whole group of new reputations, both in the past and within the modernist shift in the novel itself. This happened surprisingly late, in fact; it is worth recalling that many of these modern reputations in fiction, from Joyce to Lawrence to Faulkner to Conrad, did not really become established until the 1940s and 1950s, and that, similarly, though C. H. Rickword had been emphasizing the need for a new critical poetics of fiction in the 1920s, it was not until the late 1940s that important pieces like Mark Schorer's essay 'Technique as Discovery' appeared to change the climate of critical discussion. Up to this point the modernist novel had been regarded as something of an aberrancy, and the new 'art of the novel', celebrated in many famous journals, notebooks, and prefaces, as well as in the inward speculation of many modern novels, from *A Portrait of the Artist as a Young Man* to *Les Faux-Monnayeurs*, a special case. The prime conventions of professional novel criticism had remained those of much nineteenth-century critical assumption: the novel was eminently a copying form, a dramatic presentation in a distinct and personal 'style' that discursively explored certain sentiments, experiences, persons, and social milieux, and which could be tested as a body of awareness against men's own lives, their experience of people, and their moral stresses. These assumptions were aesthetically coherent and they led to much very fine criticism; but they were substantially disturbed by the new formalism—especially by the growing presumption that form was not an enabling but the one determining element of a fiction. The newer presumptions, with Flaubert and James and Proust behind them, could generate an extraordinary critical range—from, for example, the mythological and psychological to the rhetorical and linguistic emphases that are implicit and available in the dominant term 'symbol'.

[1] My summary here is too economical; there are many critics of fiction over this period, including those in *Scrutiny*, who had different views and a less weightily symbolist stress. But I am concerned with a climate and an approach which acquired enormous influence, shaped much of the conventional discussion of fiction, and still does so (in many respects very fortunately).

But there is repeatedly present in this criticism the presumption that, while the novel can be given the grace of art, it is nonetheless somehow inherently on the *edge* of literature—pulled by its discursive and prosy nature into the hinterland of the non-literary, towards journalism or documentary, towards the 'invisible' languages of science or report, towards language undistilled, unparadoxical, untense, and towards the formless contingencies of narrative for narrative's simple sake.

In certain of the documents of modern writing, such as Virginia Woolf's famous essay on 'Modern Fiction', the ground is prepared; there occurs the clear presumption that the novel as traditionally conceived checks both artistic and human freedom, the freedom of the creative mind and the freedom of the agents represented by it— checks them because the traditional obligation to provide narrative coherence, to give and fulfill the entirety of a story, inhibits the larger task of the sensitive comprehension of experience; and because the freedom of the life lived by the characters, freedom to grow, expand, and know the texture of consciousness, the depth of themselves, and the openness of their awareness, is at risk from the same compulsion. Plot and materialism combine to limit the texture of the fictional universe as a realm to live in and a world to be created. Through this new discourse of the novel, Forster's famous 'oh dear' from *Aspects of the Novel* sounds ('oh dear yes, the novel tells a story . . . and I wish that it was not so, that it could be something different—melody, or perception of the truth, not this low atavistic form'). Set against contingency and realism, against the novel which yielded in James's phrase to 'clumsy Life at her stupid work', the new novel seemed a fortunate evolution. By virtue of the poetics appropriate to it—the poetics of the hidden long logic, the figure in the carpet, the fiddle bow drawn across the tray delicately sanded; the tactics and orders of point of view and rhythm, of rhetorical management and symbolism—it certainly gave us a new art of the novel, and modern readers have come increasingly to see novels in their character as verbal constructs—which is what, of course, all novels are—and to evolve an articulate discourse for dealing with the verbal and procedural conduct of fictions. The costs of this discovery, which could equally be applied to novels of the past, were, of course, the demotion of the traditional poetics of 'plot', 'character', and 'moral sentiment', and a decided unease in the presence of the moral issues that fiction, by its lifelikeness, raises. It hardly needs adding that these emphases have profoundly deepened discussion of the novel, and that we cannot afford to let them go.

But what seems clear now is that realism, and narrative,[1] are coming back into the discussion of fiction; and that the poetic analogy, and its general symbolist bias—its concern with formal elegance and wholeness, its obsession with design and language, rather than with contingency and imitation, in the making of novels—is weakening or in some way shifting. This is, I think, an indication of the way in which prose itself is becoming increasingly the central object of critical attention; that in turn is part of a new interest in the social uses of language and with all structure and order-making systems in society. At any rate, many of the important works of criticism over the last ten years or so which have the resonance of general value have been about the novel—the briefest possible list would have to contain Wayne Booth's *The Rhetoric of Fiction* (1961), Barbara Hardy's *The Appropriate Form* (1964), W. J. Harvey's *Character and the Novel* (1965), Robert Scholes's and Robert Kellogg's *The Nature of Narrative* (1966), David Lodge's *Language of Fiction* (1966), Frank Kermode's *The Sense of an Ending* (1967), and Richard Poirier's *A World Elsewhere* (1967). One can sense in these books a move away from the notion of the novel as a very tight and composed structure, and an increasing concern with the general basis of organized narrative as such, of which the novel is one instance, and an instance bound in with other open fields of discourse. As for the impression conveyed by novelists themselves of their own obsessions and explorations, that too points towards certain relaxations, certain loosenings of form to admit history, free-flow confessional, or the moral opacity of persons, certain new formalisms in which nonetheless a very fluid and eclectic linguistic play is of the essence. What I think is fairly clear in all this is an element of apostasy from modernism's ways, and from the Jamesian—the adjective I use broadly; one has only to keep re-reading James to know how little of a Jamesian he is—milieu of the New Criticism of fiction. Most of the modern classics of this particular phase of novel criticism, reaching, say,

---

[1] For some of the recent discussion of narrative in fiction—which has been much invigorated by Robert Scholes's and Robert Kellogg's *The Nature of Narrative* (New York and London, 1966)—see *The Interpretation of Narrative: Theory and Practice*, ed. Morton W. Bloomfield (Cambridge, Mass., 1970) and *Aspects of Narrative: Selected Papers from the English Institute*, ed. J. Hillis Miller (New York, 1971).

from Percy Lubbock's *Craft of Fiction* in 1921 to Wayne Booth's transitional *The Rhetoric of Fiction* in 1961, were classics of the analysis of 'form' as the self-conscious and the essential controlling aspect of creation. In this line, there was a tendency to make the prototype of the novel the modernist fictions of the later James, or Joyce, and a decided tendency to underplay the fascination of the nineteenth-century realistic novel, which could all too easily be taken as a fiction of unredeemed content, a seamless web of realism or mimesis, a rawer kind of novel.

For this change of emphasis and this re-aligning of the formalistic approach, there are a number of very different reasons. One is the fact that such modernist-oriented theory favours certain types and phases of fiction over others. Thus the nineteenth-century novel demands a different kind of attention; and it is much to the point that recent criticism—even, for that matter, recent fiction (I think of John Fowles's *The French Lieutenant's Woman*)—has shown great devotion to the Victorian novel. More important, the shift which has led critics to regard the novel as *the* essential representative of the literary 'action' of the modern world, and to demote, if that term is not too strong, the poem from the central position it had held in critical attention, is part of a generally less aesthetic view of literature. If you regard novels as 'typical' forms of literature, it becomes somewhat difficult to assume that what distinguishes literary language—what makes literature literature—is those attributes of paradox and tension, those compact-nesses of self-subsistent language, that you find crucial in lyric poetry.[1] To deal with the novel form head-on, you have to come to terms with its sheer contingency and looseness, with the fact that novels cannot be possessed, in a single critical instant, as complete wholes; with the novel's traditionally large dependence on social experience, its tendency to explore and substantiate by the making of worlds containing likely persons and places and causal sequences; with its disposition to represent personages; with its narrative passion; and above all with its need to establish its credit with a reader on the basis of some form of recognition, some basic appeal to veracity. Of the three main kinds of litera-

---

[1] So Roger Fowler and Peter Mercer comment in their essay 'Criticism and the Languages of Literature' (reprinted in Roger Fowler, *The Languages of Literature: Some Linguistic Contributions to Criticism* (London, 1971)): 'there is no *aprioristic* reason why any single element of poetic language should, if isolated, be uniquely significant; that is, there is no need to set up one feature, say "paradox", as the defining characteristic of poetic structure.'

ture—poetry, drama, novel—the novel is least susceptible to formal definition or characterization; it has no distinct typographical form, or context of performance, and few recurring conventions. For this reason all theory of the novel has to be remarkably *loose* theory, and theory *about* looseness, for criticism has lost the disposition to see novels as formally tight, conventionalized, composed structures. The novel, Roland Barthes tells us, gives to the imaginary the formal guarantee of the real—which I understand to mean not simply that the novel contains human figures and doings but that it is a mode of inquiry into the knowable, analogous in its empirical modes and methods to other forms of written inquiry. Its lack of clear generic character, its length, and above all its prose nature are all aspects of its openness, and this means that it is capable of vastly more political, moral, and linguistic exposure than the poem. All of this interests modern critics. This is why Sartre, in *What Is Literature?*, makes his famous—and surely over-argued—distinction between the poem and the novel, and puts on fiction a special existential onus, an imperative to commitment, to the articulation of freedom, a freedom arising out of contingency. Finally its lack of a clear basis of structure, a recurrent or fundamental plot such as exists in tragedy, also distinguishes it; it is open to a great variety of schemes, orders, and typologies, and can draw on a wide range of modes of selection and explanation—a fact that Frank Kermode has explored fascinatingly in much of his recent criticism.

Perhaps, for definitional purposes, the best we can say is that there is in the novel—which is to say in the entire tradition of this temporally and formally very varied body of practice—a range, or a spectrum of mode, which seems recurrent. It runs from an extreme formalism, or elegant wholeness, to a contingency or looseness of narration; from romance to forms of high scepticism or high facticity; from aesthetics to documentation; from (to use Iris Murdoch's terms) crystalline forms to journalistic ones. This dichotomy you find throughout the history of the novel, redistributed in emphasis and content at different points in its evolution. There is a sharp mid-nineteenth-century version, for example, in Hawthorne, who perplexed himself frequently about the claims of a kind of fiction he called the romance, which had in it much of the marvellous, the metaphysical, history as pastoral, and a bias towards symbolism and allegory, and the novel proper which was faithful to the probable and ordinary course of men's experience, history as process, and the denuded, untextured, fleeting present of the world. Hawthorne's works are conducted in this frame of reference; he represented himself as constantly suspended between the claims of form and reality, form which was resonant but also coercive, in that it tended to transpose human agents and human matter into metaphor, and reality which was humanizing and progressive but had all the impoverishment of a history rushing into secular materialism and mechanism, like the train that carries Clifford and Hepzibah off into a raw future in *The House of the Seven Gables*. There are many present versions of this antithesis—between realism and fictiveness or experiment, say—but one of the validations of realism (as James, realist as well as formalist, always understood) was that in its empirical devotion it shattered formal sets and therefore had much to do with the freedom or humanism of a fiction. This is the sort of talk that is coming back, with new weights and emphases, and one very clear feature of it is the degree of interest that exists now in the possibilities that lie at the realistic or at any rate the uncrystalline end of this range or spectrum.

2

One reason why we so closely connect the novel and reality is that, of all the literary arts, the novel seems least given to *apriorism*. Each new novel seems to arise from a creative curiosity generated by a back-and-forth motion between the detailing and analysis of an observed, external world, or a realm of knowable experience, and an inner working process that gives formal consistency; thus each novel creates its own world afresh, and engages us for the occasion with its own laws. As for the persons it creates or copies, it gives them individually, substantially, with roundedness; the sequences and happenings through which they move seem to arise from the conditions of a world which operates much as ours does; the wholeness of the telling seems driven by experience, human understanding, compassion, so that in a great novel an extended human experience works itself out in all its complexity. In the entire activity, then, there resides a decided openness and a spirit of humanism, which have come to seem part of the form. Clearly the bases of understanding and sympathy shift from culture to culture and period to period; after all, man's conception of reality, and the primary conditions of his experience, can alter significantly. Clearly too there are novels neither open nor humanistic, perhaps more of them now than ever. Still, here is a presiding disposition in the form, and it has considerable implications for those who use it as writers and as readers. One is that by virtue of its openness the novel, and the novelist, are exposed to history: to the facts of a time, the articulable relationships of a time, the ways of knowing a time, the ideological interpretations of a time. This kinship between the novel and history has long been presumed by novelists. It is also growing a very obsessional matter for critics; and this means that, for the presiding disposition I have spoken of, we may give two basic types of explanation—one pre-eminently formal, and the other pre-eminently historical.

The first kind of explanation is primarily a definition in poetics—which means that it arises from examining the form of the novel, its tradition or traditions, surveying as many cases as possible from as many periods and creative tempers as possible, asking about the prevailing assumptions, conventions, and expectations involved in their creation and readerly consumption, and above all by posing generic questions. Here the proposition that arises is that the novel is a very empirical *form*; it gives us a world of great material and human substance and specificity, a world webbed together by a distinctive recurrent logic shaped by the arts and structures needed for exploring given experiential cases to the fullest point of their significance and narrative elucidation, to the end of their 'story', and by the capacity to make invented experience resemble actual experience in such a way that what is written has truth, aptness, and a kind of moral wisdom. But if we call these the 'generic' characteristics of novels, we compound a paradox. For Ian Watt, in *The Rise of the Novel* (1957), and Bernard Bergonzi, in *The Situation of the Novel* (1970), both argue that the species arose in the eighteenth century as a fully fledged form with —as its English name suggests—a propensity *against* generic definition, in a climate of empiricism. And, says Bergonzi, 'stylistic dynamism, or steady formal change' has always been the essential principle of the novel's development, of its interest in any one case; it is for their novelty that we value novels.

But Bergonzi also says that, as well as being very empirical, the novel has also been very liberal: its realism has represented a humanistic balance in which the claims of individuals as persons are let grow coherently in a world solid and substantial enough for them to encounter it in its force and value, so that the reality of persons meets the reality of society, or history. Thus it has sacrificed to life, rather than to form or convention. And at best—the ideal is often centred on

Tolstoy—an elegant, humane equipoise occurs, of art and life, form
and matter, persons and society, characters and story. Today, when we
consider this liberal potential, we usually return to the late-nineteenth-
century liberal social novel. At this many of our critics and some of
our novelists have lately been looking, and some of them—W. J.
Harvey, John Bayley, Iris Murdoch—have demonstrated to high
effect the operation of this particular poise, this balance between the
created opacity of persons and of the complex living reality of society
as a dense otherness, and have suggested that it is a fictional capacity
out of which many modern writers, for philosophical or theoretical
reasons, seem to have argued themselves. We should note that in these
same writers—Tolstoy and George Eliot, especially—other critics
have found almost antithetical qualities: character sacrificed to plot
or design, or to the dominant intrusiveness, or the weighty and over-
commanding omniscience, of the author—and have seen in the subsequent development of fiction a new freedom or expansiveness of
experience (this Alan Friedman suggests, in *The Turn of the Novel*,
1966). To Bergonzi, the present situation of the novel is that this
liberal realism has collapsed; the novel either seeks to hold to it, and
so loses its stylistic dynamism and its capacity to reach into modern
experience and generate the modern form experientially and morally
appropriate to it, or else it thrusts towards producing an energetic,
but an implicitly totalitarian or illiberal, fiction in which the individual
agent is dwarfed, diminished, often verbally violated. Indeed he raises
points about the fate of this primary realism which require explanations of the second type—that is, some form of stylistic-historical
explanation or, because history comes in as stress or crisis, an explanation via historicism.

   This is the view that explains the realism of the novel as the product
of sociological, cultural, philosophical, and ideological causes; a very
balanced form of the case occurs in Harry Levin's *The Gates of Horn*
(1963), but since history even more than realism is disputatiously
fought for and over, it is a case often given to extremities. The novel
by this view has a specific historical locus. It is the burgher epic; its
realism is a derivative of the materialism, specificity, individualism, and
scientism which are components of the bourgeois mind and which
produce the bourgeois 'reality'. Its tendency to regard character as a
matter of proprietary individualism and its progressive view of history
produces lively dealings between the two. Its scepticism is the product

of the perpetual attempts of the bourgeoisie to see its situation objectively. But as it enlarges its realism through expanding its social sweep, it suffers from the inevitable loss of control over reality and finds that it cannot maintain its notional community, cannot command and master experience. Hence it suffers crises of form, being unable to relate individual to society or to experience; these coincide spectacularly with modernism, which is not so much a technical or perceptual development as a discovery that reality is no more than personal. So the novel must ail or die or change its nature. Hence the paradox that informs much contemporary fascination with fictional realism; it is concerned with the novel's narrative power, its aspect as a representative language, but is also concerned with demonstrating that in many respects realism is an historically delimited world view, is infected with crisis. There is a sense in which *all* writing is created in crisis; the act of forming words and sensible and coherent structure is a struggle for meaning against disorder and a profoundly testing occasion. But as criticism bends more and more towards the historicist, it has acquired many generalizations of this sort about reality and history which pass into theory, and into current writing as well.

If you take it that the realism of the novel is important, you are likely to want to mediate between these two versions of it; but the difficulty is that hidden in them are two potentially very different views of the writer's task and his nature. In the argument by poetics there is the presumption that fiction itself is a creative power, that realism is a severe effort of mind and comprehension, a certain sort of active and moral engagement with experience; it is a complex of making, a very empirical and humanly curious fiction. In the argument by historicism another presumption is there, at any rate potentially; the writer is historically trapped, making fictions of reality not because that is his endeavour and his devotion but because that is his fate, lost as he is in the particular trap of trying to make sense of his historical situation.

This particular difference is very visible in two recent books about nineteenth-century fictional realism, both with an historicist dimension and by left-wing critics. One is Raymond Williams's study of *The English Novel from Dickens to Lawrence* (1970); the other is Everett Knight's *A Theory of the Classical Novel* (1970), a 'relevant' (i.e. far-left) critic working with Marxist and structuralist premises, and dealing mainly with the French novel 'written between the end of the picaresque and the inauguration by Kafka of the contemporary

novel'. Williams begins his book by looking at the startling emergence
of the fictional generation of the 1840s, the generation of Dickens,
the Brontës, Thackeray, Mrs. Gaskell, and Disraeli, who, in a period
of rapid industrialization and urbanization, set the novel on a course of
public and literary significance and brought it forward as the great
English form; and he ends by looking at the redirection of the novel at
the end of the century, when it becomes a more personal and more
psychological form. Williams explains the 'new' novel of the 1840s as a
burst of social inquiry with its roots in a new era of social change, and
stresses, very precisely, the sort of interaction he sees between fiction
and the social processes to which it is attentive and by which it is
undoubtedly shaped:

It was not society or its crisis which produced these novels. The society and the
novels—our general names for these myriad and related primary activities—
came from a pressing and varied experience which was not yet history; which
had no new forms, no significant moments, until these were made and given
by direct human actions.

And so the new novel was contingent, not because it was produced by
social disorder, but because it was a creative action of feeling out
through the processes, newly complicated, newly obscure, by which
society was changing.

But for Knight there is no such poise between the creative process
and the world in which lives are lived, no such direct human actions;
there is plot or praxis and there is the historical process which is in its
crisis stage—and there can, in a bourgeois society, be no coherent
relationship between the two. His 'classical' novel is a self-cancelling
form, because it is divided between criticizing that society, which
places money before people, and manifesting 'inevitably' what Knight
calls the 'annulling' assumptions of the class and the period out of
which it is written; hence the 'bizarre mixture of sense and sheer
nonsense one finds in men like Balzac, Dickens and Tolstoy'. It is not
clear whether history too explains the bizarre mixture of sense and
sheer nonsense one finds in critics like Knight. Knight's classical novel
is really realism; but realism in bourgeois society is a conspiracy, an
ideological construct imposed upon the facts under the pretence that
we can see things objectively. To this case it is essential that reality has
not yet happened, but is in store; indeed it is essential to it that, until
the great Reality bonanza occurs from the redemptive and dialectical
synthesis of the revolutionary blood-letting, the novel *must* express

false consciousness. Hence the paradox of the nineteenth-century novel; it pretends to a realism it cannot sustain, because it cannot reconcile evaluation and description; it pretends to afford discoveries of identity and truth, but identity and truth are predetermined by historical states of affairs prior to the fiction, and inauthentic. This presses us towards the inept conclusion that fiction is the product of the perceptual limitations of a society, is a symptomatic communal illusion, leaving critics with the task of unweaving the logic by which the novelist manifests the guilty perceptual system of his culture.

'Only the ministrant must really approach the altar,' said James in his essay on 'The New Novel'; many come to fiction yet get 'too little of the first-hand impression'. In this sense Knight is not a ministrant; he speaks of a novel with no empiricism, no appetite for experience as it is felt in the living, and no real creativity, the creativity which makes of all novels a *personal* forming of reality. Realism is valueless unless it can be understood as a 'direct human action'—unless we find it in some sense validated and authenticated from the author's experience and understanding, manifested and felt through the worked, the probable, likely, difficult experience of the characters in their specified historical, 'real' world. There is indeed a sense in which realism *is* an aspect of the unsigned, of what is shared and communal; for it depends on the way all acts of language and structure become real, win the nod of assent, in a given culture. Because of this realistic plots can become figurative, or paradigmatic. This is what John Bayley argues of George Eliot in a recent essay; he speaks of her use of a 'peculiarly nineteenth-century fictional form which might be called historical pastoral', and notes that her novels develop in part through feeling towards the process by which history has shape and progression. The personal case of the individual tends, in her books, to become one with the cultural, but the balance is liberally held; character is not sacrificed to the historical process, since characterness is more important than representativeness, and to make individual experience abstract would be to commit a crime against the person and the fiction.[1] A little less 'character', or a

[1] Bayley's essay—together with some others (by Arnold Kettle, Graham Martin, and John Goode) suggesting that this means that George Eliot contains, rather than fulfils, radical idealism—appears in *Critical Essays on George Eliot*, ed. Barbara Hardy (London, 1970). This is one of a number of important recent works on Victorian fiction; another of especial importance is J. Hillis Miller, *The Form of Victorian Fiction* (South Bend, Ind., 1968).

little more, and the result is abstraction, depersonalization, a violation of much concern in the moral tenor of the nineteenth-century liberal or realistic novel. It is in this sense that the realistic form can be transacted as a moral virtue; the individualism of persons, the particularity of things, is the living fictional centre that frees it from excessive historicism or over-high formalism, myth, or ideology, or compositional wholeness.

But today we like types or large-scale explanatory structures; and we like them touched with crisis. Where for the nineteenth-century novelist interest in current history was often a move away from overweening abstractions or the urgings of the inexorable, today history is increasingly our way back into them. We both like and fear large plots and schemes; and the novel form attracts and distils such plots and paradoxes. Recent criticism of fiction has given us a number of very striking stories about the coming of the novel, and its going—normally interfusions of formalism and historicism. Some of them are obvious evasions of their subject—if the novel *is* their subject. For once you start to regard the novel as a distillation of broader structures in society—myths and typologies, perceptual and linguistic crises, and the like—you are liable to think of the novelist as a man with only a limited degree of self-signature and, like him, to make reality and history themselves the object of your speculations. It is easy to end up on the one hand praising the novelist for his sheer speculative resource in exploring the complexities of human experience and rendering them as art, yet also attacking him, as Knight does, for his guilty place in the total perceptual system of a culture, which makes his realism a falsity. The fiction is a kind of literal realism, but the society itself is a fiction or crisis of substance. What James called 'the beautiful difficulties of art' become the difficulties of the substantial world, a place as apocalyptic as the most difficult, fantastic, and wild novel its best artists can create. And, as our dealings come closer to the present, where such ideas of crisis become more intensely attached to history, and also to the novel, we go further. For, borrowing from the social sciences their technique of examining present society from outside it, which historicizes everything, we demand a proof of involvement in the pressure of the times, a relevance, an encounter with history; and yet we see the results as inescapably fictional, not because the artist makes it so, but because society does. Realism becomes surrealism, and fantasy; for is not that the modern reality? It becomes compositional crisis;

and is not that everyone's crisis? The gift for creating the fictional illusion of reality is shifted from the writer—who has long thought such matters within his power—to the culture in which he practises. From the writer we require fictional evidence that the world is as it is; we require endless report. But we are loath to guarantee it; and what our newer critics tell us, and our newer novelists as well, is that the novelist needs his realism, but also that he must be the realist of a fictional world.

3

Or, to say that differently, what we seem to be in the midst of is not so much a recovery of the traditional realistic forms of the novel as a new problematics of realism. A problematics is not of itself new. We know very well that the realism of art is a made thing, and that the claim to realism or authenticity in art is a shifting claim, from writer to writer and age to age. Indeed almost every movement in fiction, or for that matter literature, from those whose prime devotion has been to extremes of determinism, naturalism, or 'research' to those which have espoused versions of high formalism or aestheticism, have called themselves 'realist' (this of course includes the exponents of modernism in literature). The front edge of realism keeps shifting, so that one generation's realism is another's romanticism or high fantasy or escapism, and the definitions are extraordinarily multiple; truth or authenticity is, just like reality and history, open to extremes of dis-putatiousness. You can always show that a work's realism is highly fictional, because that is precisely its nature, being art. None the less there is sense in proposing a mean of realism somewhere in the history of the novel, a certain sort of balance or poise in the relationship between words and what they speak of, a certain equivalence between the making and the made, a certain openness of access between the writer and his characters, which recurs with some frequency and is a characteristic way of telling stories in prose. This is the sort of realism which J. P. Stern has called 'middle-distance' realism,[1] a form of address to the material and the reader which feels no need to assert by verbal or modal self-consciousness that it is basically a construct of words and perspectivized distances; it is presumably to this that Bergonzi refers when he talks in his book of realism as a world of Nature in which we

---

[1] J. P. Stern, *On Realism* (London, 1973).

effortlessly participate. We know that the making itself is not at all effortless; much of the newer critical comment on nineteenth-century fiction has been devoted to showing just how great the effort of that making is. Once you start on this sort of analysis, you discover that no writer's 'realism' is actually like anyone else's; you also find yourself defining this realism according to all sorts of different analogues (realism is empiricism; it is moral scepticism; it is a documentary attentiveness based on research, itself perhaps managed according to hypotheses or procedural categories; it a a pursuit of a moment of authentification; etc., etc.)—which makes it very patent you are talking of a fiction. As for the presumption that reality is fleeting and hence difficult to apprehend or represent, that is hardly a discovery of the *modern* novelist; the writer has always found his dealings with experience, with the knowable and visible world, with the comprehensible and the feasible, both a shaky and a constantly reconstituted exercise. But the current problematics has its own quality, and at its centre a curious and decisive unease.

There are, I have suggested, clear signs that we have refurbished some long-standing presumptions about the novel; that it is realism, and history, and that it is a contingent and open form, seeking out the feasible and verifiable world. In a good number of our writers there is a desire to resist formal wholeness—either on the grounds Iris Murdoch gives, when she suggests that the writer must manœuvre between the philosophical implications of making 'convincingly coherent, but false pictures of the world' and outright contingency; or on the kind of grounds Norman Mailer and some of his American contemporaries have asserted, insisting on the compelling necessity for the novelist to face and become immersed in the historical and psychic drift of the times, at whatever cost to the idea of 'craft'. But this is also an age obsessed with fictions, and with what Robert Scholes calls 'fabulation'[1] —the stubborn separateness of what is written from that about which it is written, the peculiar capacity the maker of narratives has to invent a universe or remake one by writing it, the strange mystery of referentiality and separateness that is a work of fictional art. The two obsessions are now commonplace and they look very hostile; the distance, say, between Mailer's *The Armies of the Night* and Nabokov's *Ada* is seemingly great. 'Writing novels is more like writing history than we

---

[1] Robert Scholes, *The Fabulators* (New York, 1967).

often choose to think,' says Frank Kermode,[1] and that sounds realist; 'Reality is a nice place to visit, but you wouldn't want to live there,' says John Barth, and that sounds fictionalist. We see, in fact, many assertions of the power and the imperative of realism, or the collapsing of craft and formalist concerns, and equally of the power and imperative of the fictive, an intensifying of those concerns. Are there then dealings that allow us to pass between the two? The obvious answer to this is that there is common ground indeed in the fact that realism *is* a fiction; but if we consult some of the preoccupations of modern novelists and modern critics of the novel—to some of which I have already referred—I think we can see yet further ways in which that proposition has become compelling for us.

One idea that has become important in thinking about the modern novel is that there has been a profound disturbance in the relationship between writing and reality, that this disturbance is now somehow inherently 'in' the novel, and that therefore the creation of a modern novel is especially difficult. This notion arises in and has been especially attached to the modernist novel of the earlier part of the century; I have emphasized the formal, aesthetic change this brought, but that change has been currently taken as a confession of a deep cultural failure in communal language and relationship, a failure of realism. We have subsequently seen a drift back to various forms of realism in fiction; so the notion of crisis might predictably have faded too. But it has persisted in many quarters of creative and critical expectation, and the realist writer is pressed either to defend his enterprise or else articulately to manifest its difficulties. A second important idea is the growth of a usage by which fictionality is regarded as the common attribute of all forms of discourse, even when these are ostensibly factual, reportorial, or analytical, so that the constituents of fictionality are present in history and sociology, psychology and biology, report-writing and journalism. One of the powers which sustained the steady drift towards realism in the nineteenth century was in fact a move towards these languages, which were presumed to be ordered and objective. This drift was especially clear in naturalism—in, for example, the famous prescriptions of the Goncourt brothers, urging a new scientific method in the novel, or in Zola's *Le roman experimental*, which saw the novelist as experimental, but in the same sort of in-

[1] Frank Kermode, 'D. H. Lawrence and the Apocalyptic Types', in *Modern Essays* (London, 1971).

vestigatory and hypothesis-creating way as the doctor or the scientist. Now, though, there are active signs in contemporary discussion that this sort of proposition is being reversed. The activities and discourse of the human, social, and biological sciences are being increasingly considered—indeed by their own exponents—fiction-making activities. This emphasis gives an especial credit to the novelist and his peculiar expertise. A third important idea is the presumption that reality and history are themselves deeply invested with ongoing powers or plots, arising from the forces of modernization, which are inherently absurd and of a terrible enormity; they act in life like an improbable fiction rather than a circumference of reality, and outrun the limits of invention, forbidding a balanced realism, demanding an art of extremity. And the fourth is the idea of the fictionality of an entire culture or society, an idea which arises especially with new developments in anthropological linguistics and structuralism, where linguistic acts are held not simply to explore but actually to make a culture, each human language being, in the words of Benjamin Lee Whorf, 'a vast pattern-system, different from others, in which are culturally ordained the forms and categories by which the personality not only communicates, but also analyses nature, notices or neglects types of relationship and phenomena, channels his reasoning, and builds the house of his consciousness.'[1]

It is increasingly in this sort of context that contemporary theories of realism, and contemporary aspiration in fiction, arise. And it will be clear how such propositions, and the reappraisals of the very idea of fiction that they contain, tend to produce new transactions in which the polarity of 'fiction' and 'reality' is very active, but the terms frequently reversed. Novels are concerned with creating the consistent appearance of truth, though they are not true, and are known not to be. They are therefore exemplary games of human invention containing self-consciousness but being without consequence. This is much the sort of notion advanced by Michel Butor in some of his essays, with their obvious structuralist associations; the novel, he tells us in his essay 'The Novel as Research', is to be seen within the total context of narrative, of which it is one particular form:

---

[1] I draw the quotation from George Steiner's 'The Language Animal' in his *Extraterritorial: Papers on Literature and the Language Revolution* (London, 1972), a collection very pertinent to this entire argument.

And narrative is a phenomenon which extends considerably beyond the scope of literature; it is one of the essential constituents of our understanding of reality. From the time we begin to understand language until our death, we are perpetually surrounded by narratives, first of all in our family, then at school, then through our encounters with people and reading. . . .[1]

All human beings are narrators, seeking to reconcile what they see and what they say, seeking to make whole and credible the world they speak into existence. But the novel differs from all other narrative in that it gives the appearance of reality to what is not so, what is not verifiable. This makes novels into typologies of inquiry, a quest for reality and a grammar of it; hence, says Butor, the novel 'is the best possible place to study how reality appears to us, or might appear; and that is why the novel is the laboratory of narrative.' This might support the case for a novel which avoids the pursuit of essences to convey the particularity and variety of experience, the material as opposed to the formal. In fact, as we know, Butor's theory is in support of that highly reduced and formal realism known as the *nouveau roman*, a fiction of contingent *is*-ness that Alain Robbe-Grillet calls a 'destitution of the old myths of "depth"'. On this Butor's point is that in a changing world traditional narrative techniques are incapable of dealing with new relations, and that hence formal invention is the only basis of greater realism, for the inner parts of the novel—the relationships of grammar, narrative sequence, temporal order, inside the work—constitute an inner symbolism, 'certain portions playing in relation to the whole the same part that the whole plays in relation to reality.' It is through this invigilated self-elucidation that the novel leads—or should lead—us to reality.

This rightly puts a great onus on the novel, and demands of it that it should not impose a pattern prior to the occasion; that, of course, is a recurrent thesis of realism. But the attempt to avoid prefigured form or pattern can—and in the *nouveau roman* has—produced very speculative fiction about the sparsity of reality, a highly formal kind of writing in which the real seems not true and authentic but meticulously sorted and selected. This is of a piece with the fear of plots or laid-over grids

[1] Michel Butor, 'The Novel as Research', in *Inventory*, trans. and ed. Richard Howard (London, 1970); this collects essays largely drawn from Butor's two French collections *Repertoire* (1960) and *Repertoire II* (1964). Also see Alain Robbe-Grillet, *Pour un nouveau roman* (1963), translated (by Richard Howard) as *For a New Novel* (New York, 1965).

that runs through much modern writing, and may seem to stand for a new realism which is unable to find in particularity a plot, which is to say a consistent and evolving human purpose. The result, however, tends to be narrative in which there is nothing to narrate except the narrative act itself, an act busily disembarrassing itself of order and causality. The ambiguity is significant because it is widespread; we now have many novelists who would present themselves, in all integrity, as so overwhelmed by the enormity of the substantial world, of material reality, that they are incapable of producing formal order, and who yet produce a very framed and formalized art whose prime satisfactions are those of aesthetic elegance—like many 'pure' pursuits of reality. In fact, many of the contemporary assertions of realism are not direct attempts to recover the narrative empiricism of earlier fiction; they are puristic attenuations or remodellings of it. Our 'reality' seems inclined to the very great—it is that entirety of the historical process which a novelist like Mailer offers to attack with his documentary-psychic-fabulatory artistic equipment—or to the very small—those objects in a room, or episodes or fleeting interludes sought from the past, which form the elusive data of the very phenomenological universe of the *nouveaux romanciers*. In order to accept this as reality, there is much that is real that you have to dismiss: the reality of the self as an active moral agent, the reality of the culture as a place of meanings commonly accrued out of individual living and speaking. Butor's implication is that the reality of the new novel is in this sense a metaphor. So, of course, with all fictions; they can do no more than invite us in, work out their world, and ask our provisional belief that this *is* the way things are, offer themselves for assent. However, the less empirical the exercise, the harder this is to do, for the basis on which assent is being sought alters: the novel is less an articulation, a bringing alive, of the knowable world than an abstract articulation of our historical, cultural, and social situation. Such abstract articulations can be taken, of course, as enabling justifications of fiction, which affect and satisfy us primarily *as* fictions. But it is possible—I think now increasingly possible—for critics to assent to the implied history as well, to make the fiction that feeds fiction into the facts of our present situation: a state of affairs much at odds with the central spirit of fictional realism.

4

It will become apparent that in this book I am much interested in the fortunes of realism and what critics might say about it. Part of criticism's purpose is, I take it, to clarify the nature and possibilities of the forms with which it deals, in ways illuminating and invigorating, but not absolutist or prescriptive. Now criticism keeps changing, and for several reasons. One is that literature is not over yet, and the matter as a whole is not and cannot be closed; another is that criticism itself accumulates energy and possibility as literature does, and draws in fresh thought from fresh potential relationships and situations. Often this fresh thought arises from notions developing among writers themselves; and one of the commonest activities of criticism—especially that kind concerned with the comparison and relation of texts and authors, and so with epochs, periods, traditions, genres—is that of resolving the procedural reasonings, the working theories, the self-rationalizations and justifications, the advertisement and publicity, of creative artists and movements and turning them into a special form of historiography, a kind of literary-cum-intellectual history. The problems that face historians then appear; do theories and movements arise inexorably and with devastating logic, so that no other could do in that time and place, or do they arise from chance and freedom and the peculiar dispositions of great artists? At times the argument can grow very historicist, because, on the one hand, of the need of writers to justify their activities in terms of some universal, to show why their work is not an arbitrary invention but a distillation driven by onerous necessities, and because, on the other, of the critic's disposition to systematize the literature that gives him pleasure and validate in universal terms the pleasure it gave him. And some such state of affairs seems to be developing in the discussion of the novel and its realism.

On the face of it, a phase in criticism preoccupied with fictional realism ought to be one given to considering the novel's openness, plurality, and richness. The business of criticism being, as I say, inherently to maintain open and not closed definitions, this enterprise ought to be congenial. For, being a *post facto* activity, criticism should be devoted to the eclectic interpretation of the potential of any literary form, should try to pass from particular texts of as many kinds as possible to some broader working idea of the species to which they contribute. All novels are therefore a contribution to *and* an escape from the pattern of the novel; if you want there to be more novels in the future, you ought to be careful with your pattern. But the relations between patterns and the random are today difficult areas of

discourse. And it is symptomatic that in opening up literary thought
to the idea of the proliferating, contingent variousness of experience,
to the phenomenological and random, to experiential inclusiveness—
ideas which bring the novel into a place of theoretical importance—
we start to surround this inner world with an exterior plot, the plot
of history. (It is notable that precisely the same mixture occurs, as Tony
Tanner has lately suggested, in many contemporary American novels.)[1]
The fact is that the historicist is these days in all of us; one of the most
familiar and fashionable accounts of life now is that history issues formal
imperatives, closing man in a world of contradictions with limited
options, or demanding from him a particular type of act or belief. In
criticism as elsewhere, history becomes one of our most obsessive
fictions; criticism turns into a world of very elegant and very large-
scale plots which explain not only literature but man and society.
We can, properly enough, use an historical attention, an attention to
the living life of the time and the way it generates and is observed by
consciousness, to explain literature, or show why it is forceful and
illuminating to our lives. But we can also use it to see writing as an
outright, virtually an unsigned, manifestation of the times, a choric
act written by the linguistic community under defined compulsions;
this makes art sound very important, but important in a pointless way,
for the freedom and the significance of the individual creative action is
gone from it.

The matter seems compelling because the novel particularly distils it,
as Bergonzi, in *The Situation of the Novel*, sets out to suggest. In that
book he offers an enormous uncertainty in the face of historicist discussion of the novel; he sees the novel as an intrinsically liberal form,
concerned with exploring in fresh milieux the interchanges of character
and reality, yet he senses that the liberal part of the enterprise is somehow past: 'It is the fiction of the Human Condition, of existential
isolation and alienation, of efforts at self-definition and vain sisyphean
struggles, that for good historical reasons has the most direct appeal
throughout the world today.' The same historical reasons justify the
efforts of French and American novelists to write crisis fiction, and
throw postwar British fiction into historical doubt. Yet many of the
new energies in the novel—the French *nouveau roman*, the American
black humour novel—are energies arising from a sense of absolute
historical apocalypse; morever, they grow from and involve an ex-

[1] Tony Tanner, *City of Words: American Fiction 1950–1970* (London, 1971).

plicit attack on the idea of character, free action, and the rights and capacities of persons to mediate with a substantial world. That these are the novels that show fresh and salient energy he takes to indicate that liberal realism has either become formally routine or is philosophically discredited. Traditional fiction is bankrupt, though whether because it is true but boring or outrightly false is not clear; of course to say the latter would be to say we live in very bad times indeed. What underlies the problem Bergonzi poses, though, is a question that underlies much of our talk about literature in all places and at all times: when we speak of crisis or change of consciousness, as now we so much like to, do we regard that crisis as a generative principle within the arts that produces innovation; or do we regard innovation as the result of inevitable historical pressures on the culture which are binding on the serious artist, so that his form is the only one that can be made valid in his particular historical circumstances, the only one that is not, as Butor puts it, 'an image of reality in flagrant contradiction to the reality which gave them birth', and hence an 'imposture'?

Now of course if you reach the latter conclusion completely you can easily mask under an idea of historical authenticity a complete rescinding of all ideas of openness, creative and personal freedom. For that matter you also rescind what I have referred to as an obligation on criticism: that of not being predictive in this way, by too abstractly trying to determine the forms appropriate to given circumstances. This sort of historicism can apparently validate literature and respect it by giving it this provenly central historical representativeness; it is an engaging explanation for literary significance and universality, but it does precisely deny creative variation. Or, rather, it denies the most intrinsic kind of realism literature can possess: the realism by which we make fiction out of the knowledge that life and experience are always opening up towards the possibility of new orders and understandings. There is a danger now that critics can—and are beginning to—write fictions much more apocalyptic than those of our novelists: fictions which have the wise objectivity of analysis criticism can command, but are wanting that openness of sympathy which is the only real justification for criticism's existence. Moreover, because they are fictions of history, they can tend to deny the primary centre of literature—which surely lies in the creative play of individuals responding not to 'history' but to life, a response capable of generating forms, orders, or fictions of extraordinary range and variety.

PART TWO

THE NOVEL AND THE COMIC MODE

II

Fielding, Sterne, and
the Comic Modes of Fiction

I want to begin by proposing that there is a significant relationship between the novel form and the comic mode—a mode which, of course, transcends the novel, but seems to attach itself particularly closely to some of the novel's most familiar business. That, at any rate, was the belief of some of those who had most to do with this new form as it emerged: Cervantes, Fielding, and Sterne, for example. The most explicit statement of my proposition indeed occurs in Henry Fielding's 'Preface' to *Joseph Andrews*, a work which he wrote in the manner of Cervantes; that preface seems to me still one of the most promising attempts we have at the sketching of a poetics with which to explore that new and almost indefinable form that Fielding practiced, and we today call the novel. 'Now a comic Romance is a comic Epic Poem in Prose': Fielding, in using the word 'comic', takes it from the neo-classical tradition, as well as of course from its most familiar context, that of drama, and he uses it to suggest the tone, and also the type of structure, that work of the kind he was writing might contain—even as the word 'epic' suggested its spatial and its social scale. Fielding meant, in a way, what we might today call 'realism'; the empiricism and the scepticism of fiction, and hence its particular kind of moral enlightenment. What is especially elegant about the association is that it is a flexible one, broad enough to contain other propositions important to the discussion of fiction, and notably this one: that the novel is, as we now assume, disposed to both realism and fictiveness. Although these presumptions were alive close to the origins of the novel in England, they were open to some variety of interpretation or arrangement. And because that is so I want to look at Fielding and at

Sterne, two great comic writers but in different modes, who seem to
me to stand for possibilities in the fictional form that have remained
within the range of major novelists ever since.

I

There is an argument, one we all know, about the character of the
English tradition in the novel which runs somewhat as follows. The
typical species of the novel in England is the socio-moral novel, or the
novel of manners and morals, the prime theme of which is the ethical
conduct of man in a society relatively stable and secure. The novel,
taking society as substance and not as an hypothesis, and life in time as
a reality and not a deviance from the 'real' or 'higher' life of consciousness or art or symbol, expresses a particular species of moral realism. It
subjects social appearances to the tests of normal reality, and by dis-
solving hypocrisy and artifice and by burlesquing pride or vanity in the
interests of a synthesis of greater ethical solidity, it witnesses to the fact
that the social and moral world are contiguous: that the social world is
properly conceived a moral world, in which manners can be redeemed
from their apparent contingency by making them a species of morals.
This kind of novel is realistic, by virtue of its empiricism and its
concern with the particular stuff of life, particular experience affecting
particular persons; but it is often also comic, since it explores dis-
sonances between ethical absolutes or social virtues and the particular
individual experience of these, and since it ends with a restoration,
that replacement of the social norms, that giving back of sons to fathers,
of lovers to lovers, which we associate with the resolution of a comic
plot. Tom Jones becomes the good squire, Emma Woodhouse—
having completed the moral assault course Jane Austen sets for her—
marries Mr. Knightley, and the social order is somehow given back to
us, having been experienced by a hero or heroine as an individual, a
personal experience; it has been through the proofs of human reality,
and it emerges, in its subdued way, as really real. On the way we have
seen follies and deviances, hypocrisy disguised as goodness and goodness with the appearance of folly, comedy penetrating reality where it
is a disguise and romping with reality where it is a farce. But if realism,
empiricism, and historiography of the individual are a familiar
part of the novel's generic stuff, then repeatedly in England we have
seen going along with it the comic spirit; so much so that a recognizable element of the generic type is the mode of comedy and then

irony, parody, mock-heroic, burlesque, which are the formal expressions of the mode.

Or, to put this in E. M. Forster's terms, there is a basic species of the novel which regards the contingent world of life in time as reconcilable with that other element in which the novel must deal, the life by values; so contingency becomes plot, and life in time is finally teleological; the universe of chance becomes a universe of meaning, and the individual and history unite. This is apt to be a comic genre because the hero is characteristically one of us, deviating from sublime or heroic norms, but also because his capacity to draw misadventure and live through chance turns out to be a sustainable inquiry—the comic Muse and fortune are really behind him, rejoicing in his follies and making them a genuine quest. So it is not surprising that when Fielding offers to give a poetic description of the new form he is exploring, the novel novel, he speaks of that form as a comic epic in prose. 'Comic' here prescribes several things: obviously a type of diction, which is anti-heroic, not at all concerned with high sentiments or elevating action, inducing a sense of the ludicrous rather than the sublime, enjoying burlesque; obviously an inclusiveness of social range, including many ranks and many manners, many incidents and more varied characters than romance, or tragedy, or even stage-comedy; obviously an extended and comprehensive action or structure, large in social and ethical experience but also light. Indeed, judging from *Tom Jones,* Fielding seems to have taken as a representative structure for the comic epic in prose a reverse tragedy, in which the hero moves steadily downward towards a low point of fortune, and then rises again to success. Misfortune and disorder are part of the comic shape, then; but the conception of comedy is finally that of a peculiarly fortunate universe, one in which special laws operate, so that the hero's misfortunes never seem finally severe. Hence Fielding emphasizes the unreality—as well as the reality—of the invented world of comic myth. So we are aware of unusual probabilities—we know that chance works in strange ways and that coincidence is a given—and we exist in a world of double expectations, for fortune, seemingly malign, is benign in a way appropriate to the generosity of comedy. Apparently a force for contingency, it is in fact the supreme plotter, twisting contingency about to show finally that it was all the time an order in the world.

The History of Tom Jones is therefore a history of good fortune, of

chance operating in one particular set of possibilities; by virtue of that
it is—since fortune is not always good—a fiction. It is Fielding's pride
that he makes of the picaresque form of the novel, a form whose natural
sequence is 'and then', a causal form, so that the novel can be read,
backwards, as a coherence, 'because of this, so that.' That 'because'
lies, of course, not simply in the fortunes of life but in the self-consciously
commanding skill and elegance of the writer, who demands that we
notice his virtuosity. The book opens, in a familiar eighteenth-century
picaresque convention, with the birth of the hero, which starts everything; here the hero has confused and mysterious social origins,
enabling him to create for us and for the story an environment of social
uncertainty. He can thus move freely and fluidly through a great
range of experience and question and explore the various levels, orders,
and codes of society. So Tom initiates a very open society and he
moves comically about in it; still, he has a place, and the ending con-
firms it, attaching an essence to existence and a moral significance to an
open field of action. The chase was a pursuit, and the end was Sophia,
who was love but also truth and social place. One of our bases for
comic enjoyment is a delight in arbitrariness, in the manipulations of
coincidence; Fielding gives us all that joy but then insists on capping
his plot, showing that what we thought was an episodic world was
really a plot or causal sequence, a coherent formal making and a significant emotional order which had, all the time, been developing in the
society.[1] That social shape was artistic shape; it was form for the reader.
And this double aspect of chaos and order is comedy—comedy by this
view being not only a diction or a tone of voice, not only an emphasis
on the ridiculous or affected, but a special kind of action in a special
kind of universe: one with genial laws which is controlled by the
novelist who, holding fortune in his hand, can dispose it finally in an
aesthetically and morally satisfying way. Clearly it is essential to
Fielding's view (as to that of many subsequent comic novelists of his
kind) that the universe is special, which is to say fictive, having its
own orders and improbable probabilities; hence we recognize that

---

[1] It is appropriate that one of the best discussions of plot in fiction that we have is a
discussion of *Tom Jones*: R. S. Crane, 'The Concept of Plot and the Plot of *Tom
Jones*', in *Critics and Criticism*, ed. R. S. Crane (Chicago, 1952), is an admirable
account showing that the notion of plot has been limited in critical discourse to
the point of being a misleading account of the way in which story creates
coherence in fiction.

comedy is not finally realism but a self-conscious fictive stylization. Social comedy, comedy of manners in this sense, may then engage us with duplicities and disguises, rogues and impostures, eccentricities and unearned punishments; it may create a sense of the falsities of the social fabric, or produce devastating exercises in irony, such distances between action and author as we find in Jane Austen; or it may involve us in mock-heroic and parody, and have a highly intensified fictiveness. Yet it may still be disposed towards the subject-matter of the social interaction of men, develop through their interaction and give social meaning to it, and restore the social order at the end (which is to say it may close its universe in a mood of social satisfaction).

But clearly this kind of comic novel, a kind which tends in the end to stabilize the familiar social reality and throughout to explore the follies within it, is not the only one there is. This description hardly suggests the comic forces at work in Dickens or Melville or the modern ironists; and we make a mistake if we suppose that the eighteenth-century novel, in searching out its modes and its business, produced only that species. We sometimes take *Tristam Shandy*, which is a subversive novel, to be simply subversive of the generic type, a parody of it, of the rules, the beginnings, middles, and ends, the typographical presumptions, the conventional procedures of argument and discourse of the extant novel: 'I shall confine myself neither to his [Horace's] rules, nor to any man's rules that ever lived,' says Tristram/Sterne. But *Tristram Shandy* is more than an anti-novel; it is the working out of a different comic typology, and it is this aspect of the book I want to look at.

2

What kind of structure and procedure might a comic novel have if it is not of the species of social comedy? There are many such; but *Tristram Shandy* is an exemplary case. It is a comic novel; but it is not a novel in which fortune is finally benign or in which restitution of place is to be won—where unlucky Tom Jones or unlucky Jim Dixon becomes Lucky Tom or Lucky Jim—because it does not see comedy as a form but a condition. Tristram says of himself,

I have been the continual sport of what the world calls fortune; and though I will not wrong her by saying, She has ever made me feel the weight of any great or signal evil;——yet with all the good temper in the world, I affirm it of her, that in every stage of my life, and at every turn and corner where she could fairly get at me, the ungracious Duchess has pelted me with a set of as pitiful misadventures and cross accidents as ever small HERO sustained.

So comedy is rather the good temper with which we bear the ironical universe, and enables misfortune to take on a comic guise. *Tristram Shandy* is not a fiction in which the expectation of good fortune is established, and it hardly can be—since the misfortunes of the hero derive not from an uncertain place in the social order (a mystery, say, about his birth) nor from a moral incompleteness which would send him out on a moral quest, but from nature itself. Sterne must create both the misfortunes and that temper that will bear them like Beckett's Murphy: 'And life in his mind gave him pleasure, such pleasure that pleasure was not the word.' The narrator is a small hero established as a farcical victim within the novel, unable directly to dispose of the fortunes of his other 'characters', for they are his 'real' companions, nor indeed of his own fortunes, since these have already been determined from outside the action by the *true* novelist, Sterne himself, who has set this farcical world into motion and predetermined its society, logic, and laws.

Of course Sterne makes this fictional world penetrable in all sorts of ways; there is that curious and fascinating interaction between Tristram inside the story and Sterne outside it; the first-person narrative Tristram tells is one carefully made in order to be open to the novelist. So, for instance, experiences and ideas conceived subsequently to the initial creation of the novel can get in, while the book's peculiarly open-ended form is itself proof against that kind of fictional writing that sets up a world of expectations and tones which persuade us towards a view not only of the characters and events but also towards a sense of predetermined structural rhythm, a mental pattern of beginning, middle, and end. The structure we are invited to accept in *Tristram Shandy* is perpetually kept on a provisional basis, with constant permissions to reader and for that matter writer to leave the room at any point, so precluding a comic *action* as Fielding means it, a shape predetermined in the direction of an ending. Sterne leaves us precisely without that sense of an ending, that drift towards apocalyptic conclusiveness, that gives most novels their air of performing integrally as opposed to incidentally; and he does so in such a way as to create not only an accidental view of life but an accidental view of fiction, making his art open to superb serendipities. But as I have said the work allows for another kind of penetration, that of the coalescing and separating of narrator in the fictive world with and from narrator outside the fictive world, Shandy and Sterne, victim and maker. And so if one aspect of irony is distance between narrator and world, Sterne is free to play with it not only mimetically but at the core of his narrative situation: letting Tristram be ironic about the world he is in, but letting Sterne be ironic about Tristram.

So the freedom of telling the whole tale doesn't make Tristram entirely a free agent in the novel. The book makes him to begin with a victim of a preordained world ('this vile, dirty planet of ours') rather than the direct determinant of his own fate. His *life* is made for him—and not as a *history*, a life through event and society. It begins at the beginning, *ab ovo*, where lives usually do begin but not most plots; it begins not with a birth but a conception. Indeed it begins, as Andrew Wright has observed,[1] *in flagrante delicto*, in a joke about the inadequacy of all beginnings. A birth is usually a start into a system of adventures enacted through society and individual will. Tristram's fictive life starts prior to the existence of will; existence precedes essence in a very total sense; and fortune determines a fatality consonant not only with Tristram's subsequent career but with the total vision of the book. For Tristram's conception is the book's conception, the start of the telling. Tristram's is an incomplete conception—a botched performance mismanaged because progression and digression, physiology and chronology, intersect; not only must the character be created but the clock wound up. And the novel itself proceeds appropriately, by a principle of literary *coitus interruptus*, of questioned progression, half-negated fulfillment. The divergent worlds of personality and time then go on diverging and intersecting, here and there; not so as to suggest that the linear development of time holds the real meaning in life, and divergence is a comic episode of spectacular fictive freedom from the condition of time, but to suggest that the two worlds of life in time and life in mind are intersectional. As Tristram, speaking now as novelist, says: 'I have constructed the main work and the adventitious parts of it with intersections, and have so complicated and involved the digressive and progressive movements, one wheel within another, that the whole machine, in general, has been kept a-going;——and, what's more, it shall be kept a-going these forty years, if it pleases the fountain of health to bless me so long with life and good spirits.'

[1] Andrew Wright, 'The Artifice of Failure in *Tristram Shandy*', in *Novel: A Forum on Fiction*, II, No. 3 (Spring 1969), 212–20.

Digression is not divergence only, but provides an interlocking logic and illuminates the life in time with the life by opinion, or wit, or ideas. It is indeed opinion that rescues life from its contingency: 'It is the nature of an hypothesis, when once a man has conceived it, that it assimilates every thing to itself as proper nourishment; and, from the first moment of your begetting it, it generally grows the stronger by every thing you see, hear, read, or understand. This is of great use.' Opinions in *Tristram Shandy* are not of course truths but redemptive mechanisms; they are ideas as sensations and as personality. 'But I say, *Toby*, when one runs over the catalogue of all the cross reckonings and sorrowful *items* with which the heart of man is overcharged, 'tis wonderful by what hidden resources the mind is enabled to stand it out, and bear itself up, as it does against the impositions laid upon our nature,' says Mr. Shandy; and, resisting Toby's desire to identify these resources as religion, he attributes them to 'that great and elastic power within us of counter-balancing evil, which like a secret spring in a well-ordered machine, though it can't prevent the shock——at least it imposes upon our sense of it'. Mr. Shandy's 'transverse zig-zaggery' is obviously such a survival mechanism; thus the mind does stand it out. And this it does, not only because it is the focus of sensations, but also the active creator of opinions and ideas, which can themselves become objects of comedy, parody. The procedures of the mind, whether these are personal hobby-horses or traditional intellectual or rhetorical strategies, whether they are trains of association provoked by fictional events or by the comedy of the story-telling situation, give us the method of *Tristram Shandy*.

On the one hand, then, the farce of a life; on the other hand, the comedy of ideas. The penetration of the two worlds yields irony in another sense: a context of multiple presentation. *Tristram Shandy* as a telling has at least two beginnings before the one which sounds that linguistic register that has the feel of fiction: 'I was begot in the night, betwixt the first *Sunday* and the first *Monday* in the month of *March*. . . .' And once we have that, we revert to the digressive question of how the date is arrived at in a world in which such information is not a given, but exists in a context of surmise and investigation. It is not ideas as such, but the way in which surmise and the determinism of opinion work, which gives *Tristram Shandy* its theme and progression; intellectual procedures substitute for narrative procedures, but intellectual procedures *encounter* narrative procedures and so can be violated, parodied, mocked. So these frames of ideas, these schemas of association and wit, these species of argument as rhetorical mode, create a context in which we can judge the narrative, but not find in it a single belief that is the author's belief, a permanent wisdom. The comedy of ideas becomes a comedy of ciphers; and that is how it is, I think, that we come to regard *Tristram Shandy* as doubly an ironical novel—a comedy of ideas which is also a comedy of misfortunes, a novel which ironically distances its world and then ironizes again about the procedures by which this is done.

In this lies, surely, the beginnings of a new ironical mode in fiction. When we speak of irony in *Tristram Shandy* we therefore mean the word in a much more total sense than we do in speaking of the irony of Jane Austen or Henry Fielding, or even of Swift. It is not a species of presentation used towards the gaining of a comic resolution or the establishing of a vision, and it is not a moral instrument. It is rather a total vision, or itself a plot. It is that in *Tristram Shandy* which creates the world that might have been there if time and opinion were consonant, if the world was a meaning; and which then shows that meaning is in essence a fiction. It is that in *Tristram Shandy* which regards the real as an alien system of contingent things, having no consistent order to itself, but only that order which perceivers perceive in it, and then goes on to show that there are many perceivers. So the world is lapsed or lost in time; and it is discovered again and made gay by that art which matches the powers of the mind of perceivers, in short, by fictiveness—seen not as the possession of an author only, but as the active making of a world by its citizens, a world that is the context for myth but which cannot be given as one myth. The agents in *Tristram Shandy* are all fictionalizers; they create stories to assuage the mind. But it is not the nature of invention or fiction or discourse to discover or order reality. Rather it flees it, and takes us into the self; the verbal operation is incomplete. That is Tristram's own dilemma. In *Tom Jones* there is a history to be told; Fielding tells it to us, demonstrating his own linguistic and creative presence, yet expressing the presence of a subject outside himself in reality. In *Tristram Shandy* there is a substantive reality presumed to be there, and indeed there is a particular tale to tell, but it is virtually impossible for man to reach it.

The one significant variation between this speculation and much that is current in contemporary comedy is that in Sterne it is very explicitly a species of *gaiety*. It is the incoherent distance between the action of the individual mind and the world of general order and general experience which gives grace, making the 'wheel of life run long and chearfully round'; the obverse gesture to Swift's irony, which deals with a universe equally ambiguous, but with a seriousness that is not ironic but satirical. Swift can never take the powers he has to annihilate his own opinion through irony as the end of the affair. But that is precisely, I think, what Sterne does. That is why he is finally an ironist and not a satirist, that kind of ironist whose vision is bleak but whose mode is benevolent. His enemy is not affectation or hypocrisy but finally gravity itself—which is why he can identify himself finally with the gay small hero, comically afflicted, who is able to forgive Dame Fortune because he is her joke, a human joke who like Yorick claims as his supreme gift the power of seeing himself in 'the true point of Ridicule'[1] where human affairs and destinies stand.

[1] *Letters of Laurence Sterne*, ed. L. P. Curtis (Oxford, 1965), 74.

III

'The Most Interesting Moving Picture':
Fanny Hill and Comedy

I

Though a few years back it was a *cause célèbre* and an outrage, John Cleland's *The Memoirs of a Woman of Pleasure*—better known as *Fanny Hill*—can only seem today a modestly pornographic book. Indeed the category of pornography is receding, moving from being an outrage to a style and perhaps even fading beyond that, so that students of generic classification who find the term useful as a definition of an aesthetic procedure had better be on their mettle. Criticism now is clearly baffled by the anti-humanist character of many works that seem important; we have developed a large modern literature of dehumanization, and resuscitated a whole tradition in the past; from Swift, Voltaire, and de Sade to Nathanael West, Burroughs, and Genet, we can find significant lines running which lead us further into that universe of fantasy (if fantasy is the right word for a process also recognizable in history) in which the human self is dwarfed, violated, perhaps destroyed, physiological functions dominate, man (or woman) is put into thing-status in, often, an apocalyptically surreal universe, and in which both social protest and a patent emotional perversity can coincide. We cannot take such works as part of the humanist canon of literature, but, by a transitional fiction of our times, one we ought to examine more than we do, we can find qualities of literary and emotional merit in them. We sometimes postulate that once a certain level of literary excellence has been achieved the disturbing or pornographic elements somehow, like the state after the revolution, wither away—a piety that has been transferred into law and proved unsatisfactory. For of course it is hard to claim that literary virtue is redemptive, giving another value that improves on the perverse or the kinetic aspects of a work. Indeed often the literary endeavour is devoted to the best achievement of the pornographic, to producing erotic stimulus and a sexual sublime. And when criticism loses not only its moral but also its generic hierarchies, success in any sphere can constitute merit. We may still feel that certain kinds of literary proceeding—the detective story, pornography—are inherently inferior. But without a clear moral referent we cannot be sure; and in the novel the sheer proliferation of types and species—from realism to romance, facticity to fabulation—helps us not to be.

Part of the complexity of *Fanny Hill*'s pornography is that the book comes out of such a situation of generic uncertainty, and marks an interesting stage in the rise of the novel. The form developed in England in a neo-classical climate in which generic norms were both called on and sceptically questioned by practitioners in the new form. It is fairly typical of the eighteenth-century novelist that he immerses himself freely in the contingencies of contemporary experience; he specifies, grows sceptical, ranges 'epically' through the classes, uses multiple levels of diction—yet he also promises some over-all effect or single moral end in the classical way. Criticism has now overemphasized the empiricism, realism, and verisimilitude of early fiction in the interests of defining the new form. Still, a dissonance between ends and means, arising from this, is familiar to us in these novels, given to prefatory promises not quite lived out in the narrative. As cultural sophisticates, we discount the ends and explore the means, proposing a conscious or even—as with Defoe in one critic's account[1]— an 'unconscious' irony of method. This dissonance has a recognizable place in pornographic writing; it is certainly there in *Fanny Hill*. The explicit moral end is based on Fanny's discovery that normal marital love is richer than any other mode of pleasure; but *en route* we are entranced by a sequence of episodes developed, to use the appropriate metaphor, up to the hilt. We have this in much other contemporary writing too; but the dissonance is clearer when the episodes are sexual, and when Cleland creates them, as I want to suggest, according to another aesthetic principle he gets from the age's neo-classical temper—that of kinetically involving his audience in his pastoral and sexual sublime. Cleland was probably partly parodying

[1] Dorothy Van Ghent, *The English Novel: Form and Function* (New York, 1961).

the literary and aesthetic principles of his day. But his book is a sophisticated, formally complex work, and he is clearly engaged in the aesthetic fascination of his enterprise; the result is a book that—while one wouldn't want to claim it as startlingly good—has its distinctive merits, and obviously opens up a number of striking and unconventional possibilities in the working of that new form, the novel.

Part of Cleland's effort in the book is clearly that of politely covering up what he was doing, and he parodies literary seriousness in order to serve the erotic and pornographic possibilities of his story. He promises to anatomize the life of pleasure and show its dangers—a familiar period theme—but busily explores the erotic resources of literature, especially drawing on the romance tradition from which the new novel form partly derived, partly diverged. A similar effort led in many eighteenth-century novels to a comic mode and diction, as new matter is related to old literary strategies, and mock-heroic methods are used to break up traditional hierarchies, with high events presented in low language, or the reverse. Cleland engages in several such tactics; he is given to a sceptical realism and a playfulness about relating his matter to his tone. Of course there are reasons for not taking this as seriously as we do in Fielding or Sterne. For one thing, Cleland's first-person narrator, Fanny, is an *ingénue*, an instrument of the narrator in several senses; for another, the comedy is partly that not uncommon in the pornographic novel, where we can gain amusement from the fact that all the literary devices seem finally occasioned by the need to allow the participants, emotions, and postures involved in each sexual episode to change in the interests of maintaining erotic variety. But the book is modally very self-aware. On the event of its much-publicized reissue Brigid Brophy reviewed it as 'art of an artless kind'. One sees what she means; there is a patent manipulation in the novel, an avoiding of the general human requirements of the felt moment ('I skip', says Fanny of the death of her parents, 'over the natural grief and affliction I felt on this melancholy occasion'), familiar enough in cheap writing, though also in much episodic fiction. But such artlessness can be naïve or deliberate; and *Fanny Hill* is in fact rather artlessness of an artful kind.

One can see this by comparing it with the more patent naïveté of Defoe's *Moll Flanders*. Defoe has a similar kind of heroine, similar types of narrative device, and uses the familiar eighteenth-century mode of a basically episodic narrative line, with heavily worked set scenes but with flimsy and clearly functional connective links. Both books have heroines who move from poor births to wealthy penitence; both begin their actions when the heroine reaches self-awareness —in *Moll Flanders* class and monetary awareness, in *Fanny Hill* sexual awareness. Both women are at first simple, ingenuous, and easily tempted to depravity, which they espouse less by intention than through influence from people and circumstances; and both tell their own stories, as retrospective first-person narrators giving a 'moral' account of their lives, so mixing realistic documentary telling with interspersed, *post facto*, penitential reflection. But their creators are after opposite effects: Defoe's aim, which explains some of his simplification, is to limit the suggestiveness of his narrative, while Cleland's is to intensify his. Defoe therefore pursues verisimilitude: his preface asserts a factual source for the book as Moll's 'own memorandums', and he claims that his own skill as novelist lies in applying to that a moral control by managing a potentially titillating narrative ('There is in this story abundance of delightful incidents, and all of them usefully applied'). His self-conscious art therefore lies in inventing incidents which appear true and pleasing but are also instructive; they are varied and sensational, but muted by plain style and moral management. We may read ironies into this, but we do so afterward; Cleland, on the other hand, designs his.

He too claims realism and verisimilitude—in a figure typical of the whole book: 'I will not so much as take pains to bestow the strip of a gauze wrapper on it [Truth]', writes Fanny, 'but paint situations as they actually rose to me in nature, careless of violating those laws of decency that were never made for such unreserved intimacies as ours....' This is a traditional tactic, and points up the fact that, though Cleland is actually interested in creating social and environmental verisimilitude, he is mainly concerned with exploiting the possibilities in the basic kind of incident, which is sexual incident, he limits himself to. Moll's story is the story of a human life; Fanny's is the stylized tale of an ever-elaborating set of incidents in a single universe narrower than— and at times outside—human probability. Defoe clearly shares some of Moll's ingenuousness, and does not make her experience or judgements absurd; Cleland exploits his heroine both in her experiences and her judgements. His posture is urbane—the urbanity both of the narrative manager and the socially experienced individual. He takes his norms of sexual behaviour from an urban, aristocratic milieu, that world of pleasure, fops and wits, urban sexuality and experimentation, that he shared with Richardson and Fielding. Fielding took the comic view of that world, seeing it as the place of follies; Richardson took both a more sentimental and a socially more mobile view of it, placing his lower-middle-class heroines in redemptive tension with it; both enter it fully, if finally to discard it. In this they differ from Defoe, and Cleland is closer to them: partly, perhaps, for chronological reasons. *The Memoirs of a Woman of Pleasure* was putatively published in 1749.[1] *The Fortunes and Misfortunes of the Famous Moll Flanders*—often called the first English novel—came out only 27 years before, in 1722. But by 1749 *Pamela* (1740) and *Clarissa* (1748), which probably much influenced Cleland, had appeared, and *Tom Jones* came out that year. The one real difference between Cleland and Richardson and Fielding is that the first shows no interest in social or in moral *tensions*. His book is without those variations among the classes, or the related moral hierarchies, which are the normal sources of conflict and development in eighteenth-century fiction. In this it approximates rather to the condition of romance or pastoral.

Cleland's urbanity is a sort of social and moral inclusiveness; Fanny moves through a social world that is classless in the sense that the world of sexuality is a genial democracy. She is a pleasure-advocate, a member of a stylized world of rakishness by which she is not really corrupted but matured. She explores, albeit at first passively, her own propensities, and actually values them; in certain respects she becomes a sophisticated heroine, making interesting judgements about her experience (though never as sophisticated as her author's). 'The inflammable principle of pleasure so easily fired at my age' is her only principle; she becomes a scientist of, an expert in, a moralist about, pleasure. Because of this there is an absence of any critical explanation of, any textural density arising from, those socio-moral matters so recurrent in eighteenth-century writing, as one might expect of titillatory fiction; and the book is thus relatively static, bearing considerable resemblance to the earlier form of romance, likewise little concerned with the collision of values. Of course it states what much earlier romance implies, and intrudes a species of realism: a realism of tone that becomes comedy. But my point is that it is very much part of the general climate of the new novel form, and offers an interesting redistribution of

[1] Peter Quennell's preface to the Putnam edition shows the difficulties of dating undercover writing.

prevailing constituents. Cleland's real problem in the book is to work out these constituents effectively: and, like most of his contemporaries, he is much more aware of his rhetorical means and the fictional game than we often care to say.

2

How does he do it? Cleland makes the book a first-person narration in the form of two letters to a female correspondent who has asked Fanny to recount the story of her life of pleasure. The first letter deals with the innocent Fanny's rapid involvement with sexual emotion, the pleasures of enjoyment, and the chief erotic rewards, taking her to the point where she is compelled to submit to prostitution. The second deals with her life in a brothel, her rise to wealth, and her marriage to her first lover, to whom she presents the riches she has acquired. She starts her story by claiming the value of her wide experience; she also says that by leaving the life of pleasure she is the better enabled to think and reflect about it. The result is that she is put in the narrative position both of reporting the episodes, all essentially sexual, and offering some sort of judgement on and organization of them. Thus made pseudo-author as well as heroine, she comments on the narrative problems as such—particularly strikingly at the beginning of her second letter, where she writes to 'Madam':

I imagined, indeed, that you would have been cloy'd and tired with uniformity of adventure and expressions, inseparable from a subject of this sort, whose bottom, or groundwork being, in the nature of things, eternally one and the same, whatever variety of forms and modes the situations are susceptible of, there is no escaping a repetition of the same images, the same figures, the same expressions, with this further inconvenience added to the disgust it creates, that the words JOYS, ARDOURS, TRANSPORTS, ECSTACIES, and the rest of those pathetic terms so congenial to, so received in the PRACTICE OF PLEASURE, flatten and lose much of their due spirit and energy by the frequency they indisputably recur with, in a narrative of which that practice professedly composes the whole bias. I must therefore trust to the candour of your judgment, for your allowing me the disadvantages I am necessarily under in that respect, and to your imagination and sensibility, the pleasing task of repairing it, by their supplements, where my descriptions flag or fail; the one will readily place the pictures I present before your eyes; the other give life to the colours where they are dull, or worn with frequent handlings.

Nothing, of course, could be franker about the difficulties of the species. Though an odd inruption into an ostensibly factual narrative, it draws attention to the artful skills of the book. Limited as it is in subject-matter, it can vary 'form and mode' —which it does, treating the different sexual episodes with a variety that derives not only from the kind of congress involved or the kind of people participating, but also from the sentiments and literary treatment employed.

One can see this early in the book, when Fanny, still a virgin but living in a brothel, witnesses two sexual encounters. The treatment of the first, between a fat old lady and a Horse-Grenadier, is brisk, comic, spoofing: 'Droll was it to see that clumsy fat figure of hers drop down on the foot of the bed, opposite the closet-door, so that I had a full-front view of all her charms.' The second scene, between an attractive girl and a young Genoese merchant, dusky and handsome, is attentive to features of physical charm and presented in a heightened, romantic, sentimental tone. Limited in language, the writer can employ his skill in varying images and expressions in order to gain requisite variety and hence sustain continuing interest. According to this modest aesthetics of pornography we can work out the appropriate Aristotelian permutations: the plot is episodic and repetitious; the diction—as she goes on to suggest—falls in the mean, tempered by taste, between 'vulgar expressions' and 'mincing metaphors'; 'the forms and modes the situations are susceptible of' afford the basic area of variation; and the effect on the reader, the kinesis, depends on imagination (to realize the scenes) and sensibility (to invigorate the language).

The book actually works close to this literary prescription, using much variation of form and mode. Despite its realism, it is notably figurative, especially in the second letter where Fanny becomes a devotee of the pleasurable life. She becomes the celebrant in a poetic exercise she herself is offered as describing. She lives in an idyllic brothel, to which she is initiated by elaborate, formal sexual rite, and passes 'from a private devotee of pleasure into a public one, to become a more general good'. The brothel is a 'secret institution' and those in it describe themselves humorously as 'the restorers of the golden age and its simplicity of pleasures, before their innocence became so unjustly branded with the names of guilt and shame.' Throughout this section, from the elegant artifice of the initiation rites onward, the style is elevated and courtly, celebrating 'the liberty of nature'. After various episodes involving sharp variations of tone and modes of description, there is a further ceremonial scene, a pastoral bathing

scene, suddenly cut short: 'nor indeed', says Fanny, 'were we long before we finished our trip to Cythera, and unloaded in the old haven;
but, as the circumstances did not admit of much variation, I shall
spare you the description.' She then apologizes

for having, perhaps, too much affected the figurative style; though surely,
it can pass nowhere more allowably than in a subject which is so properly
the province of poetry, nay, is poetry itself, pregnant with every flower of
imagination and loving metaphors, even if the natural expressions, for respect
of fashions and sound, necessarily forbid it.

The reader might sense a touch of desperation here, but Cleland appears
serious about his association between his subject and poetry; and his
pursuit of lyricism—the flowers of imagination and loving metaphors—
seems conscious and purposeful. 'Fanny's' vocabulary is dense, energetic, evocative; and if she is in some of her adventures an innocent
heroine she is quite a learned one—indeed, the language of the book is
a fascinating mixture of realistic vernacular and the heightened and
witty tone of the lightly learned.

In fact it is finally in the maximization of the possibilities of language,
in creating the variations with which the book progresses, that Cleland
shows his powers. Of course he employs graphic physiological detail,
exploiting the kinetic effect of imitating sexual characteristics, sexual
sensations, and the various dispositions of the sexual act, including both
the abnormal and the fanciful. But he also has an elaborate vocabulary
of response and of neo-scientific observation, of kinesis and emotion,
by which erotic sensation and perception can be linked with intellectual, aesthetic, and to a point moral experience. And then there is the
figurative structure he derives from classical learning, scientific speculation, and philosophical discussion, especially in such areas of contemporary debate as about the sublime and the pleasurable.[1] In short,
Cleland consciously and complicatedly exploits, in accordance with
various assumptions and theories about the means by which art can
affect readers, the variations between appropriate involvement and
appropriate distance that can make his fable most effective.

The Memoirs of a Woman of Pleasure is about aesthetics as well as about
sex: this is the basis of its remarkable quality of literary vigour. We
might say that the book is about the synaesthetic process in Fanny, her

[1] Hence the courtroom point that the book offers many interesting first usages
of words.

growing sense of the poetry of sexuality, of the value of vigour and transports; and is also a conscious effort at creating a like sense of intensity, aphrodisiacally conceived, in the reader. For Cleland assumes that poetry and love-making are essentially analogous—involving imaginative variation on a theme, invention allied to energy, sequences of intense sensation. Both are essences or universals in nature —part of a universe seen in terms of its springs of energy and forces of passion. The result is a vigorous energy in the writing, though Cleland's view is an abstract, sophisticated, and witty one. The book isn't of course a Lawrentian hymn to energy and force; it is fairly firmly located in its convention, dependent on a reserve of wit which may derive partly from Cleland's sense of the limitations, and profit, of his enterprise but has also to do with a sceptical temper in the telling. A growing element of qualification runs through the book, and this finally gives it its pornographic as opposed to romance texture; the lyrical-erotic is qualified with a comic self-consciousness.

In many scenes Cleland's forceful use of the tradition of amorous and erotic writing is clear. For instance, Fanny's first love-making is with a youth who is described with romantic attentiveness. There is a long listing of bodily characteristics, highly dependent on romance-writing:

... besides all the perfections of manly beauty which were assembled in his form, he had an air of neatness and gentility, a certain smartness in the carriage and port of his head, that yet more distinguish'd him; his eyes were sprightly and full of meaning; his looks had in them something at once sweet and commanding. His complexion outbloom'd the lovely-colour'd rose, whilst its inimitable tender vivid glow clearly sav'd it from the reproach of wanting life, of [being] raw and dough-like, which is commonly made to those so extremely fair as he was.

This is a detailed, vigorous treatment in the romance tradition, and the sensations aroused in the characters are appropriate: 'to find myself in the arms of that beautious youth was a rapture that my little heart swam in. Past or future was equally out of the question with me. The present was as much as all my powers of life were sufficient to bear the transport of, without fainting.' The emotions of love, which are eventually the refiner of lust and the culmination of pleasure, are not only piously desired but supported with stylistic energy. When Fanny is taught late in the book by an elderly philosophical lover that the pleasures of mind are superior to those of body—'at the same time, that they were so far obnoxious to, or incompatible with each other, that, besides the sweetness in the variety and transition, the one served to exalt and perfect the taste of the other, to a degree that the senses alone can never arrive at'—this is more than pretentious décor. The romantic first lover returns, and this is the culmination of the action. Yet the very fact that this is a kind of philosophical achievement creates an odd modulation in the romantic sensibility.

For the book is about Fanny's efforts not only to achieve the pleasurable sublime but also to define it. Capable of romantic feeling, she is also presented as an analyst of the way in which feeling is promoted. Fanny is the whore as philosopher. This is hardly calculated to make her believable as a character; it means that the author's hand is everywhere apparent. The book is structured on a sophisticated proceeding whereby Fanny is granted a working mind to speculate about her impulses; she speaks of herself as one 'whose natural philosophy all resided in the favourite centre of sense'. She sees herself as analogous to the musician, the painter, the statuary, because she is concerned not just with imitating nature but finding its force and fire, the spirit of its being. She possesses, in fact, a sophisticated version of eighteenth-century pre-romanticism. At one point she describes the male organ as 'the most interesting moving picture in all nature', appreciated only by those who have the real fire of the imagination, the sexual correspondent breeze within. It is preferable to art in being 'nature's unrivalled composition', a sort of sensualist's Aeolian harp. She makes a similar point, about sexuality being nature's art, when she speaks of her general philosophy: she prefers the real pleasures offered by nature to oblique ones, and complains of philosophies which overlook the significance of pleasure and so 'for ever mistake things the most foreign of the nature of pleasure itself'. Fanny's empirical enterprises into the kinetic joys and transports of the sexual act are a 'study' as well; her final aim is both a satisfactory sexual relationship uniting mind and body and a satisfying general theory of pleasure. Hence Cleland can make his novel a pornographic idyll in which realistic appreciation of erotic sensation is linked with a romantic dream of the good life of superaesthesia. The sexual organs being 'the seats of pleasure', the universe of pleasure can be explored not only with titillating variation but according to a principle of development, as Fanny moves through partners who afford considerable social, sexual, and psychological range towards the sexual utopia. But inevitably her observation, her often highly scientific language, her wide range of metaphorical reference, are all touched with an obvious absurdity. The absurdity lies, of course, in the improbable assimilation of the author's mind as speculator into that of his character as agent, and it results in a Boswellian dimension, a kind of comic self-consciousness familiar in an age in which paradox and dichotomy thrive and in which man is both animal and rational being, lecher and philosopher. Some critics have read the book as a piece of mock-science, mock-learning, and mock-romance created really to fill out the spaces between the sexual episodes, an elaborate piece of fakery with a marked discontinuity between the sexual sections which are the book's *real* purport and the other parts which are there to allow these sexual episodes maximum effectiveness. The book is more rounded than that, however; it has behind it the force of a particular cultural style, the style of the rational ideal under pressure, which creates a distinctive comedy of mind throughout the entire work.

Nonetheless, it is founded on a dissonance.[1] To make the book into a unity, Cleland would need to sustain the integrity of Fanny's personality, sustain a continuing psychological as well as sexual interest in the characters, and set the episodes in a significant order of development. To a decided extent, he does do this. The sexual episodes are related to Fanny's personality, and they characterize quite carefully her sexual partners. They tend towards a significant pattern of development; and they anatomize pleasure misused as well as used, show 'barrenness' and 'self-loathing'. There is a steady gradation of erotic content, exploring first the extent of the pleasures, and then the limits. The limits are trespassed, but Fanny regrets this; of course Cleland still depicts such scenes. Hence though the progression serves the obvious purpose of opening up new kinds of sexual situation, it also sustains a thematic development with evaluative overtones; experience is being qualitatively examined, as well as erotically extended. Because of this sense of design, there is a certain rhetorical convincingness about the conclusion, where Vice is sacrificed to Virtue. For Fanny's final love-

---

[1] It is a dissonance I find extremely interesting, since it seems to me to have a lot to do with the spirit of modern intellectual comedy, as well as with our fascinated return to writers who in some ways resemble Cleland or are vastly nastier to man than he is—not so much Swift, who seems finally humane in expectation, as de Sade and some of the intellectual gothicists.

making with Charles, her original lover, is in more than one sense the consummation of all that has happened:

. . . as our joys grew too great for utterance, the organs of our voices, voluptuously intermixing, became organs of the touch . . . and oh what touch! how delicious! . . . how poignantly luscious! . . . And now! now I felt to the heart of me! I felt the prodigious keen edge with which love, presiding over this act, points the pleasure: love! that may be styled as the Attic salt of enjoyment; and indeed, without it, the joy, great as it is, is still a vulgar one, whether in a king or a beggar; for it is, undoubtedly, love alone that refines, ennobles and exalts it.

The passage—with its witty metaphysical intensity, its mixture of the vernacular-exclamatory and the literary—represents the end of a systematic quest. Of course there is the characteristic gap between the aptness of the sexual metaphor applied to speech and the final moral phrases; Cleland hardly finds the language for moral intensity as readily as he does that for sexual intensity. Still, he tries hard: the final passages are well done: 'Thus, at length,' says Fanny, now married, 'I got snug into port,

where, in the bosom of virtue, I gather'd the only uncorrupt sweets: where, looking back on the course of vice I had run, and comparing its infamous blandishments with the infinitely superior joys of innocence, I could not help pitying, even in point of taste, those who, immers'd in gross sensuality, are insensible to the so delicate charms of VIRTUE, than which PLEASURE has not a greater friend, nor VICE a greater enemy.

It has a certain ring of truth, precisely because virtue is transposed into a species of pleasure—not a limitation of it, but the most delicate form in which it can appear. It is what the sexual aristocrats, the persons of taste, prefer, on aesthetic and synaesthetic grounds; it is the fulfilment of the aristocratic stance towards which Fanny has been developing.

3

Yet of course it can't be entirely convincing; and it makes for a comic suspension. For the problems are two. However consistently Fanny is drawn, we cannot but be aware of her unlikely status *vis-à-vis* the author. Her pretensions, when set against what she is and what she does, become ironic. This is not really because Cleland is joking throughout—he seems perfectly interested in questions about how life might be led according to a pleasure-principle, and puts a lot of creative and linguistic energy into the effort. But he faces the inevitable difficulty of the 'serious' pornographic novel, which is that the sexual scenes tend to have an interest in excess of other elements—for the writer as well as the reader. Pastiche occurs; then the very plurality of his tones, his way of exploiting the 'comic'—lower-class, vernacular, a-heroic—areas of literary art that lie outside and beyond romance, as well as his proliferation of varied sexual detail, throw the quest into doubt. Not only is Fanny an unlikely philosopher: the philosophy itself is creatively inconsistent. It is, of course, a point he doesn't miss, and on which Fanny goes on at the end to comment:

You laugh, perhaps, at this tail-piece of morality, extracted from me by the force of truth, resulting from compar'd experiences: you think it, no doubt, out of place, out of character; probably too you may look on it as the paltry finesse of one who seeks to mask a devotee to Vice under a rag of a veil, impudently smuggled from the shrine of Virtue. . . . But . . . such a supposition is more injurious to Virtue than to me: since, consistently with candour and good-nature, it can have no foundation but in the falsest of fears, that its passages cannot stand in comparison with those of Vice; but let truth dare to hold it up in its most alluring light: then mark, how spurious, how low of taste, how comparatively inferior its joys are to those which Virtue gives sanction to, and whose sentiments are not above making a sauce for the senses, but a sauce of the highest relish. . . .

This is in its way quite a rhetorical triumph, an effective and witty conclusion to the persuasive dimension of the novel, that dimension which organizes and theorizes about the significance of what has been given it and the reasons why it has been given. But of course it won't quite do. It won't do because it can only be an intellectual delight, a witty resolution, like some of Donne's. It won't do, then, because of the ends-and-means split which invests the whole tactic of the book, making it an extreme case of the problem that exists with many novels; experience is instant and local, and interpretation structural and general, and given what experience *is* in a pornographic novel like this the mind cannot place and shape it. With the kind of relationship that exists between the author and his narrator-agent, a relationship in which she is both immersed performer and emotional philosopher, Cleland's own kinetic success as author comes over most strongly in passages quite different from the ones where Fanny asserts *her* own emotional success to come. In his pre-romantic and pre-Paterian day, Cleland has no language of the romantic senses that would allow him to give an immersed, psychologically convincing status to Fanny's final position, even if he wanted to. Inevitably, then, it is the sexual episodes that dominate the book: it is in the nature of things for Cleland that he cannot give the same kinetic force to the representations of the 'tasteful' and selective aspects of sexual pleasure as he can to the more inflammatory passages where the descriptions of sexual organs, sexual acts, and observed sexual ecstasies come powerfully off the page. What in fact he does is to offer us a pretty pure case of a recurrent and well-recognized crux in eighteenth-century fiction, that of relating the power that resides in individual episodes to the generic and emotional unity of the work as a whole.

Of course what Cleland does do—and it is this that makes the book a modest *tour de force*—is to *recognize* the dissonance, and write a comic sexual romance in which it is wittily alive. The organic, kinetic dream of the book, which Cleland seeks in language and Fanny in the ultimate marital fornication, is made artificial and mechanical; it fulfils, in effect, the recipe of Bergsonian comedy. Cleland's treatment of the book is derived from a steady and consecutive fascination with emotional and imaginative intensity, from a lyric impulse. But he puts that activity into the context of a sophisticated eighteenth-century aesthetic debate about the way which both art and nature can move us. The mixture of lyrical and intellectual becomes a complex rhetorical strategy; and it produces an imbalance with profitable comic dividends. A vigorous book both intellectually and emotionally, it plays happily along the borderline where the worlds of mind and body meet. It is in fact a very Cartesian comedy; and today, when the species has returned with some force in the work of a novelist like Samuel Beckett, we can see something staple about it. It sets up possibilities in the new form of the novel, an area of relationship between romance and comedy, which later writers were to come back to. The result is as lively a disposition of those aspects of aesthetics and creative feeling which produce the pornographic mode as one could wish to find. 'Artless' is the last thing one can call it. It lives vigorously among the forms and mental and aesthetic sets that compose the eighteenth-century novel, and creates its own distinct possibilities; and for that, minor *tour de force* as it is, it deserves a solid place in fictional history.

IV

Persuasions:
Moral Comedy in *Emma* and *Persuasion*

I

'Jane Austen', said that great expert in the sophisticated arts of the novel, Henry James, in one of the few large misjudgements we can lay at his door, 'was instinctive and charming. . . . For signal examples of what composition, distribution, arrangement can do, of how they intensify the life of a work of art, we have to go elsewhere.' We do not, of course: modern criticism has shown us what a conscious artist Jane Austen was, as a formal designer and a manager of the sophisticated arts of tone. What makes James's judgement of Jane Austen so surprising, though, is not that it was made but that it was James who made it—James who seems so exactly in the same tradition, and whose novel of social comedy read through moral irony appears, especially in his early work, so like hers. *Washington Square*, for example, seems inconceivable without Jane Austen—not simply because of its drawing-room milieu, and its concern with emotional impoverishment, but because it is an epic of irony to be read with balance only by an iron-ically disposed mind. Irony is its subject-matter, Sloper's main weapon in and against a provincial American world; irony is the basis of its structure; irony is the tone of the telling. Admittedly, in James's case it is a long irony, filtered through geographical and historical distance; in Jane Austen the distance is or seems to be from one end of the drawing room to the other. And in James irony frequently adminis-ters emotional loss, while in Jane Austen it frequently elicits emotional and moral growth; still, both are novelists active in the moral sphere. But what James seems to have felt was that Jane Austen was not active

in the aesthetic sphere too; as her characters lack James's form of
consciousness, the search for aesthetic validation, the compositional
sense of vision, so she lacked it too. 'Why shouldn't it be argued
against her that where her testimony complacently ends, the pressure
of our appetite presumes exactly to begin?' he asks; it is a complaint
about both social and aesthetic provincialism, about the kind of distance an artist should have from his society. Jane Austen is clearly an
artist who depends on the guarantee of society to bring her fictional
world into being. James was that too (he once reminded us that the
world is no illusion and 'we can neither forget it nor deny it nor dispense with it') but that much more uneasily. 'The moral is', he said,
writing of Hawthorne, 'that the flower of art blooms only where the
soil is deep, that it needs a complex social machinery to set a writer in
motion.' But we know that his society was something both carefully
and consciously chosen in life, and very formally made in art. In that
sense 'composition, distribution, arrangement' were thrusting forces
against any facile taking of society as simply 'given'. But what James
seems to miss, what throws his judgement off, is that this was surely
true of Jane Austen as well.[1]

   The presumption that Jane Austen observed rather than composed
is in part a judgement about a kind of novel, the novel of realism.
What I want to propose for this essay is that her fiction is best considered
as one in which nothing is given—that, as a conscious artist, her society,
her moral world, her compositional form are made, and made as in all
good novels for the purpose of persuading us into a total, coherent
impression in which arrangement and authorial management are of the
essence. In a sense I am saying something I believe to be true of all
interesting novels; something that, because we have become much
disposed towards symbolist and aesthetic notions of fictional creation,

---

[1] Richard Poirier's comparison of Mark Twain and Jane Austen in *A World
Elsewhere: The Place of Style in American Literature* (New York, 1966; London,
1967) valuably extends this point. Distinguishing between fictions which tolerate
an environment already credited by history and society, and those which create
imagined worlds elsewhere, he notes that the structure of Mark Twain's novels—
and also Henry James's—'are symptoms of some larger distrust of social structures
themselves.' Thus *Emma* restores 'to social intercourse the naturalness temporarily
lost through artifice', while *Huckleberry Finn* presumes that 'what is natural for
society is nothing but artifice, games, and disguise'. The problem for criticism of
fiction, it might be added, is to preserve a discourse capacious enough for the
discussion of both kinds of fiction; this is part of the theme of the present essay.

we are apt to forget. For not only are they verbal constructs, so that the society they create and body out, the shape they make, must be a fiction, a fleshing out of a world whose existence and coherence is made by and of which we are persuaded by the novelist alone, but their creation is self-evidently 'compositional'. Because nearly all novels are explorations of persons in possible milieux living out relationships that are probable to experience and guided by shared norms and expectations, social and psychological laws and customs, they create society: the making of a novel is the making of a world—a persistently developing, changing world—in language and the persuasion of the reader into the practices and principles by which it supports itself and remains coherent. Our means of engagement with that world is through a running act of persuasion which may be stabilized as a 'tone', a rhetorical wholeness or narrative posture devoted not only to convincing us that there is here a whole world operational and worth attention but that it is assessable and comprehensible only if a certain attitude is taken to it. The society of a novel emerges coherently from a developing action which brings it into existence; it is not there before the novel begins, though by the time we put the book down the effect of verisimilitude may be such that we feel it has always been there. What *is* there before the novel begins is the social character of all our experience and discourse, the common web of language which means that the reader does share a sense of the probable and the coherent, a knowledge of the likely forms of human conduct, of moral dilemmas, of the form and imperative of social institutions, codes, roles, and duties. There are novels which appeal to the socially normative or comprehensible more than others; novels of manners rather than romances or existential novels or works of high aesthetic composition. But in all novels the task of creation and composition involves in some sense the organization of society, the creation of a social and moral life; and the task of criticism is surely to recognize this as an essential act of endeavour as severe and demanding as any other. This is generally necessary for the reading of fiction, but in Jane Austen's case it is especially necessary, for it is here that she shows herself to be of very high artistry, an exemplary performer in the possibilities of the novel.

If it is true that Jane Austen is a very conscious novelist, a writer of great formal expertise, then we are concerned with a way of using and embodying that expertise not to make it formally dominant, a radiating aesthetic power, but rather—as in most novels, though with a higher and finer sureness—as a making and managing instrument subtly employed to persuade us into seeing the 'reality' of certain people and events and making sense of them, into judging their own capacity for dealing with their experience and testing our own as readers. The social world of Jane Austen's novels is not only very probable but very onerous: for those who live in the novels, for those who read them. Society—narrow in social spread, formal, conventional—is the source of expectations and the place of fulfilments: a testing ground for sense and emotion, a living centre of experience. She is not then a novelist who, in the modernist sense, structures her works for form so that the prime source of coherence is the aesthetic object as such; her form is the derivative of an elaborate rhetorical compendium, whose purpose is to elicit from a structure of carefully managed episodes and a pattern of social and emotional relationships the maximum sense of what the most sceptical mind can find of living value. But this means that society in her novels is the product of a very complex creative achievement, possessing in each book its own occasions, and constituting a made life for particular people presented to us in that particular compositional enterprise. As with Fielding, the area of Jane Austen's formal self-consciousness is managed through the aesthetics of a comic realism, moral as well as social in emphasis. Her language is very little figurative, or symbolic, or psychological; it takes society into consciousness, and consciousness into society, letting the characters distil virtue out of a very possible and recognizable world. To account for the structure of her works, then, we have to look at the society she makes: or rather the societies— for it is within choices that taken conventionally or literally can prove extraordinarily deceptive that she establishes both the possibilities for growth in her characters and order in her fictions. We might indeed propose that in most of her novels the central figures, those central heroes and heroines, have first to experience society as false, a mockery or masquerade, before they go on to realize and live out a real one. It is to that particular realization that the thrust of each of her books is directed: to a self-awareness and awareness of others in the central characters which is for them a form of rediscovery and for us a re-discovery of form.

And we must also say that if society is discovered in her novels it is discovered in each one in a different way, in a different set of compositional arrangements, social and moral meanings, postures of relationship between writer and reader. Though there persist certain presumptions we think of as Austen-like, no one society in her novels, false or true, is ever quite like that in another. Each is the society of these words made for this occasion, made and felt differently, so that even the norms and standards, the prime moral terminology, come out quite other from book to book. The social geography is a freshly made landscape; and it serves fresh emotional ends. To suggest the difference of compositional practice I want to take two of her books, *Emma* (1816) and *Persuasion* (1818), where the differences are very visible. 'I am going to take a heroine whom no-one but myself will much like,' she said of *Emma*; she said of Anne Elliot, the heroine of *Persuasion*, that she was almost too good for her. This implies two very different tasks; in *Emma* she must shape and order to forestall the moral objection she proposes, embodying her audience, might be held against the heroine; in *Persuasion*, there is little to amend—which is why the book has been found uncomplex and disappointing—but much to show about the consequences of virtue. The result is two very different economies; new dispositions of design, new relations of author to characters, and, indeed, new social and moral worlds to be made. It is at those two forms of making, at the kinds of making they are, that I want here to look, in the belief that her art is precisely an art of composition, distribution, and arrangement, of experience intensified by form and perspective, of, in fact, a central enterprise in fictional creativity; and that one main business of criticism is to find the angle of approach to it.

2

What Jane Austen must do both in *Emma* and *Persuasion*, as in any serious novel of social and moral realism, is to create and complexly to connect a society and a moral life. In each novel, the social world is carefully and substantially given, a world elaborate in detail if narrow in population and class, so that we can feel its weighty ecology. The action of *Emma* takes place in Highbury, 'a large and prosperous village, almost amounting to a town', sixteen miles from London, at a time around the time of writing (i.e. 1814–15). The landscape of Highbury is a landscape of property; its main landmarks are Hartfield, the home of the Woodhouses, 'the first in consequence in Highbury'; Randalls, the home of Mr. Weston, 'a little estate'; Donwell Abbey, 'in the parish adjoining, the seat of Mr. Knightley.' Highbury, despite the glimpsed presence of London, is a more or less self-contained social unit; and it contains nearly all the action. Its upper-middle-class citizens—landowners with tenant farmers, persons of private income— form a small society held together by stable links of kinship and common social duty. It is from their level that we see in this novel. There are persons of higher rank (the Churchills, the great Yorkshire family), but we feel them to be high; there are characters clearly 'below' the social balance of the book (the tenant farmer Robert Martin, the former Miss Taylor, Mrs. Goddard, Miss Bates); and then there are the socially indeterminate, who in fact precipitate much of the action (Miss Harriet Smith, illegitimate, of obscure origins; Frank Churchill, split between families; Jane Fairfax). But even these people, coming from outside and existing in uncertain relationship to the stable life at the centre, are related to it by credentials and connectives; nearly all the characters in the book exist in some kind of established relationship to the heroine or her immediate friends. The result is a form antithetical, say, to the picaresque structure; a world founded in a homogeneous society, taking its standards essentially from within itself and what works best for its own relationships, emotional needs, and duties, and maintaining, throughout, certain determining social presumptions, above all about rank. The Highbury equals are capable of intimacy; but rank governs the relationship to the Woodhouses (the vicar is not close, the schoolmistress is received, the poor are visited), and there are places to be known and kept in. The constraints of a fixed society are firmly felt, and in this book Jane Austen doesn't—as she does in *Persuasion*— measure the values beyond the milieu in which they are possible and functionally significant. There is, indeed, no need to; for in this rural, hierarchical society, with its ascribed roles and assents, she finds a context in which the values can be put to the most extensive test.

The society that generates and supports the moral action then is a local, limited, and self-consistent world. It has its own operative values and occasions, provincial and unpretentious. People meet over dinner or in Ford's shop; encounters occur by formal arrangement; there are few accidental meetings, and those few are of high significance (Harriet meeting Robert Martin in the shop). People stand large, families stand whole. Our own sense of propriety is demanded and engaged; so when Jane Fairfax and Frank Churchill are accidentally left alone with the sleeping Miss Bates, only we as readers are capable of observing the 'breach'. And the degree of social stability, the preciseness of social expectations, the limitations on extreme or eccentric behaviour, reinforce and make significant the moral order. They involve a high degree of consensus, a high demand on maturity and responsibility, provide a closed, rounded world in which, once a level of adequate living has been acquired, it can be reinforced by society—a society in which the future will seem reasonably like the present (as it does not in *Persuasion*). But this society also throws up a wide range of values; from these the tensions of the novel arise. The characters think about similar things; they think differently about them. They consider the importance of rank, the relative value of taste, courtesy, honour, the weight owed to reason or emotion in conduct. Though they commonly frown on frivolity and value goodwill, they weight their expectations differently; and out of this fact arises much of the management, the persuasive register, of the story. For these variations are tested in action, in incidents small or considerable, in turns of thought or general acts of feeling; and as these occur we perceive in the book an alternative scale of superior and inferior people, a moral hierarchy superseding the social. The morally inferior tend in fact to be socially high (a classic but still dramatic literary effect): Emma herself in the opening sections is so, Frank Churchill as well, while by contrast the Martins and Coles elevate themselves by their actions. And as the sequence of actions extends certain values acquire weight, especially values having to do with care and respect for others, the decent discharge of one's duties, the scrupulous improvement of oneself. Frivolity diminishes, but accomplishments are meritorious; they evidence self-discipline, self-enlargement, and they please others. A friendly social disposition is valued, within limits (Emma's criticism of Jane Fairfax's reserve comes to tell more against Emma herself than Jane); goodwill and contented temper matter, but can lead to easygoingness (Mr. Weston) or false indulgence (Emma herself). To be 'open, straightforward and well judging', like Martin, is important, though not as important as the valuable side of Knightley's more closed, critical temper. Birth weighs, but only when supported by manners and responsibility.

These values arise naturally within this particular world, but they are lived out actively in it and they also preside over it, to the point where by virtue of their selectiveness and their humanity they become a vigorous, liveable standard. In this sense the book is an education, the education of Emma, an education in judgement and right awareness, and also an education in emotions. In both forms of this education Mr.

Knightley is a central figure, and pre-eminent in the story is the way in which he shifts from being influential on the first count to being a probable lover and husband for Emma. As for the moral education, it is a careful matter of adjusted weights and stresses ('No, Emma; your amiable young man can be amiable only in French, not English,' says Mr. Knightley of Churchill. 'He may be very "aimable", have very good manners, and be very agreeable; but he can have no English delicacy towards the feelings of other people . . .'). In Emma's own case, it means a careful balancing of her virtues and her propensities. The range of variation is narrow, but it is also fine; and the moral life is in the front of the characters' minds throughout. It is linked with class (thus the description of the estate at Donwell Abbey belonging to a family of 'such true gentility, untainted in blood *and understanding*'), but understanding is clearly prior to blood, and a notion of gentility begins to take on ideal shape. This is a primary part of the rhetorical texture of the book, and is established in the opening sentences. Emma's situation is socially a happy one:

Emma Woodhouse, handsome, clever, and rich, with a comfortable home and a happy disposition, seemed to unite some of the best blessings of existence; and had lived nearly twenty-one years in the world with little to distress or vex her.

But the diction hints that the best blessings of existence only *seem* to be hers, that, moreover, she has been *too* little vexed or, in short, over-indulged; and the hints are soon converted into an explicit moral observation from the narrator: 'The real evils, indeed, of Emma's situation were the power of having rather too much of her own way, and a disposition to think a little too well of herself.' More instances of the fact that social blessings are not always moral ones are shortly adduced by tone and instance—so the history of Mr. Weston's previous marriage, one into a family of higher rank which 'did not produce much happiness': 'Mrs. Weston ought to have found more in it, for she had a husband whose warm heart and sweet temper made him think everything due to her in return for the great goodness of being in love with him; but though she had one sort of spirit, she had not the best.' And through many such instances, not simply from the surroundings of the story but from the centre of it, there emerges a very detailed and considered moral scale—a scale of fine distinctions based, though, very particularly on what is reasonable, desirable, and most richly liveable in a social life whose basic unit is the family, whose basic relationship marriage, and on what makes for good and open dealing between people and makes them both generous in their emotional contact and just and delicate in their public actions.

All Jane Austen's novels are really domestic novels, novels with marriage at the centre—not only of the story but of the household and the society. They usually deal with marriage as a disturbance in the settled world, a prime moment of creating effective life; and most of the effort of design, the management of the commentary or moral tenor, the handling of episode and tone, is devoted to defining the conditions, social and emotional, of the one good marriage which usually contrasts with all others in the book, and certainly dominates it. Marriage is a social pact and must answer to the public dimension; it is also a definition of self, a realization of inner knowledge, a metaphorical fulfilment of being. In all her books the presumption is that people make the marriages they deserve. Most do not deserve well; and much of the action is concerned with the deservings. Thus the pursuit of marriage is the pursuit of society and both are the pursuit of a precise moral discourse. But the society, the marriage, and the discourse all differ from book to book. In the case of *Emma* the plot turns on the question of who Emma will marry; the development is that of an imperfect heroine who is brought towards all three of these things. It is a plot, then, about a girl of many fine qualities and much force and charm, but of certain considerable errors deriving from the misuse of her own powers, who creates a false society, a set of false relationships; but she realizes her errors, perceives that these have led her to false judgements, harm to people in her circle, and misused emotions, and, in the course of her repentance, finds both emotional enlargement and a more accurate view of the world in and through the man she chooses finally to marry. The telling starts with Emma at the height of her errors and concludes when she seems about to amend them, an emendation we have been led to hope, partly because of the intimacy we have acquired with her, will not be excessive.

The action is told chronologically and falls into three fairly clear phases, like an Aristotelian beginning, middle, and end. In the first, Emma is the detached agent in someone else's destiny, attempting to intervene in Harriet Smith's life by marrying her to Mr. Elton, and by chapters 16 and 17, where we see Emma's regrets, we have the book's moral direction: Mr. Knightley's judgements now seem better than

Emma's, and we can see those faults, especially of snobbery and whimsy, which make her misread situations. Being illegitimate, Harriet is an excellent test of the accuracy of social and moral judgements, and two totally different sets of judgements can and do accrue around her, with each of the parties—Emma and Mr. Knightley—potentially appearing snobbish. To Emma, Harriet has the virtues—beauty and good nature—which commend a woman to men; to Mr. Knightley, marriage needs more: 'Men of sense, whatever you may choose to say, do not want silly wives.' Eventually it is Knightley's judgement of Elton's intentions that proves accurate, and his criticism of Emma morally apt: 'If you were as much guided by nature in your estimate of men and women, and as little under the power of fancy and whim in your dealings with them as you are where these children are concerned, we might always think alike.' The situation in turn generates the comedy of the scenes founded on the ambiguity of Mr. Elton's supposed wooing of Harriet, and the ensuing irony when Mr. John Knightley points out to Emma that Elton's interest is in her:

She walked on, amusing herself in the consideration of the blunders which often arise from a partial knowledge of circumstances, of the mistakes which people of high pretensions to judgement are for ever falling into. . . .

It is here that her ignorance acquires the stature of a moral fault. The 'middle' of the novel is devoted to Emma's mistakes about the characters of Frank Churchill and Jane Fairfax. Though the circumstances are more complicated Emma makes similar pre-judgements; but here her own destiny is involved, she is drawn into a false style and set of social habits, and we see her capable of falsifying and misusing herself. The 'ending' is consequential on Emma's crucial discovery that she is in love. The resolution here is delayed until the moral lessons are laid bare, and involves Emma affected, committed, and pressed into realization of her follies; it involves her growth and self-discovery, which is a discovery of true style in relationship. With understanding comes marriage, a right resolution to the plot in that it distils the significance of emotional and moral understanding, and managed with extraordinary compositional pacing, elegantly enforcing the weights and meanings of the book.

It is at this point that the tactical indirection of the novel becomes clear. The most complex device is that of seeing action through the eyes of a character of whom that action is implicitly critical; this involves a very precise management of the criticism, partly through the pedagogic role of Mr. Knightley, though he is not incapable of error, and partly through the values that emerge when we have taken away the irony from the treatment of events seen through Emma's eyes. And Emma is not always in error; she is indeed right on nearly all the occasions where she is not given to the faults I have mentioned of whimsy, snobbery, or pre-judgement. This in turn means inventing many scenes devoted to presenting her in a good light. The result is *Tom Jones*-like; we look towards Emma coming to grief and trust that it will be the grief that leads to blessings, which is what happens. The artistic problem is to make us care for her in such a way that we wish her well without subduing our feeling about her faults; this is a classic comic form. And the novel is a comedy, a comedy of manners, a comedy of morals. Its modes are broad, but they are shapely. There is straightforward humorous treatment; so Mr. Woodhouse and Miss Bates are comic 'characters', though of course their humours actively fit the moral line of the book: Mr. Woodhouse's indulgence is an apt cause of Emma's nature, and Miss Bates's absurdities make her a test of Emma's critical responses. There is much tactical comedy, as in the early scenes, where Emma, Harriet, and Mr. Elton, playing at picture-making and with riddles, lead the reader on towards a sense of operative irony as he sees that there is an explanation quite other than Emma's for Mr. Elton's actions. And that irony dominates the novel. Concerned, almost always, with the difference between what a character sees and comes to judgement about and other potential readings of the incident, it is conveyed by a variety of methods, largely arising from the deft use of authorial omniscience. One instance is the change in point of view which lets us, at the beginning of chapter 20, see Jane Fairfax independently of Emma's judging eye. It tells us not that Emma is wrong, but that she might be; and it characteristically works in favour of empiricism, of possible variety, of a more complex view than that yielded up by Emma's eye. Events, as episode after episode teaches us, will bear at least two interpretations; the tension between events as they seem and events as they might be gives the ironic dynamic of the novel.

The novel completes this ironic shape and fulfils it, closing on a final ironic stasis. One of Emma's most obvious follies has been her external view of persons, her willingness to interfere in others' lives without involving herself. Marriages are to be made only for others.

In being forced into feelings of love, she is released and opened out; this is the final testimony of her development. She concludes the book by taking on the final commitment of the Austen universe, marriage; she has opened out into tenderness of heart, a tenderness without weakness or sentimentality. If there are other follies to recover from, this will come; it is a union of 'perfect happiness'; the shape of the book is complete. It began by delineating various contesting moral viewpoints; it ends by clarification and wholeness. We have learned our way through the experience by the perception of Emma's faults, and we finally accept their fundamental significance. Emma's aloof relation to others, her willingness to treat them as counters, her over-practical view of good qualities, her snobbish self-enclosure, are betrayals of human possibility:

With insufferable vanity she had believed herself in the secret of everybody's feelings; with unpardonable arrogance proposed to arrange everybody's destiny. She was proved to have been universally mistaken; and she had not quite done nothing—for she had done mischief. She had brought evil on Harriet, on herself and, she too much feared, on Mr. Knightley. . . .

It is here that the social and moral worlds take on their potency; these are violations of an entire worthwhile universe. And the book's method is to draw on our moral stringency and humane responses to the point where this insight is essential and recantation necessary. The agents of retribution are Knightley and Jane Austen herself, and they are commonly, in the end, genial: the lesson Emma learns is an intensification of her own best self, and this is a recovery of society, leading to the capacity to commit herself in life, love, and marriage. What, on the way to that point of achievement, has been rendered for us are the vivid consequences of falsity within those values—snobbery, social theatricality and over-elegance, goodness seen as simply a thoroughly *marriageable* trait—which are sometimes thought to be the prevailing values of the author herself. We have, then, been persuaded progressively, by an intensive process of rendering and illustration in an expansive formal order, managed through a skilled employment of the disposable means of the story, towards a final effect—one that substantiates and fills out the full human being as a fine, emotionally rich, morally serious, totally responsible creature, in a world where every human action has come to seem a crucial and committing act of self-definition.

3

Two years after the publication of *Emma*, Jane Austen's last full-length novel, *Persuasion*, appeared posthumously; it remains still a book of very mixed reputation. It is usually read as a novel about an intelligent, mature young woman, Anne Elliot, who succumbs to bad advice or persuasion about marriage and then learns better, achieving, after various complications have been cleared away, the conventional benison of a good Austen marriage. But because the action begins with Anne's adult maturity, and because her virtue is constancy rather than change, it is often thought a book without development or tensions, a book in which 'nothing happens'.[1] Anne does not, like Emma, have to learn her way to amoral society, or even find her way to love; she does not change internally or discover herself in any fresh way, experiences no great emotional or moral revelation, or even suffer or enjoy a great change of her external fortune. *Persuasion* is also sometimes said to be a less genial, more savage book than the others; and it has been claimed that Jane Austen attempts, by dealing with scenes more dramatic and violent than usual (above all the scene at Lyme and Mrs. Smith's story), to pass beyond her effective range. Moreover, two of the book's apparently central episodes—Anne's first falling in love, and her 'persuasion' by Lady Russell—are not made part of the 'discriminated occasion' of the telling, but are retrospectively reported, and placed prior to the narrative time of the novel. And so, if we take for our measure of the value of a novel the degree to which characters alter and develop, encounter adventure, startling choice, or fresh inner experience, or if we regard life rendered and made vivid as the test of a novel's interest, we may well have qualms about *Persuasion*. What does happen? An engagement and a love-relationship is broken, by outside interference, and is finally renewed,

[1] Andor Gomme strongly argues this case in 'On Not Being Persuaded', *Essays in Criticism*, XVI, 2 (April 1966), 170–84, urging that the book's development is largely mechanical or haphazard; 'character is frozen on each appearance, and human relations [are] either perfectly predictable or quite arbitrary'; the whole action takes place under conditions of nearly complete moral stasis; and of the characters only Captain Wentworth—who is seen externally and obliquely, from Anne's limited point of view—is more than momentarily affected by what he sees and learns, and actually changes significantly. There is a directly antithetical account—the most sensitive and deep reading of the creative structure of the book I know—by R. S. Crane, '*Persuasion*' in his *The Idea of the Humanities and Other Essays Critical and Historical* (Chicago, 1966), II. 283–302.

by luck. A relatively mature heroine grows—by contrast to Emma—
only a few faint gradations in maturity; but mainly she suffers in
circumstances that could apparently be resolved at almost any point
in the action. She is deprived of the family home, but the fact is not of
importance to her. She witnesses a violent incident, but maintains
equanimity. She is attracted to a dishonest man, but her caution is
considerable and the danger conveniently interrupted. If divisions,
misfortunes, and accidents occur, Anne can endure; if mistaken relationships take place, Anne is too sensible to engage in long-term follies.
Jane Austen's description of Anne as a heroine almost too good for her
suggests why the book can seem thin; there are few grounds for positive conflict, and this can make the action seem a collection of chance
incidents and mechanical confusions finally put neatly right by the
author. At the level of rendering, of sustaining conflict, of moral poise,
the book can, by the standards Jane Austen herself sets for us in novels
like *Emma*, be found too abstract, too stoical, or too savage to be a
well-composed whole.

My proposal is that it is precisely that, but on terms other than those
set by her other novels. One way of saying this is that the making of the
social and moral worlds of this book is a very different act of persuasion.
Like any new book by any writer, it is a set of new tasks, a new world
contingent on the possibilities arising from the decision to explore
a particular sort of experience by particular means, such decisions
presumably being faced fairly early in the creative process and affecting
what has to be undertaken. A writer may construct and conventionalize
the world according to his own cast of consciousness, and that gives
us an *œuvre*; but he will do this too in particular ways on the separate
occasions of each novel and so encounter new problems and engage
in new activities, problems and activities which are the very centre of
the task of undertaking to write fiction at all. The meaning of a scene
lies in the writer's interest in the scene as well as what he elicits from it;
criticism, in looking at what he elicits, normally deals with the persuasion that shapes events, rather than the way the felt experience
shapes the persuasion. In the case of *Persuasion*, critical experience of
earlier novels may actually mislead us. For example, Lionel Trilling,
in the course of some delicate observations on Jane Austen's novels,
remarks, rather as Poirier does, on the way that natural emotion and
sincerity are directed into society, and says: 'With what the great
houses represent the heroines of the novels are, or become, wholly

in accord.'¹ But in the case of *Persuasion* this is not the emotional outcome; the book turns on a relationship between a girl whose ties with her aristocratic family are critical and a man whose profession is dependent on chance and luck, and moves its weight towards the value of the latter.

It has also often been suggested that the inner life, the primary emotional action, of Jane Austen's novels is the discovery of love; this book turns on love already felt, and it therefore presumably lets the author explore matters other than love. But what matters, and on what basis of relevance? Certainly, as before, she is devoted to the question of marriage and aims to persuade us that it is in various terms the ideal reward for two people whose maturity, whose capacity to act and value, has been shown to us at length and, in this case, over an extended period of time. As before, marriage is both an affectionate relationship involving the moral regard of each partner for the other, a recognition of some difference in function and sensibility between male and female, and a form of stewardship, involving the tending of a household or estate. Usually the view is developed by distinguishing the heroine from others who fail in appropriate maturity or moral balance, or else by showing her growing towards maturity through events which reveal relative success or failure, and the events of the novel seem to be chosen and explored with these ends in view. But in this novel the events seem to follow a different line. For one thing, there appears to be an emphasis on the emotional value of delaying the fulfilment of love to the point at which it can be most maturely felt, when the characters are 'more equal to act, more justified in acting', with the benefit of contrast with less satisfactory experiences; but for another the main processes of discovery in the novel seem to have little directly to do with love, rather with the meaning and the moral and social significance of experiences of other kinds.

Something of this difference of weight can be seen as soon as we attempt to describe the action of the novel. A young sea captain, Wentworth, who has no ship and no fortune, and a girl of nineteen, Anne Elliot, of patrician family which has little fortune either, fall in love and wish to get engaged. Anne is dissuaded by her father, a man vain and self-conscious about his class, on the grounds that the marriage is degrading; and more influentially by a friend of the family and mother-substitute, Lady Russell, on the grounds that Anne's suitor's expecta-

¹ Lionel Trilling, *Sincerity and Authenticity* (London and Cambridge, Mass., 1972).

tions are based primarily on his confidence in the future, which she thinks excessive. Wentworth departs; Anne remains at home for eight years, somewhat regretting her prudence in being persuaded, and fading in looks. The family fortunes deteriorate; Anne's sensible suggestions about retrenchment are ignored. After eight years—the point at which the 'narrative present' of the telling starts—the suitor returns at the moment when the family must let the house and estate to an admiral become wealthy from his profession, though he is without inherited social rank. Wentworth's confidence has been justified, his luck good; he is now a Navy captain, and rich. He and Anne move together through a society linked by family connections and the letting of the house; they meet occasionally, though without seeking this. Each has retained his love, though neither knows the other has. Wentworth must rediscover his love, and so must the reader, for we see from Anne's point of view. The two become more and more divided. Anne is growing away from her own family, because of their extravagance in poverty. Wentworth is drawn towards another woman who is of strong will; Anne is drawn towards another man who is of the family and can solve its problems. But circumstances allow Anne and Wentworth to discover they are still in love; and the action concludes with their re-engagement and marriage and Anne's effective severance from her family bonds.

Now if this is the primary story as Jane Austen seems to have conceived it, it contains a good deal of matter attended to to such an extent that it seems beyond a simple complication of the love story, and it is matter unlike that in the other novels. One central feature is Anne's movement away from her family. Andrew Wright has said that the book is marked by a faith in society, that the measure of a person is not isolation but integration, that Jane Austen is untouched by any awareness of radical social transformation.[1] But that does not seem true of this novel. Socially and morally there are embodied in the novel two different groupings or classes of people, and two different codes; in the course of it, as Anne moves emotionally towards her mature love for Wentworth, she moves towards those with whom he is associated and away from association with her own family. At the same time she moves from an attachment to a certain kind of prudence and caution towards an appreciation of values associated, as I have said, with luck, self-confidence, and new forms of stewardship. The landowning

[1] Andrew Wright, introduction to *Persuasion* (Riverside ed., Boston, 1965).

virtues are not to be had here among the class that should embody them —among the Elliots themselves. They are not, directly, to be had among the second main group in the novel, the seafarers who take on Kellynch, the captains with their luck and pluck. But underlying the story there is a comprehension of a quiet social supersession taking place, indeed what in the fashionable vocabulary we might like to think of as a 'revolutionary' situation. And it is Anne who, in accommodating the new complex of values raised by that situation—the pressure of new values, new social needs—brings the action into focus at the proper point of vision. In short, Jane Austen again seeks to persuade us that the moral life and the life of the classes are intimately connected, but in a way that she has not so presented the matter before. For she is interested in the ways in which the co-existence of two carefully defined social groupings—the world of the inherited aristocracy, the world of the seafarers—extends our notion of what the moral life is, and sets up, in society, contrasting areas of value. In order to engage interest in this and to make these connections urgent, she has used certain new methods of deploying her material—to the extent, indeed, of shifting her entire scope. She creates, as she always does, a very full social world with its elaborate conventions and manners, a world whose norms we are led into with elaborate caution, through ironical tones of narrative voice and overt statements and an implicit recognition of the constituted barriers. But these ironies and conventions—always ordered somewhat differently from book to book—here have numerous fresh intonations.

These are especially evident in the larger blocks of presentation, the structural elements of the novel, which makes them difficult to judge and weigh. For instance, Jane Austen chooses to show us several representatives of each of the two groupings I have mentioned, doing this, by comment and less direct methods of presentation, in such a way as to make them significant *as* groupings. For this reason there is a strong case for supposing that these differences have a more crucial function than simply to provide a division of background and values between the lovers, separating them at first but being at last overcome. It is not just that Wentworth is insufficiently appreciative of the merits of caution, prudence, and duty in a girl of nineteen, or that Anne thinks too little of Wentworth's confidence in his future to take the risk of marriage. These are themselves important reasons for the delay on which the book turns. But the pattern is more elaborate; we are persuaded to see that there is a significant set of social and moral contrasts, of different types of social relationship, to be found by contemplating these groupings. The one we see first is that of the Elliot family, aristocratic, landowning, ancient, respectable, but now in different ways inclined to vanity, extravagance, social irresponsibility. The other group, composed around Admiral Croft, who becomes the tenant of Kellynch, consists of a number of high-ranking sailors, their wives and friends, who are not, in Sir Walter Elliot's strict use of the term, gentlemen. They are presented as a variously intelligent group of people, to a point cultured, who have risen rapidly in society as a result of having served and defended it; their wealth comes from capturing sea prizes, especially in battles with the French. The groups are connected through the Musgroves and Hayters and also through the renting of Kellynch itself. Between them certain effective distinctions are made by the author—for example when Mrs. Clay, flattering Sir Walter, comments on the value of not having a profession, and Sir Walter makes his double complaint against the seafarers:

' The profession has its utility, but I should be sorry to see any friend of mine belonging to it . . . it is in two points offensive to me. . . . First, as being the means of bringing persons of obscure birth into undue distinction, and raising men to honours which their fathers and grandfathers never dreamt of; and secondly, as it cuts up a man's youth and vigour most horribly. . . .'

The sailors are a force of change in society, as Sir Walter sees; so does Anne, but she sees both the social and the moral dimensions of the matter. Not only are they freer and easier, but they keep up estates better; Anne's severance from her family largely arises from this sort of insight and the realization that the sailors possess more supportable values, values consonant with her own growing moral insight. The significant moment in the moral action *is* a discovery of knowledge by Anne, at the moment when she returns from Lyme to see the Crofts at Kellynch, having meanwhile learned more of the lives and attitudes of the sailors, and feels that the Crofts have more right there than her own family:

. . . she had in fact so high an opinion of the Crofts, and considered her father so very fortunate in his tenants, felt the parish to be so sure of a good example, and the poor of the best attention and relief, that however sorry and ashamed for the necessity of the removal, she could not but in conscience feel that they were gone who deserved not to stay; and that Kellynch-hall had passed into better hands than its owners'.

Since one of the presumptions the novel fosters is that, in this particular created society, the administration of estates is a social and moral duty, the Crofts maintain values for which Anne's own family once stood but in which they have now failed; and she bestows the favours that in this world can be bestowed—for her a good marriage and a good home—on those who have so deserved them.

There are other moral reasons why the sailors deserve the implicit favour of history that the novel grants them. For all the associated moral values of the book have real analogies with this particular supercession. The sailors are carefully shown to have a more open, freer set of values, a demonstration which is encompassed by the moral stretch of the novel and given an important, indeed conclusive, place in the moral equilibrium of the ending. The contrast between the groupings is given in many ways: in Captain Benwick, with his romantic reading, and Captain Harvill with his fitted-out house at Lyme, showing both the effect of his profession and his own labours. They are shown not as social climbers but as a class making the best use of their opportunities in matters of domesticity and culture as well as defence. What is very clearly established is the merits of the people among whom Anne is at last to find herself: 'These would have been all my friends', she thinks, and finally they are. The moral level of the action supports all this, giving high regard to somewhat exceptional virtues for Jane Austen— energy and steadfastness, but also will and luck, when the last takes the form of 'honourable toils and just rewards'. And since what is behind Anne is perhaps mistaken biddability and status unearned, we must see the value of will (but not, as Louisa, wilfulness) and luck earned. This extends the testing place of value; it remains rural-domestic and genteel, but stretching beyond that are questions of national importance, of the claims that professions have on society, and the evolving need for moral virtue in an evolving society. There are other fields of action than the country and Bath; and there are heroic virtues. This touch is of the greatest importance and it becomes essential to the ending:

His profession was all that could ever make her friends wish that tenderness [which Anne and Wentworth, married, have for each other] less; the dread of a future war all that could dim her sunshine. She gloried in being a sailor's wife, but she must pay the tax of quick alarm for belonging to that profession which is, if possible, more distinguished in its domestic virtues than in its national importance.

Jane Austen makes a world in which energy, confidence, fortune, above all warmth, are vindicated on the chosen ground of the action, the domestic world; Anne's association with it, her becoming part, in effect, of that profession, is the vindication. And this weight too makes the novel different from all her others.

It must be said that this is a theme pointed, as usual in her work, in the direction of a finally personal and emotional wholeness; though the moral values of the novel are affected by a more than passing concern with the values of a new and emergent class, and this produces an underlying structure of social fluidity not previously there in her fiction, that is not to say that this is the basic theme; this is not a novel of social symbolism as is, say, *Howards End*.[1] She takes the matter only so far; Wentworth, for instance, does not inherit Kellynch. The point is that Anne, originally persuaded towards rank and security, accepts the world of energetic uncertainty. Security proves false, morally and financially; the promise justifies itself, morally and financially. Anne's development in the novel—it is much more substantial than most critics allow—is a coming to maturity by acting on this. She accepts as a given standard of her social world the dangers of lowering herself; she sees the obligations of Kellynch but will not marry for them— it is Walter Elliot's role in the book to show us that. For this reason we see that Lady Russell's 'persuasion' was rightly accepted by her; and it is subsequent events, in turn indicating a lack of insight into character as a possibility rather than a fact, which prove Lady Russell wrong—Anne comes to an understanding more radical than even a good woman like Lady Russell can conceive of. Most of the events, therefore, are surely chosen to develop Anne's understanding of this situation. Anne's temptation is Kellynch: that she is willing to remain there and accept retrenchment shows her worthy of it; but the second part of the book, in Bath, shows that it is not worthy of her, for it is

[1] R. S. Crane strongly stresses this point in the essay cited above, and, discussing these contrasted groups, says, 'It is not at all a question of a decaying feudal class on the one hand and a rising middle class on the other, as several recent critics in love with abstractions have wanted us to believe.' He stresses that the sailors stand in analogical relation to Wentworth himself, afford 'goodness by association', and are the structural consequence of a narrative method in which Anne's attachment to Wentworth has to be vindicated despite his behaviour. I am sure this is an essential function of the groupings; but I am equally convinced that the social contrasts, while finally pointing to liveable moral values, are of considerable significance and give the novel a much more fluid social form than any earlier one.

inheritable and to belong to Walter Elliot. By the end of the action, she has moved out of the world of stewardship we are familiar with in Jane Austen ('Anne had no Uppercross-hall before her, no landed estate, no headship of a family . . .') and the reader is persuaded that this is to the good. This is more than an historical myth; history favours the good in Jane Austen, even when compared classes are not involved; this is part of the undertaking. The social and moral themes run together to the end; but the effect of course is to realize a moral and emotional rather than a directly social good, and it is in marriage and marriage alone that it will be realized. Two essential lines of possible development—the progress of a heroine towards social status, and to-wards self-awareness—diverge, in such a way as to show self-awareness incompatible with a social inheritance. The rewards then are of an unusual kind, and the main effort of literary management in this novel must be towards persuading us that Anne does, significantly, grow—does extend in moral and social awareness, advance from a biddable acceptance of duty and 'persuasion exerted on the side of safety' to a conscious appreciation of the virtues of risk-taking—this movement being justified by discoveries about the nature of the family and society she belongs to, and about, not so much Wentworth's character, as the environment in which it takes on moral force.

This is the action imagined by Jane Austen and the emotional effect produced by it, an action entirely achieved in the feelings of the final marriage. The material is worked towards our belief in the joy the lovers feel when finally they are reunited; and the pursuit of that climactic effect is surely what helps determine the shape and order of the work, its tactical means or what are often thought of as its formal attributes. In this respect there are, as R. S. Crane points out, a number of essential tactical decisions of the first importance: the use of retro-spect for the early part of the action, the use of Anne's consciousness as the centre of the telling. A large part of the action, including the original engagement and act of persuasion, is presented in short compass and in retrospect. This leaves the present of the novel to deal with a relatively short period of time in which the complications deriving from that situation are worked out with close attention—complications involving the separation of the lovers and their final reconciliation, and involving the divorce of Anne from her family. The novel begins at a point where the latter must be the prime point of attention, since Anne has few grounds for thinking she will regain Wentworth: thus the main

action is concerned not with her falling in love or feeling new emotions, but with recreating *old* emotions under the stimulus of Wentworth's return and with showing Anne pushed towards a situation of
critical independence *vis-à-vis* her family. This gives much greater
weight to the class theme of the book. So, too, does the decision to
present the story through Anne's consciousness; thus we do not know
that Wentworth has retained his love for Anne (indeed Jane Austen
artfully shifts the point of view in chapter 7 to indicate that Anne's
power with Wentworth is gone forever), and we see that Anne's
separation from her family is disinterested and prompted by moral
necessity. So too we can appreciate those crucial virtues of constancy
and steadfastness which are primary in the moral meaning of the final
alliance. This tactical decision drives part of the emotional action
underground, so to speak; it delays much of it, including Wentworth's
emotional story, to the final explanations. But it is necessary if we are
to retain the feeling that Anne is constant, steadfast, and mature, is,
as Wentworth paradoxically sees, unalterable, yet matured by making
her own free choices, and when, at Bath, she is faced with a refigured
version of the initial act of persuasion, able to act both with strength
and emotional fullness, and to find the realization of all her acts and
values, the justification of her fortitude and suffering, in a final 'warmth
of heart': 'Anne was tenderness herself, and she had the full worth of
it in Captain Wentworth's affections.'

If, as Poirier says, Jane Austen's final marriages become not only
meaningful acts of choice but unions of social and natural inclinations,
this is managed by making us aware, in the discovery that two people
have made a good marriage, that they have realized much else in the
way of social and moral experience. In this book that culmination is an
act of persuasion surely focused on the way in which Anne's constancy
enforces on her and on us discoveries that she could not possibly have
made had she sustained the engagement eight years before (and it can
thus be measured by the distance Anne moves from Lady Russell's
view of her). The book is more than simply a triumph of constancy,
then, as the scene where Wentworth and Anne restore their engagement makes clear:

There they exchanged again those feelings and those promises which had once
before seemed to secure every thing, but which had been followed by so many,
many years of division and estrangement. There they returned again into the
past, more exquisitely happy, perhaps, in their re-union, than when it had been

first projected; more tender, more tried, more fixed in a knowledge of each other's character, truth, and attachment; more equal to act, more justified in acting.

The action of the novel is, we might say, a patent validation of this last claim, and especially with regard to Anne. There are proper qualifications here ('. . . more exquisitely happy, *perhaps* . . .'), logical enough in view of the joy felt by Anne in her first love; but the focus of our understanding of that has been to relive that feeling in the context of a bettering of it. This is surely why Anne can justify her previous yielding to persuasion—for Anne, by being constant, has changed. This, as I say, is the paradox Wentworth dwells on at the end; she has remained the same, but she has acquired new extensions of character. She has re-realized her virtues as well, and they have been thrown before him in a new light (mainly through the comparison with Louisa). This explains, in turn, his growth and his story; his long pursuit of Anne, his coming to Bath. The result is a fresh and not a repetitious moral energy at the end, a compound of Anne's social independence and her new resources of tenderness, an energetic warmth of heart inconceivable in relation to their first encounter. This is why the novel is about growth, a growth of a remarkably delicate kind, and of, I think, a decided element of—for Jane Austen—moral radicalism.

Emma's 'perfect happiness', Anne's 'warmth of heart', are two very personal, and also two very different, achievements. They are that because the heroines are two quite different people, but they exist in two quite different worlds as well. *Persuasion* is a softer novel; it is indeed an autumnal comedy in which, though a pointed savagery is used in dealing with several characters, the main ones are narratively less directly pressed and challenged. Jane Austen's way of patterning and structuring, of placing and concealing, of judging and sorting her characters, of standing values in relation to other values, is here done quite differently, and it invokes a different kind of human concern. To grasp that means reading her in a certain way, a way in which we relate formal decisions and procedures to human and moral matters as we can only learn to do from the books themselves. The learning involves a locally specific sense of what the writer feels has to be achieved, involves an understanding of the distinctive balance of ends and means employed in the writing. There are standards and expectations common in novel criticism—ranging from expectations about 'consistency' of point of view to assumptions about the need for all scenes to be vividly rendered, through to assumptions about the artifice of any fictional society—which may tempt us to reverse the weight of those ends and means. But if, as is surely clear, Jane Austen's novels, these extraordinary moral comedies, are a crucial centre in the novel, then her successes are neither innocent nor uncomposed. Today as critics we have acquired an admiration of performance, of artistic skill, however directed; and this makes it harder to realize that centre. Jane Austen is a novelist of a composed realism, a novelist of skilled intentions; the business of critical discourse must be to retain the actual and the theoretical capacity to talk of such writing in all suppleness and sympathy.

PART THREE

MODERNISMS

V

Phases of Modernism:
The Novel and the 1920s

I

One of the most important assumptions in modern thinking about the novel is the notion, prevalent among novelists and critics alike, that sometime in the concluding years of the last century or the early years of this one, at a point which is not exactly sensitive but is nonetheless there to be felt, there occurred a change, a redirection, a re-emphasis or a 'turn' of the novel. It is a turn which distinguishes, say, the later work of Henry James from that of George Eliot, or separates the work of Lawrence from the work of Hardy. This change is not of one kind and is not total or inclusive, for some novelists seem not to be touched by it; nonetheless it brought about an enormous alteration in the novel's nature, structure, and mode of activity, so that a new period or phase of style seems to emerge. The change has something to do with the fortunes of realism and liberalism in the novel. Both George Eliot and James merit the name of realists, but at different levels of comprehension of the term; George Eliot's is a realism of the middle distance, a realism in which the embodied life of society was both inescapable and a condition of personality and growth; James's, not so much a substantiation of reality as a questing for it, as if its substance were always provisional, so that all insight into it must be perspectivized, and the relation of those perspectives to the author himself managed with an utter care, intensely demanding on the logic of art itself. It is with this perspectivism that one essential aspect of the modern novel makes its presence felt. An essential feature of the twentieth-century novel is the presence of a new kind of self-awareness, an introversion of the novel to a degree unprecedented in its fortunes. This gave a stylistic milieu in which some practices which had been very close to the centre of fiction as a story-telling art were brought into question; it seemed that certain well-established types of narrative presentation, certain kinds and modes of realism, certain poised relationships between the story and its teller, certain forms of chronological ordering and particular views of character, even the belief that a form does not need to exceed the working needs immediately occasioning it, were being restructured to fit the form of a new world.

One of the characteristics of style, of any community of aesthetic perception and mannerism, is that the same sort of aesthetic phenomena, the same species of technique, can occur for a wide variety of different reasons; and can be explained, by their creators or those who later wish to criticize and elucidate their works, from an enormously different range of assumptions. Such is the case with the modern 'turn of the novel', for many different versions of it exist. To some writers, like Virginia Woolf, what was happening was the dissolution of a material reality which had fixed the novel substantially in a single mould; it was now free to be more itself. To Henry James, the novel seemed to be reaching a new level of social acceptance and hence potentially a new level of self-realization; 'It has arrived, in truth, the novel, late at self-consciousness; but it has done its utmost ever since to make up for lost opportunities,' he said in his essay 'The Future of Fiction', written at the century's turn; and he suggested that much higher 'ministrations'—though at the same time a decided expansion of the commercial level of fiction, and hence a bifurcation of intent—might be about to occur. To both these writers, the change was associated with a freeing of consciousness in general: 'The centre of interest throughout *Roderick [Hudson]*', James noted in his preface to that novel, 'is Rowland Mallett's consciousness, and the drama is the very drama of that consciousness'; Virginia Woolf also spoke of consciousness, though as something else, 'this, the essential thing', 'whether we call it life or spirit, or truth or reality . . .'; Lawrence pursued yet another consciousness, the flux of experience according to which character is 'unrecognizable'. We can propose that what, among some of our most striking novelists, is evolving is a new content for fiction, a new inner life for the characters, a new order of experience arising, in part, from the breaking down of traditional social forms, the growth of cities, the power and pressure of new styles of life, the emergence of a more fleeting and fluid view of the world, perhaps a general moving inward of experience.[1] Or we can propose that what is welling forth is a new form for it, a new means or manner, a much more symbolist kind of novel. We can propose, as Alan Friedman does, something in between the two:

The shift to which I refer was gradual, but it took place, I will suggest, with greatest velocity at about the turn of this century. . . . It was not merely plot, or characterization, or technique, or point of view, or thought, or symbolic organization that changes; it was not a matter of irreconcilable meanings, conflicting themes, or difficult problems. The change in the novel took place at a more fundamental level than any of these; it left the novel 'open' in another sense and in another respect, though in a respect that inevitably touched, now here, now there, all other matters. The process which underlay the novel was itself disrupted and reorganized. The new flux of experience insisted on a new vision of existence; it stressed an ethical vision of continual expansion and virtually unrelieved openness in the experience of life.[2]

The different emphases give us different priorities, different essential forms of explanation; but whether we take the change to be one mostly of matter or mostly of means, what is clear is the presence not only of new intensities of experience but new intensities of technique; and the novel's subject does become increasingly the novel itself.

There are periods in art—we may be entering another now—when modal speculation and mannerism become of great concern, giving an air of anti-realism to prevailing practice; such periods are usually represented as eras both of artistic growth and artistic crisis. Crisis adds another dimension to the explanation, a historical one. The novel come 'late at self-consciousness', the newer, freer, more poetic novel, was also the novel afflicted—as Virginia Woolf said in 'How It Strikes a Contemporary'—with the dilemma that the modern writer 'cannot make a world, cannot generalize'. The notion that the new novel was also the novel of stress in the culture, and perhaps at odds with history, that it was related to cultural and epistemological collapse was vivid in criticism then and has remained so since. And according to whether you see the modernist novel—which, it must be said, remains only one part of the *modern* novel—as a novel of new possibility or a novel of crisis, you may well date differently the high point of modernism, the

[1] The question of the relationship between the causal background and the forms of modernism I have discussed extensively in my book *The Social Context of Modern English Literature* (Oxford and New York, 1971).

[2] Alan Friedman, *The Turn of the Novel: The Transition to Modern Fiction* (New York and London, 1966), 14–15.

central phase of significance. To some critics the real 'turn' occurs around or before the turn of the century; others have looked much later and seen the heart of things in something else. So for Harry Levin the epicentre of modernism lies in the 1920s; in 1922, he reminds us, there appeared *Ulysses*, Proust's *Sodom and Gomorrah* (and the translation of his work into English), Lawrence's *Aaron's Rod*, Virginia Woolf's *Jacob's Room*, Katherine Mansfield's *The Garden Party*, Eliot's *The Waste Land*, Yeats's *Later Poems*, Rilke's *Sonnets to Orpheus*, Brecht's *Baal*, while 1924 offers a similar list including the Surrealist Manifesto, *The Magic Mountain*, and *A Passage to India*.[1] This is obviously *a* high point of modernism, and the list speaks to the idea of modernism as crisis art. But the question of whether it is the centre depends on the kind of account you give of its nature and its causes.

We often take modernism to mean the internal stylization of the arts, the distortion of the familiar surface of observed reality, and the use of what has been called 'spatial form'[2]—a disposition of artistic content according to the logic of metaphor, form, or symbol, rather than to the linear logic of story, psychological progress, or history. The artist is thus radical in a particular sense: he is concerned not so much with revolution in the world as with revolution in the word. It is not exterior crisis that prompts him or shapes him; he is radical in his primary environment, that of art itself. Modernism hence has oblique relations with the modern world; and its works make oblique report on it. In them, modern history or reality does not give a proper field for the enactment of events, or a structure; they deal rather in a contingent and fallen world stuck in a chaotic or circular history, a pointless time, and lacking order, structure, or myth save when these are created by the artifices of fiction or the transcendent power of form. But to transact too directly with history was, as Joyce once suggested, to risk form.

If modernism is mainly this, then it considerably pre-dates the twenties, and the main changes in aesthetic assumption occurred a good deal earlier, when what we might call a symbolist mode, a fresh tactical logicality, entered the novel in the middle career of Henry James, in the early writings of Conrad, in—now in another form—the

---

[1] Harry Levin, 'What Was Modernism?', in *Refractions: Essays in Comparative Literature* (New York and London, 1966).

[2] Joseph Frank, 'The Dehumanization of Art', in *The Widening Gyre: Crisis and Mastery in Modern Literature* (Bloomington. Ind. and London, 1968).

new novel of Lawrence. Indeed from the 1890s onward a succession of writers and movements had laid down, in an enormous variety, a modernist mode. Gradually there arose a model of artistic creation in which art was the product of creative ferment, analogous indeed to rebellion in other spheres, but distinguishable from it, and the artist was an isolated figure in communion not with his gross and material milieu but with an artistic utopia, hints of whose existence lay in aesthetic consonance, the epiphanies of form. And in the novel by 1915 there was a body of inescapable performances—the novels of James, George Moore, Conrad, Ford, Stephen Crane, Dorothy Richardson, Lawrence, Joyce—pointing a direction, as well as a mass of aesthetic statements suggesting what it might be. There was, too, a group of basic intellectual influences—from William James and Bergson to the unmaskers of process like Darwin, Marx, and Freud, as well as the cyclic historiographers Vico and Spengler; the French formal realists, especially Flaubert, and the Russian novelists of consciousness, especially Dostoevsky; the Post-Impressionist painters whose modes seem to offer literary analogues; and so on. The emphasis on technique, or on the perceptual resources of the artist himself as a high subjective consciousness; the emphasis on rendering, or the heightened resonance that might be attached to certain observed objects; the emphasis on tactics of presentation through the consciousness of characters rather than through an objective or a materialistic presentation of material; and the emphasis on the medium of art as the writer's essential subject-matter—these were all laid down before the First World War. And yet there remains with us, I think, the sense that there was another phase of modernism, that there is a crucial temper of the twenties, a finalizing of something, and also a turning point.

The twenties, I suspect, exist for us today as the period when something happens to modernism's fortunes—when its opportunities and limitations are simultaneously explored, with the result that we are led towards the sort of art we now have, the sort of possibilities we sense. In a series of primary and major works—*Ulysses, A Passage to India,* Lawrence's later and more symbolist novels, the works of his most apocalyptic phase, the finest books of Virginia Woolf, Wyndham Lewis's *Tarr* (1918), *The Childermass* (1928), and *The Apes of God* (1930), Ford Madox Ford's *Parade's End* tetralogy (1924–8), and so on —many of the best propensities of modernist writing were realized in fiction, establishing the already-extant tradition of experimental fervour not so much as an eccentricity but a style. Yet, too, the tradition of the new seems to weaken; and though there is *Finnegans Wake*, and Durrell, and Beckett, and much today still to come, another kind of modern novel seems to take shape. We often presume, in modern criticism, that in the English line the experimental tradition did shift or lapse, a lapse usually identified with the thirties, when realism and politics came back, and a generation less certain of its artistic role—writers with the Silver Age presumptions of Waugh's Gilbert Pinfold, or the uneasy anti-aestheticism of an Orwell, the guilt of a Virginia Woolf, the self-diminution of an Isherwood, sacrificially offering sensitivity to an overwhelming historical experience—gives us a 'contemporary' rather than a 'modern' fiction.

This belongs to the 1920s too; a new kind of modern writing, devoted not so much to realizing modern forms as to engaging with the extraordinary, strangely ungraspable experience of the modern, or the modernizing, world, comes through: in Waugh's comic surreality, the guilty existentialism of Greene. For by the end of the war something seemed to have happened to the modernist internationalism that ran through London in the immediately pre-war years. For one thing, Paris reverted to being the modernist capital. Pound went there in 1921, as did Ford; Joyce and Lawrence were already expatriates; James had died in 1916, and Conrad's best work was done; the experimentalist ferment seemed a foreign tendency that after a brief visit was departing again. It did not, of course; for in the twenties the real assimilation of modernism occurs, so that it becomes artistically not an individual eccentricity or innovation but almost an artistic necessity; as Virginia Woolf put it, in 1910 'human character changed', and with it all relationships and forms of consciousness. In the 1920s the assumption that the material fabric on which the 'materialist' novel depended was not stable but shifting became commonplace; so did the psychological presumptions of Freud and the formal consequences they carried for fiction; so did the symbolist norms that are transmitted, say, in Percy Lubbock's *The Craft of Fiction* (1921) or Forster's *Aspects of the Novel* (1927).[1] But modernism's stylistic availability itself changed the situation; and so, even more, did the sense that the

---

[1] One might also note the importance of C. H. Rickword's 'A Note on Modern Fiction' which appeared in *The Calendar of Modern Letters* in 1926, and is a very early instance of the taking of modernist assumptions into the professional criticism of fiction.

modern was not simply an exciting, fresh, and poetic literary form but a prevailing social environment: modernism crossed with an inescapably modern world.

2

Towards the end of the 1920s, D. H. Lawrence wrote the book finally called *Lady Chatterley's Lover*; it was not an easy book for him and it went through three very different versions, which we can now inspect. Lawrence clearly intended to make the novel very modern—a postwar-age book about brooding modernity, impending cataclysm, emotional void, class conflict reaching towards extremity, increasing mechanism and materialism in all classes, the growing triumph of an egoism urging man deeper into cold will. He also needed a figure for resurrection, of what might lie beyond: it might be social recovery, a world of touching and tenderness with economic motives and class barriers gone, or it might be a lonely and local achievement of emotional survival in two special individuals, while the world goes down into hopelessness. But it was above all a novel about a tragic age not taken tragically, and in all the versions that theme survives, in the form of reflections on modern relationships and affections, fashionable styles of living and loving that hide the split of mind and body, the emptiness beneath, in a stubborn stoicism of which Sir Clifford is exemplary. The book is dominated by the 'bruise of the false inhuman war', which is partly the cause of the thin, modern, post-cataclysmic sensibility that can only look to the next cataclysm—the bad time that Mellors says is coming. Lawrence's judgement of the situation and sensibility of the 1920s is very much of a piece with present ambivalent assessments of the period. For it is clearly the first recognizably modern decade we have behind us, organized around modern communications, production, and consumption, and behaviourally modern—a period of emancipated modes, an urge to freer behaviour, a preoccupation with personal styles and fashion, an appeal to the temporary, the hedonistic, the sensational. It is an age that, by virtue of the radical change of war, is preoccupied with its initiation, its newness, and it ends with another radical change, the slump, which brought back politics and looked back on the twenties as empty, 'a period of irresponsibility', said Orwell, 'such as the world has never before seen.' Yet its very preoccupation with style, with proliferating expression, with new forms, new music, new dance, new media, new amusements, is clearly linked

with the accelerated mood of aesthetic exploration in the arts, arts nonetheless decidedly critical of the experiences that they also in some
sense release and embody. Moreover the arts of the twenties tend at
once to report the modern and to enact it. Modernism and modernity
converge; and from the mixture arises, I think, a new sense of literary
form.

An important element that runs through the writing of the twenties
is the deepening distrust both of history and progressivism, a mood
perhaps implicit in earlier fictional symbolism, but substantially
extended in the literary spirit of the 1920s. In particular the war gave
writers a specific event to be apocalyptic about, fixed the point in the
cycle where transition occurred, a point of severance, social, intellectual, moral, and experiential. Hence the famous comments of Henry
James's letter of 1915 to Howard Sturgis about the war, where he
speaks of the plunge of civilization into the abyss of blood and darkness
as the 'thing that so gives away the whole long age during which we
have supposed the world to be, with whatever abatement, gradually
bettering, that to have to take it all now for what the treacherous years
were all the while really making for and *meaning* is too tragic for any
words.' James perhaps misses the extent to which a new, crisis historiography—apocalyptic, pessimistic, recognizing transition, anarchy, the
destructive element—had, as I have suggested already, become part
of symbolist typology, of which his own fiction partakes. His distinction between 'clumsy life at her stupid work' and the artistic construct, taking order from the artist's technique and fine consciousness,
is consistent with the symbolist conviction that history and society do
not give a sense of reality. But this can be viewed positively as well as
negatively, as a joyous expansion of art, or an exposure of the failure
of history and politics; it was the twenties that tended towards the
latter view. The large progressive element in earlier modernism,
touched by the spirit of the Nietzschean superman who will unite man
and society in a new world, darkens. The transition into the modern
now seems to have occurred, but it is a bleak initiation, producing
disillusion and a sense of living between disaster and disaster. And this
seems to enter the form of fiction. For Lawrence, the war was the
obvious end of something ('The old world is gone, extinguished') but
also a beginning, a phoenix rebirth ('I know we shall all come through,
rise again and walk healed and new in a big inheritance here on earth').
In his postwar novels the notion of the last days rather than the first

gets stronger, and *Lady Chatterley's Lover* is the clearest example.[1] But Lawrence is not alone; the same notion of double cataclysm recurs in Huxley and Waugh, for example, where the primal modern transition into change leads to a universe of continuous flux threatened by further disaster. The past being gone, men must be modern; but they as much as the novelist are in a world in which time ceases to progress, in which history is Stephen Dedalus's 'nightmare from which I am trying to awake'.

The problem of structuring and mythologizing a modern history which is—in the words of Eliot's famous comment on *Ulysses*—'an immense panorama of futility and anarchy' is primary in the art of the twenties. *Ulysses*, with its formal plurality and parodic relation to myth, is a classic instance; there is in it an echo of nothingness behind form that reaches over to the Marabar caves echo of another central work, Forster's *A Passage to India*. But there is also another form prevalent, one which seeks to enact fiction through the novelties of the age—its new generational sense, its exotic pleasures, its urbanized, modernized ferment, its orgies, cynicisms, and despairs. One mode of this is a partial giving up of the writer's self to the intensifying stress of history (as, classically, Scott Fitzgerald did); this can produce the smart exoticism of a Michael Arlen, the febrility of a Ronald Firbank, the mixture of comic involvement and satirical detachment we have in Huxley or Waugh. The sense of flux and provisionality can themselves become elements of the characters, as they do for Calamy in Aldous Huxley's *Those Barren Leaves*:

'I don't see that it would be possible to live in a more exciting age,' said Calamy. 'The sense that everything's perfectly provisional and temporary—everything, from social institutions to what we've hitherto regarded as the most sacred scientific truths—the feeling that nothing from the Treaty of Versailles to the rationally explicable universe, is really safe, the intimate conviction that anything may happen, anything may be discovered—another war, the artificial creation of life, the proof of continued existence after death—why it is all infinitely exhilarating.'

'And the possibility that everything may be destroyed?' questioned Mr. Cardan.

'That's exhilarating too,' Calamy answered, smiling.

Yet in most of the novelists of the twenties there is an attempt to show

---

[1] Frank Kermode discusses this admirably in 'D. H. Lawrence and the Apocalyptic Types', in his *Modern Essays* (London, 1971).

that this provisionality and contingency are historically novel and put a painful strain upon art, on apprehension and order. The feeling of surveying an existence without essence, a continuum without a structure, runs deep in the art and gives it a sense of internal strain—a certain terminal quality in the writing which reveals that it is attempting to reach towards the limits of language, the ultimate possibilities of form, the extreme of an aesthetic order beyond time and history. The dilemma of the novelist in the twenties seems to be to express the double pull upon him—the desire to witness to the modern as an extraordinary and new historical environment; the desire to create from history an aesthetic consonance of some sort. And one consequence of that is an ironic phase in fiction—a phase in which the epic of contingency, like *Ulysses* or, in another way, *A Passage to India*; or the lyric of personal consciousness and self-generating form, like *To the Lighthouse*; or the surrealistic cool comedy of novelties, like *Antic Hay* or *Vile Bodies*; or the plot of modern chaos left to die, while two retreat towards personal salvation, as in *Lady Chatterley's Lover*, become typical modern forms.

VI

E.M. Forster as Victorian and Modern:
Howards End and *A Passage to India*

I belong to the fag-end of Victorian liberalism, and can look
back to an age whose challenges were moderate in their tone,
and the cloud on whose horizon was no bigger than a man's
hand. . . .
>   E. M. Forster, 'The Challenge of Our Time', in
>   *Two Cheers for Democracy*

I

Modern literature seems to have given us great writers of two main
types: the masked and impersonal, the withdrawn guardians of the
powers of art, and the prophets of stress, anguish, and extremity. Of a
third kind of writer, that kind who compel us as men, by virtue of the
centrality, decency, and humanity of their values, their capacity to
embody the moral best of culture, we have seen rather less. But there
is E. M. Forster, a writer who still—despite the impact of his posthumously published writings, where the element of homosexual
apologetics necessarily qualifies that famous liberal disinterestedness
and stress on personal relations—stands exceptionally for the virtues
of moral reasonableness, moral passion, and their artistic embodiment
in a fictional form. If other writers have risked themselves at the
extremes, Forster seems to have held the centre, exploring it, for its
moderating virtue, with a complex mixture of commitment and
scepticism. These are the admirable qualities of the liberal humanist,
convinced that art is a species of active morality as well as of magic;
but both the conviction and the style have come to seem in many eyes
derivations from traditional art. In cultural judgements we have

learned to support the logic of extremity and alienation; in the growingly impersonal milieu of modern criticism we are readier to ascribe
worth to structural performance in the text than to look to the moral
world to which it refers, especially when the values prized seem reconciling virtues of poise and sanity. As for Forster's kind of socio-moral
novel, the novel that mediates spontaneous passions and social realities,
that too we find harder to talk about as the prime tradition of fiction.
For these reasons the critics have shown a fondness for identifying
Forster as a late Victorian writer, a writer decidedly less radical artistically than, say, Virginia Woolf, with whom he shared the Bloomsbury
milieu. Forster came forward for attention with the great modern
writers of the generation of which he was a part, the generation of the
1910s and 1920s, along with James, Joyce, Conrad, Lawrence, and
Virginia Woolf—the novelists who, in short, established a new modern
form of the novel. But set against the self-consciously emancipated and
avant-garde thrust of that writing, Forster has always looked a little
less modern, his reputation a little less certain; and the critics have been
unsure where to place him, whether to consider him their spiritual
coeval, or the coeval of earlier writers like Meredith and Samuel
Butler, to whom he asserted his debts. The latter view of him as
'technically, . . . a throwback'[1] is, I think, something of a mistaken
judgement, though it is not hard to see how it comes about. It is
indeed a judgement in which he has partly concurred, and our unsure-
ness undoubtedly stems from an obvious dividedness in his work—
his attempt, appropriately liberal, to reconcile two very different sets
of fictional and cultural forces. It stems, too, from Forster's own somewhat ironic disposition to present himself as historically at risk, to
show himself maintaining values which exist, somehow, against all
the logic of the times, the logic that depersonalizes the very notion of
man and assaults the idea of human individuality.

Forster thus once explained his early withdrawal from writing
novels—though he died in 1970 his last full-length novel was *A Passage
to India*, published in 1924 (the posthumous *Maurice* was for the most
part written before that)—as the consequence of the passing of the
old-fashioned world about which he wrote. In a famous phrase, he
also spoke of himself as belonging to the 'fag-end of Victorian liberalism'—a phrase that has been taken very literally and applied against
him. His belief in the redemptions of the intellect, in personal relation-

[1] Walter Allen, *The English Novel* (Penguin ed., London, 1958), 333.

ships and the heart's affections, have been held to arise from the a-
historicism of an upper-middle-class upbringing and a Victorian
Evangelical and liberal tradition, attitudes that in turn have been
attached to that strange death of liberal England which historians
date around 1914, when the equation of economic individualism with
social progress lost political force. If we can explain historically, with
hindsight, the exhaustion of that political liberalism under the pressures
of the second-stage industrial revolution, so critics have felt that
Forster's own moral tenor—which is in fact a very different affair, a
distillation of values and priorities which touch the essential questions
about our hopes for man and culture, and hence have vastly longer life
than a political conviction—can also be held in doubt. Forster has
suffered from our predilection for substituting, in Karl Popper's
phrase, 'historical prophecy for conscience'; but we ought to add that
Forster always believed in history, in the relation between ideology
and power, and that his spirit was always ready to administer the
irony, to comprehend and deal with his own victimization. Indeed it
was his devotion to history that made him an uneasy modernist, and
was to Virginia Woolf the problem of his novels; admirable as she
found them, they were 'extremely susceptible to the influence of time',
and split between the higher modes of symbolist poetry and the lower
ones of realism and history. For Forster, in fact, this was the crucial
dilemma of modern art, divided as it must be between life by time and
life by value; and it is precisely this that, in his best novels, he writes
about. The result is, in those novels, a dualism, a sense of two versions
of literary possibility; the compelling, and modern, strength of *A
Passage to India* comes from the author's attempt to reconcile the ideal of
artistic wholeness with a comic vision of human muddle, a muddle
that comprehends what Forster, in *Aspects of the Novel*, calls 'the
immense richness of material which life provides', but which presses
against, puts the highest historical pressure on, the timeless completeness of art.

The idea that Forster's work *is* built on a traditional intellectual and
literary inheritance is, of course, a perfectly real one; the problem is to
see the complexity. What the tradition is he himself has brought alive
for us by showing, in many essays and in books like *Marianne Thornton*,
his own intellectual origins and lineage, which go back to the world of
the Victorian upper-middle-class, Dissenting intelligentsia from which
he descended, and beyond that to Romanticism. To the cultural

historian the fascination of this intelligentsia lies in its responsible and unconditioned spirit, its capacity to act beyond interest and to embody without a sense of radical alienation the critical intelligence in society, the demand for culture and wholeness. This in turn goes back to the beginning of the nineteenth century, and especially to that engaging synthesis, in Wordsworth and Coleridge, of the romantic imperative of the imagination and the social imperative to right reason and moral duty. There could be, then, a romantic critique of society, a critique which took it as solid, real, and worthy, which is precisely what Forster's kind of novel assumes. His novels also assume the compelling power of the imagination in human dealings; he demands a personal connection between inner and outer worlds, demands that both man and society be whole, which is why his novels are about individual redemptions and personal relationships and at the same time very social novels, in which the passion to see life steadily and see it whole provides the moral thrust, in which the object of criticism is those 'vast armies of the benighted' who fail not only the heart but also the brain. The assault, in his stringent novels, is mounted now from the standpoint of intelligence and right reason, now from the claim of the heart and the visionary imagination that can testify to infinity and wholeness.

But I have said that Forster is an historical ironist; he knows the problems of his lineage very well. His last two novels, and his finest works, *Howards End* and *A Passage to India*, are both about that—which is why they are, differently, complex modern works. *Howards End* (1910) is a romantic novel about emotional and social wholeness, the reconciling of the prose and the passion, the commercial bourgeoisie and the intellectual, the material activity of society and the ideal of felt, living personal relationships. A classic kind of comedy which is also a deep inquiry into the state of the nation and the state of the culture, it is a very central and exemplary kind of English novel. *A Passage to India*, which comes fourteen years and a World War later, is about human and cosmic wholeness, the reconciling of man to man in a global sense, and then of man to the infinite. A book of decidedly symbolist aspirations, its world is one in which social existence is dwarfed and made a feeble invasion on the surface of a harsh, implacable, yet also spiritually demanding earth. But the difficulties are patent and turn ironically back on both books, so that the thrust of their values is unfulfilled. In *Howards End* Forster touches in with the greatest power those processes in history which will destroy the favoured world and cannot be gainsaid; the proliferating energy of urbanization and industrialism attacks his own metaphors and symbols, and the spirit of a pastoral England which seems the one offered base for wholeness. *A Passage to India* contains one of the most powerful evocations of modern nullity we have in our literature: the worlds within us and without, at the extreme of romantic dejection, echo together the sound of *boum* from the caves; visionary hope faces an alien, unspeaking, self-reflecting nature. In both books the will to vision, the liberal drive to right reason, the urgent claims of the holiness of the heart's affections, are confronted with unyielding forces in history; it is the irony resulting from that confrontation that makes Forster's works so very modern, a modernity that intensifies as we read his novels in sequence. In the early ones irony operates as a principle of moral realism, a pressure against the romantic liberal wish for wholeness; as Lionel Trilling puts it, there is an ironic counterpointing whereby while 'the plot speaks of clear certainties, the manner resolutely insists that nothing can be quite so simple.'[1] But in the last two books this becomes a primary irony of structure, a mental and aesthetic possession of two colliding views of the world, with the thrust of values coming up against history, and with, correspondingly, the thrust of form facing some extraordinary qualifications.

In our century critics have increasingly accepted modernist norms for the judgement of literature; of course not all our writers have been modernists. Forster is in this respect a decided paradox; he is, and is not. There is in his work an appeal to art as transcendence, art as the one orderly product, the view that makes for modernism; there is also a view of art as a humane power and a realistic narrative instrument, which qualifies the first view and partly contradicts it. In asserting his own literary debts Forster has particularly named three writers: Jane Austen, Samuel Butler, and Marcel Proust. The indebtedness to the first two of his species of moralized social irony is patent, and it is not hard to see why critics find him the technical coeval of his nineteenth-century predecessors. In his novels the omniscient author mediates, with the voice of the guidebook, essay, or sermon, the proffered material—as much to sustain fiction's place in the realm of intelligence as to establish dominance over the plot. But the resemblance to Proust is apparent too, especially in *A Passage to India*, a book which in turn

[1] Lionel Trilling, *E. M. Forster* (Norfolk, Conn., 1943; London, 1944).

draws on already existing propensities. And his symbolist bias, very congruent with Bloomsbury, is clear. In *Two Cheers for Democracy* he tells us that a work of art is 'the only material object in the universe which may possess internal harmony', in *Aspects of the Novel* he consistently attempts to reconcile the modes of symbolism and Post-Impressionism and the 'traditional' story-telling function. The novel tells —not *is*—a story; and it lives in the conditioned world of stuff, event, material reality, history; hence Tolstoy finally stands, for Forster, above Proust. But it has transcendent purposes; art, 'the one orderly product which our muddling race has produced', has Platonic powers to touch infinity, reach the unity behind all things, prophesy, as well as to produce those elegancies and 'openings out' Forster calls pattern and rhythm.[1] In all this he is as post-Paterian as anyone else in Bloomsbury; the novel is shrouded in the material world but is poetic, its final field of action the unseen, its energies symbolist and musical, its wholeness arising from aspects outside and beyond story, from thematic recurrence, leitmotif, pattern, rhythm, prophetic song. The question of whether what this does is to make life whole or simply art harmonious, an elegant fiction, is of course crucial to modernism; and Forster talks of that too, noting art's impulse to faking, its way of turning contingency into completeness. The encounter between the formally transcendent—the epiphany, the unitary symbol, the light behind the veil—and the world of history recurs throughout modernism's works, with different weights and stresses. But Forster's view—like Thomas Mann's, for instance— is both dualistic and dialectical. Art may reach beyond the world of men and things, which is the world of realism and also of story, but it may not leave it behind, and its connections, meanings, and redemptions must take place within it. And by retaining his hope for story, and for history, Forster clearly puts himself on the quizzical edge of modernism.

Thus he stands in the midst of some of the main intellectual, cultural, and aesthetic collisions that occur at the turn into this century; the result is a complex version of modern literary disquiet. But also it is possible to read his work in two very different ways, according to which stress one lays on what he is doing, or else to find his work very inconsistent within itself. So, for example, Lord David Cecil sees Forster's problem as that of harmonizing realism and symbolism; he

[1] E. K. Brown, *Rhythm in the Novel* (Toronto, 1950), admirably discusses this dimension of his work.

depends, he says, on creating an illusion of everyday reality, but at certain moments—one case is Helen's 'unlikely' seduction of Leonard Bast in *Howards End*—he risks probability for symbolic purport. And Virginia Woolf accuses Forster of being a 'materialist' instead of the poet he has aspirations towards being; so, at the moments 'when the uncompromisingly solid should become the luminously transparent . . . he fails, because the conjunction of the two realities casts doubt on both.' F. R. Leavis says that with the earlier novels a simple formula proposes itself: 'In his comedy, one might carelessly say, he shows himself the born novelist; but he aims also at making a poetic communication about life, and here he is, by contrast, unbelievably crude and weak.' Leavis qualifies the point but allows it to stand, even with regard to *A Passage to India*—which he says is, all criticisms made, a classic.[1] This matter of duality is very close to the entire question of Forster's temperament; he is obviously a writer who, like Hawthorne, finds the stressful division between the realistic view of the material and substantive world and the symbolist but potentially abstract and illusory wholeness of romance a matter of concern—a writer busy at strange mediations both moral and formal. But of course he is a comic writer as well, and hence typically not a novelist of solutions but rather of the reservations and contingencies that inhibit spirit, an explorer of muddle as well as an explorer of mystery. The muddle arises in part from the strange obstructability of the material world, which is given to not yielding what the romantic asks of it, and also from the more ominous and extensive processes of history itself, and the emptiness and anarchy, the vision of pluralism and the vision of evil, that it compels on those who contemplate it in the desire for wholeness. The problems of this aesthetic mixture are considerable, and they are surely best looked at in *Howards End* and *A Passage to India*. For the two books, so very different in terms of that spectrum of realism and symbolism which concerns Forster, each contain large elements of the qualities I attach to the other; the critical problem is to describe and balance, and to consider whether Forster does achieve an art which is in its own terms successful, and in a broader sense very modern—modern precisely

[1] Lord David Cecil, *Poets and Story-Tellers* (London, 1949); Virginia Woolf, 'The Novels of E. M. Forster', in *The Death of the Moth, and Other Essays* (London, 1942); F. R. Leavis, 'E. M. Forster', in *The Common Pursuit* (London, 1952). The debate can be seen in the essays in my collection *E. M. Forster: A Collection of Critical Essays* (Englewood Cliffs, N.J., 1966).

because the tension of comedy and symbolism seems to be resolved as an essential human and creative insight.

2

Forster's first three novels were social comedies with romantic moral implications, works set in a relatively stabilized world in which the bearers of the Forsterian virtues—the virtues of the developed heart, spontaneous passion, trust in the imagination—battled with the armies of the benighted and won their illuminating moral victories. So is *Maurice*, mostly written in 1913–14. But *Howards End*, though still very much concerned with a mode of social comedy open towards the world of the unseen and the visionary, turns on a new historical acceleration, an instability in the world order; the relationship between the formal world of art and the historical world of time is central. Hence the book has been seen as divided inside itself; the social metaphor Forster distils in connecting two of his central characters, Margaret Schlegel and Henry Wilcox, and the spiritual metaphor Margaret inherits from Wilcox's previous wife, seem imposed on the worked and felt life of the novel.[1] So *Howards End* raises the problem of a false wholeness, and this makes it very difficult for critical discussion.

One thing is clear about Forster's task in *Howards End*: it is a large and ambitious one. He is attempting no less than a 'condition of England' novel in which the concept of culture at stake is rich, vast, and in certain obvious respects impossible of resolution. But into this task is also drawn a deep concern with the spiritual and the unseen, and its precarious standing with relation to society and history. The critical views of the novel which see it as a visionary work with too much social detailing, or alternatively as a social novel with damaging poetic aspirations, thus touch on significant energies in its matter, and the relationships between them, and raise two questions—whether Forster succeeds dramatically and technically in relating or connecting these elements, and also whether his character Margaret does, in the apparent symbolic reconciliations of the ending. One must consider the means used to produce that mediation, and the degree to which Forster's efforts are devoted to producing it. I would propose that he is *not* entirely devoted to producing it, for Margaret at any rate, and pre-

[1] On this see especially the essay by Leavis, cited above.

cisely because he sees such wholeness as founded on extraordinary irony. One of his main concerns in the novel is with the sense of an enormous historical acceleration, and the desire somehow to amend it, replacing a 'sense of flux' with a 'sense of space'. But, since he believes in history, the only way he sees to achieve this is through the creation of an obvious fiction. And the way Forster deals with the inevitably ironic relationship between 'life by time' and 'life by value', is to produce a mediating tone in the book, a comic tone with strange tasks to perform.

The task of criticism being, I believe, to attempt a definition of the work which sympathetically includes as many parts of the book as possible and indicates how in their coherent relationship they act as a whole—rather than, as so often happens, to reconvert some significant but partial aspect of it, such as the main thread of the story, into a totally other discourse which may render it fashionably negotiable but says little about the specifics of the creative act—let me propose an over-all characterization of *Howards End*, and try to suggest the tasks of proportioning and mediating Forster appears to have been involved in to make it so. *Howards End* I take to be a novel, treated in the comic mode, about the circumstances in which the moral life, which is also the full life of the imagination, can be led in society, about the compromises it must effect with itself in order to do so, about the moral and imaginative value of making certain compromises, and about the historical pressures underlying them. The concerns here are deeply associated with Forster's 'liberalism'—his devotion to what is decent, human, and enlarging in daily conduct, to personal relationships and responsiveness to life, to finding that truth and goodness coincide— but the book also considers questions of whether this moral life can become transcendent, and by what means reality may be known. There is in the novel a push, on these lines, towards wholeness, and contact with the infinite; and Forster's liberalism apparently proposes to justify itself when it mirrors infinity—intimations of which can reside in personal relationships, harmonious living, and contact with the earth. Hence Margaret's 'sermon' to her 'lord', Henry Wilcox: 'Live in fragments no longer.' It is thus possible to read the novel as a dialectical work moving towards synthesis, which is spiritual complete-ness.[1] But to see *Howards End* like that is to underplay what is also in

[1] Cyrus Hoy, '"The Mild Intellectual Light": Forster's Metaphysical Novel', *PMLA*, LXXV (March 1960), 126–36, gives a very good reading of this kind.

it: a real devotion to society, an ironic spirit, an ambiguous ending. For the book is also concerned with the necessary conditions of life in a particular community, and indeed with those 'great impersonal forces' that Mr. Wilcox complacently appeals to when he wants to purge the personal from conversation. This makes Forster very quizzical, and one of the main functions of the comic tone here is surely to enforce this, indeed to let Forster be sceptical about his spiritualizing thrust. This makes *Howards End* more ironic than the very positive interpretations the novel has earned suggest; and that irony is of the essence, for it is a mediating presence between the parts of the book that are pre-eminently social comedy and those concerned with the poetic, which is also the infinite.

The result of this is a particular use of creative proportions, a particular relationship between the action and the means the writer can employ for its assessment. One aspect of this is that the start of the action is delayed until the complexities of manner and perspective by which it might be judged are established; the action itself is also concerned both with social and with spiritual developments. It tells of a girl, imaginative, intellectual, middle-class, of German stock, who becomes engaged to an English businessman, a widower with children, unimaginative, practical, effective, and then finds that a chain of indirect responsibility links him, and even indirectly herself, with the misfortunes of a lower-middle-class clerk and his wife, a responsibility her fiancé is too unimaginative to recognize and she too in love to disentangle. The heroine's impatient sister then sleeps with the clerk in an act of sympathy; her consequent pregnancy reintroduces the moral dilemma in new form. The couple, now married, become divided, the husband insisting on standards of social propriety, the wife on those of personal sympathy; subsequent events, involving accident and coincidence, reinforce her view, so that the husband accepts it, under duress, and the action ends with his making the sister's illegitimate child heir to part of his estate in preference to his own children. The action turns on a moral issue, though the husband, Henry Wilcox, never fully recognizes it; hence it depends on the authorial inference that there are outright moral imperatives arising from the imagination which must be served whether men understand them or not, and whether this violates their social duties or not. The social facts of inheritance are thus made to yield to the moral and spiritual priorities: the worthiest should inherit the earth. But if it is true that in this sense the personal must precede the social or the public, that, as Margaret says, 'any human being lies nearer to the unseen than any organization,' there are also weights in a different direction. Margaret loves and marries Henry, who, though unimaginative, is productive; Margaret and even more her sister are capable of moral romanticism; the book's theme of connection and its scrupulous capacity to analyse and question apparent liberal virtue are of the essence. It is this that leads to the complexity of treatment and tone.

The book in fact contains a moral action treated in a sophisticated framework of reference, in a world where the unseen competes with the seen, as the private competes with the public; and a social action, seen within an equally broad framework of speculation about who should inherit England. For these ends, an elaborate discourse of assessment is created, and the development is slowed, turned occasionally from its chronological order, treated from various points of view, presented by indirection, in order to create a subtly questioning tone, modulating between the comic and the poetic—the former having most to do with the social, and the latter most with the moral and spiritual, events. The book, then, represents various differing interpretations of the world, and it stands above them, seeking to show the social conditions in which they arise, the contradictions among them, and the extent to which each in its different way falls short of a complete or a connected account of experience. The two main attitudes are presented early and are associated with two distinct groups of people, each socially and morally very well-defined: the Wilcoxes and the Schlegels. Both groups belong to the middle class ('we are not concerned with the very poor'), the Wilcoxes with that part of it concerned with business, the Schlegels with that concerned with culture. Each group has its own distinctive history and status. The Wilcoxes are modern businessmen, though they bear, especially through the figure of the first Mrs. Wilcox, a deeper traditional, little-understood association with the yeoman past of England. They live in a world of 'telegrams and anger'; they are sharp to the lower orders, deferential towards social propriety, respectful towards machinery; pragmatic, predatory, expansionist, their spirit is the spirit of Whiggery, their social and moral philosophy *laissez-faire*. Their household is pre-eminently male, active, energetic, which is why, when Helen Schlegel goes to stay at Howards End, she falls in love with them as an institution:

The energy of the Wilcoxes had fascinated her, had created new images of beauty in her responsive mind. To be all day with them in the open air, to sleep at night under their roof, had seemed the supreme joy of life.... She had liked giving in to Mr. Wilcox, or Evie, or Charles; she had liked being told that her notions of life were sheltered or academic; that Equality was nonsense, Votes for Women nonsense, Socialism nonsense, Art and Literature, except when conducive to strengthening the character, nonsense. One by one the Schlegel fetishes had been overthrown, and, though professing to defend them, she had rejoiced.

By contrast the Schlegels are emancipated, modern, humane, thought-ful, concerned with the arts and the unfortunate, and predominantly female. Their heritage is *deraciné*; their German background gives them a distance on English life, but also associates them with the international idealism of their father, who is seen as 'the countryman of Kant and Hegel, as the idealist, inclined to be dreamy, whose Imperialism was the Imperalism of the air.' A former soldier, he had left Germany because of its commercial and political imperialism, hoping 'that the clouds of materialism obscuring the Fatherland would part in time, and a mild intellectual light re-emerge'—in that light his daughters and son believe.

Wilcoxes and Schlegels are thus given as two different principles, and the contrast between them animates the book, generating dialectical contrasts of intellectual, moral, and social attitude, in which national contests with international, seen with unseen, practical with romantic, prose with 'the poetry and the passion'—the expectation raised, from the epigraph onward, being of conflict leading to possible synthesis. So, though the novel is primarily concentrated into these two families, it has an extraordinary range of contrasts, and an extraordinary social sweep. Though the settings are domestic, there is a great amount of travel and movement to different parts of England and briefly to the Continent. Though the cast of characters is small, there are many very different types of relationship among them. The book is deeply set in the Edwardian period and among the forces of change active in it— the economic race with Germany, which was to lead to war, the processes of imperial and economic expansion, the intellectual stresses that were shifting people from liberalism to socialism—a period when the questions of the 'ends' of life, raised by G. E. Moore's *Principia Ethica* (Desmond MacCarthy saw three main 'ends' being sought: 'the search for truth, aesthetic emotions and personal relations—love and friendship'), were active matters of debate. In each of the three main milieux in the book—the intellectual urban milieu of the Schlegels, the country commuting world of the Wilcoxes, the suburbia of the young clerk Leonard Bast—social change and development are taking place. A major theme in the book is moving house and rebuilding, for this is a great, expansive phase of urbanization. Wickham Place, where the Schlegels live, is to be pulled down for flats. 'To be parted from your house, your father's house—it oughtn't to be allowed. . . . Can what we call civilization be right if people mayn't die in the room where they were born?' asks Mrs. Wilcox; but the 'civilization of luggage' insists on movement. The London of the Schlegels is not only the milieu of the arts but also of rampant expansion, as Margaret sees. Hilton, the station for Howards End, shows the same process at work further out: 'The station, like the scenery, like Helen's letters, struck an indeterminate note. Into which country will it lead, England or Suburbia? It was new, it had island platforms and a subway, and the superficial comfort exacted by business-men. . . .' And the novel acts *against* the suburbanizing movement, which is in part why so deep a symbolic significance attaches to Howards End. What underlies the novel is in fact a notion of a changing England, an expanding commerce, an altering economic structure, and a cultural and intellectual life which has its roots threading down into these forces.

That cultural and intellectual life is something very strongly evoked in the novel, something central to the lives of all the characters, even to Leonard Bast. To all the middle-class people of the book cultivation and taste are part of their natural experience, through which their lives intersect (the Schlegels meet the Wilcoxes looking for a Rhineland cathedral, Leonard Bast at a Queen's Hall concert). The various ways in which art serves each one of us differently is amusingly evoked in the passage comparing responses to Beethoven's Fifth Symphony. But what is clear is that cultural responsiveness—and what in part derives from it, the essential and humane spirit of liberalism itself, a kind of full-blown moral and imaginative realization of that responsiveness— is seen to be based in the class arrangements of the society; hence the very realistic assessment Forster offers of Leonard Bast's incomplete cultural aspirations. I think Forster details these social arrangements not in order to expose them but rather to suggest that they dramatize a moral incompleteness which only a greater imagination can alter. For the book grows out towards a standard other than—and more than

—the political. *Howards End* is indeed one of the great cultural novels, in that it does most powerfully explore a profound qualitative demand made upon the social life of the community, a community created for us as a fully made, historically exposed, contemporary world.

In this respect it appears that the controlling values of the story—the 'novelist's' values—are very close to those of the Schlegels. Forster represents the Schlegels very precisely, showing both their strengths and their limitations:

In their own fashion they cared deeply about politics, though not as politicians would have us care; they desired that public life should mirror whatever is good in the life within. . . . Not out of them are the shows of history erected; the world would be a grey bloodless place were it entirely composed of Miss Schlegels. But the world being what it is, perhaps they shine out in it like stars.

Their interests nonetheless constitute the interests of the novel in general, and fill out the meanings and the life behind its humanist intent, its concern with good and evil, with civilization, with responsible living. To a considerable extent, the narrative method of omniscient telling works to let us see the world through their—and particularly through Margaret's—eyes. The opening paraphernalia of letters and telegrams lets us filter our first judgement and impression of the Wilcoxes through Schlegel values, as well as reinforcing those values by showing how easily private things are made public and distorted. It also shows carefully how Margaret can be distinguished as the ethical centre for the Schlegels by virtue of her scruple and responsibility, and how Mrs. Wilcox can be distinguished from the other Wilcoxes and be their distant ethical origin. Chapter 2 turns us further in Margaret's direction: 'Away she hurried, not beautiful, not supremely brilliant, but filled with something that took the place of both qualities —something best described as a profound vivacity, a continual and sincere response to all that she encountered in her path through life.' But the novelist's half-comic tone of regard for and criticism of Margaret is better seen in another passage where he again intervenes, using Margaret's awareness both to set and to ironize his controlling discourse:

To Margaret—I hope this will not set the reader against her—the station of King's Cross had always suggested Infinity. Its very situation—withdrawn a little behind the facile splendours of St. Pancras—implied a comment on the materialism of life. Those two great arches, colourless, indifferent, shouldering between them an unlovely clock, were fit portals for some eternal adventure, whose issue might be prosperous, but would certainly not be expressed in the ordinary language of prosperity. If you think this ridiculous, remember that it is not Margaret who is telling you about it; and let me hasten to add that they were in plenty of time for the train.

It doesn't, of course, set the reader against her, but it does show how Margaret's own capacity for romanticism, which is not very far away from the author's, gets dissipated into a genial common sense, though it doesn't gainsay the concern with infinity itself. Margaret's taste for Infinity, her continual and sincere reverence for life, are notions that take an active, dramatic force. This is partly because she is distinguished from Helen, who also speaks for Imagination, for spontaneous emotion and the feeling that people matter more than any organization, but who has a 'more irresponsible tread'. Helen romanticizes; Margaret, less beautiful, more sober and intelligent, sees the object as it is, sees things steadily as well as whole—and as we pick up her tone, we pick up much of the narrative tone too.

Yet Forster's narrative posture is such that the two contrasting value-systems, the second arising from the Wilcoxes, are allowed seriously to challenge each other. Especially this is true of Mrs. Wilcox; when she comes to Margaret's disastrous luncheon party, we are asked to see what she criticizes, and why. This is more than the self-criticism Margaret has up to now been capable of, as she contemplates Bast and recognizes that her cultivation is partly the result of her economic position; she must also see her own thinness and incompleteness, the things that are later to make her wish to be the successive Mrs. Wilcox. When Mrs. Wilcox's delicate imaginings are withered by the clever talk, when Margaret feels compelled to confess to her her 'inexperience', and to say: 'We live the lives of gibbering monkeys. Mrs. Wilcox—really—we have something quiet and stable at the bottom', we sense her to be in the presence of a forceful if almost silent criticism:

Margaret, zig-zagging with her friends over Thought and Art, was conscious of a personality that transcended their own and dwarfed their activities. There was no bitterness in Mrs. Wilcox; there was not even criticism; she was lovable, and no ungracious or uncharitable word had passed her lips. Yet she and daily life were out of focus: one or the other must show blurred.

The criticism focused in Mrs. Wilcox arises in fact from two sources, from the standard of a cultural stability and rootedness that contrasts

with the intellectual cosmopolitan life, with its uneasy associations
with urbanism and rapid change, and from a standard set beyond daily
life and in infinity, a standard that questions the apparently real and
substantial and evokes its 'panic and emptiness'. And it is thus that
Margaret comes to sense that in the daily world the unseen cannot be
expressed adequately, that it is 'personal intercourse, and that alone,
that ever hints at a personality beyond our daily vision', that the
human task is not to contrast unseen and seen, but to reconcile them.
Margaret herself must join life's prose and its poetry; and the filling
out of that insight is the basic principle of development and expansion
in the novel.

In life, in personal relationships, that reconciliation comes to depend
on Margaret's movement from the cosmopolitan to the honest-
English vein, to her spiritual acceptance of a taking of England whole,
to a reconciliation with the land and those who embody its force and
its activity; and this means her discovering an essential kinship between
the Wilcoxes and herself, founded on the fact that cultivation is not
an act of separation from but an imaginative activation of society, and
that England belongs both to those who can see her *sub specie aeternitatis*
and those who have made her powerful. D. H. Lawrence accused
Forster of mistakenly 'glorifying' the business people in *Howards End*;
and in his own treatment of Sir Clifford Chatterley in *Lady Chatterley's
Lover*, his lack of sympathy drives him into symbolically castrating his
character. But Forster is intrinsically more liberal in his creative action,
even if he does finally distinguish between his moral sheep and goats;
this is seen in his complex way of interpenetrating his two modes, the
social-analytic and the romantic, an interpenetration that puts a strain
on the narrator—'the commentator', as Forster calls himself at one
point—whose function conspicuously varies, and whose rhetorical
mode or controlling language undergoes complicated modulations.
There are extended essayistic passages—for example, the eulogy of
'preparedness' where the commentator intervenes to observe that life
is romance, its essence romantic beauty (Chapter 12), or the central
evocation of the English landscape (Chapter 19)—which serve to
extend the action well beyond its social horizons; there are other
passages in which the authorial point of view is close to Margaret;
there are yet others which maintain the comedy (as when we learn that
Mr. Wilcox did not kiss Margaret 'for the hour was half-past twelve,
and the car was passing by the stables of Buckingham Palace'). But

especially this use of the essayistic enables Forster to manage and evaluate an action which he makes very disconnected and mobile, and which involves odd and sudden shifts in point of view as well as of tone.

A clear example of this is at the beginning of chapter 11, where Forster suddenly divests himself of several characters who have given him his angle and point of vision, and at the same time oddly turns his narrative chronology for an extreme dramatic effect. In the last scene we have just had Mrs. Wilcox alive and talking with Margaret; the new chapter begins, 'The funeral was over.' The tone alters, and the chapter proceeds to reveal, not only that Mrs. Wilcox is dead, but that her death is a ritual intimately related to the land; so the countryman lops off the bough, and reinforces Mrs. Wilcox's place in a symbolic structure surrounding the house, the wych-elm, and what follows— the woodcutter's night of 'mating'. With him all the human figures are removed from the scene, and there follows 'silence absolute', with the church seen as a ship, 'high-prowed, steering with all its company towards infinity.' Then in another rapid shift of tone we return to the social level of the action ('Up at Howards End they were attempting breakfast') and a semi-comic scene in which Mrs. Wilcox's last wish, that the house should go to Margaret, is questioned by the Wilcox 'committee':

Considered item by item, the emotional content was minimized, and all went forward smoothly. The clock ticked, the coals blazed higher, and contended with the white radiance that poured in through the windows. Unnoticed, the sun occupied his sky, and the shadows of the tree stems, extraordinarily solid, fell like trenches of purple across the frosted lawn. . . . Evie's fox terrier, who had passed for white, was only a dirty grey dog now, so intense was the purity that surrounded him. . . .

To follow it is unnecessary. It is rather a moment when the commentator should step forward. Ought the Wilcoxes to have offered their home to Margaret? . . . The practical moralist may acquit them absolutely. He who strives to look deeper may acquit them—almost. For one hard fact remains. They did neglect a personal appeal.

The commentator steps forward, and he does so, for the first time, from a perspective in which the Schlegels are absent. And, striving to look deeper, he identifies himself with the pure light, the church sailing towards infinity, the colouring of life, the significance of Howards End itself. The standard is transcendent but it is also pastoral, which is to say that it has an imaginable social form, as Margaret senses: 'The feudal ownership of land did bring dignity, whereas the modern owner-ship of moveables is reducing us again to a nomadic horde.' The house with its Hellenic and Druidic spirit is still attached to English social forms: 'House and tree transcended any simile of sex. . . . Yet they kept within limits of the human. Their message was not of eternity, but of hope on this side of the grave.' That temporal hope depends on an imaginative richness and 'understanding', in the colloquial and intel-lectual sense of the term, drawn from the 'peace of the country', which reassures man that life goes on in forms transcending his indivi-dual existence. And it is around the house and the tree that those characters who, in their development, bring the development of the novel forward, come to change—Helen, Bast, Henry Wilcox, and Margaret herself.

Towards the end of the book the poetic aspect of the story grows denser, even as the plot rushes forward in a series of rapid events which 'succeeded in a logical, yet senseless, train. People lost their humanity, and took values as arbitrary as those in a pack of playing-cards.' Action and change being the means by which the sensible order of life is violated, working, like London's 'flux', against the truth of things, the reinstatement of truth depends on reasserted stability. It produces the failure of Henry's fortress, and Margaret's realization that it is through the Wilcoxes and their house that she can possess it, that her way of life is well chosen. Yet her solution is makeshift and temporal; and, by affirming this as the book closes, Forster turns to criticizing his 'poetic' self. Howards End cannot solve the problem of the present, of the 'civilization of luggage', and Margaret sees that the places of an unmelted life are 'survivals, and the melting-pot was being prepared for them. Logically, they had no right to be alive. One's hope was in the weakness of logic.' The novel's concluding vision is of a world in decline, precariously balanced against a paradoxical act of hope on Margaret's part:

'. . . This craze for motion has only set in during the last hundred years. It may be followed by a civilization that won't be a movement, because it will rest on the earth. All the signs are against it now, but I can't help hoping, and very early in the morning in the garden I feel that our house is the future as well as the past.'

The buoyancy at the end fulfils and realizes the novel at various levels of notation, fulfils its domestic action and its broader intimations, suggesting that the cultural problem can be solved and the rhythmic pattern of the novel, with its many motifs and 'little phrases', be realized according to the ideal Forster was to propose in *Aspects of the Novel* ('Expansion. That is the idea that the novelist must cling to. Not completion. Not rounding off but opening out'). Yet if in one sense Howards End makes coherent the meaning of the book, in another it does not, for there is no necessary perpetuation of Howards End. As for Margaret herself, she does not so much come to terms with 'infinity' as allow room for it. Her 'uncanny' sense of triumph lets her dominate the situation, become the radiating moral centre, and the mantle of Mrs. Wilcox falls symbolically as well as actually upon her; yet she can hardly 'inherit' England, for England is changing, and the red rust of the modernizing process presses towards the kind of life she values and speaks for.

The strongly poetic note of the last chapter therefore has its ironies, and they are consequent on the entire manner of the book. For Forster has been writing of history too, of commercial growth, imperial competition, the industrial city, the pervasive motor-car, the movement of the world towards a logical future through the impersonal processes of modern development. The ending that opens out the book towards infinity also sets it ironically against this, making it a compromised hope that 'all the signs are against.' And because this is a moral novel with a value to attach to the temporal and social world, a book in which society is established in its historical as well as its personal or spiritual significance, the voice of irony is persistent and relevant throughout, pulling everywhere against the poetic impulse. The comedy that speaks of muddle, arbitrary events, and even the bleaker spaces of 'panic and emptiness' touches in a disturbance that is critical and inescapable. If the question of the book is a romantic one —can society, like a good man, 'live in fragments no longer'?—it is located deeply in a modernizing world. The conclusion is ironic because the book's most valued centres can be given spiritual and moral, but not temporal, justification; the timeless hope of the novel depends on a 'weakness of logic' in history, and unity can only be a symbol. This is the theme that returns, with even greater force, in *A Passage to India*.

3

A Passage to India (1924) is Forster's most ambitious work, and surely
one of the classic modern novels. The echo in the Marabar caves
levels all meanings to one, declares that 'Everything exists; nothing
has value,' enforces that 'twilight of the double vision' in which the
Janus-face of the universe is visible, where the horror and smallness of
the universe are simultaneously known, where 'we can neither ignore
nor respect Infinity.' At the same time an ambition to symbolist
cohesiveness seeks to unite the book and make it into a resonant unity.
It is the work of Forster's that most deeply embodies the neo-symbolist
preoccupations he was to set out three years later in *Aspects of the Novel*,
and behind it runs an oblique debt to Proust, who helped clarify for
Forster the idea of 'rhythmic' composition as a modernist substitute for
linear plot towards which in *Howards End*, without benefit of Proust,
he had already been moving. This gives it an imaginative texture
different from that of the pre-war novels, though many of the earlier
themes and problems continue: here again are those rival claims upon
men and nature which divide the universe and urge reconciliation—
the claims of seen and unseen, public and private, social needs and conventions and those ultimate mysteries for which institutional forms
never serve. Forster's basic sympathies persist, and the book is centred
in the testing-ground of human relationships, in the 'good will plus
culture and intelligence' needed for honest intercourse, in the need for
the liberal mind to transcend the grids of interest and custom which
divide men from men. So too do his basic modes, his way of modulating between a poetic evocation of the world of mystery and infinity
and the comic world of muddle, its obverse, and the normal state of
human affairs; of maintaining both symbolism and a social form of
fiction.

But clearly the balance has changed; and this, too, has divided the
critics, though less in judgement than in interpretation. To some, this
is Forster's largest because most affirmative novel—the book which
most suggests, says one, that 'unity and harmony are the ultimate
promises of life. ... The theme which this book hammers home is
that, for all our differences, we are in fact *one*. ... Physically of one
environment, we are also psychically one, and it is reason's denial of
our commonality, the repression of that *participation mystique*, which
has caused man to rule his Indias and himself with such futility and

blindness.'[1] But others have seen in the book the precise opposite, reading it as a work about the final dissociation between the chaotic life of man and an intractible eternal reality.[2] These problems arise partly because some critics have read the novel as pre-eminently a social novel and others as pre-eminently a symbolist one; but even if one takes the latter emphasis, and assumes that though the world of men, politics, human action divides, the work itself as a single orderly product involves profound inner correspondences and growth, the question persists, as Frank Kermode has pointed out, as to whether this is more than a rhetorical 'faking', a unity of life as well as of form.[3] The problem arises because the book has, as Lionel Trilling says, an unusual imbalance between plot and story: 'The characters are of sufficient size for the plot; they are not large enough for the story—and indeed that is the point of the story.' But it is typically in such contrasts of time and transcendence that Forster deals; the problem, again, is to arrive at an effective description of the over-all working of the novel.

On one level, *A Passage to India* is once more a social comedy, concerned with manners and morals and life in time, though with an extraordinary extension of social range and experience. It is not only more than what *Howards End* was, a national novel; it is more than that form that James so finely aspired to, the international novel, the novel attempting to resolve contrasting value-systems from a cohesive cosmopolitan standpoint of value. *A Passage to India* is, as the Whitmanesque overtones of the title may convey, a global novel, a novel that attempts inclusively to survey mankind. The contrast of England and India is primary, and it produces detailed, and sometimes local, social comedy, but that is not all, in part because India is seen as both eclectic and divided within itself—so that its challenge is that of a multiverse: not unlike the challenge Henry Adams faced on encountering the dynamo and the twentieth century. What the city is as metaphor

[1] Wilfred Stone, *The Cave and the Mountain: A Study of E. M. Forster* (Stanford, Calif. and London, 1966), 344, 339.

[2] See, for example, James McConkey, *The Novels of E. M. Forster* (Ithaca, N.Y., 1957). I have represented the range of this debate in my collection *E. M. Forster, A Passage to India: A Selection of Critical Essays* (London, 1970).

[3] Frank Kermode, 'The One Orderly Product (E. M. Forster)', in *Puzzles and Epiphanies* (London, 1962). Kermode admirably stresses the extraordinary effort at inclusiveness underlying the book: 'All that civilization excepts or disconnects has to be got in for meaning to subsist.'

in *Howards End*, India is in *Passage*: a figure for contingency. And Forster's interest is not just in the social-comic irony of confronting one social world with the standards of another; he stretches across the social and political implications to religious and mystical ones, and finally to the most basic question—how, in the face of contingency, one structures meaning. So the geographical scale of the book is supported by the vast scale of its standpoint. Forster attempts a structure that will include the range of India, and the judgements of the book are reinforced by the rituals and festivals of three religions, by the heterodoxy —racial, political, cultural, religious, mystical—of this multiple nation, and by the physical landscape of a country which both invites meaning ('Come, come') and denies any. 'Nothing embraces the whole of India, nothing, nothing,' says Aziz; the landscape and the spirit of the earth divide men ('Trouble after trouble encountered him [Aziz], because he had challenged the spirit of the Indian earth, which tries to keep men in compartments'); the sects are divided within themselves just as the earth is: 'The fissures in the Indian soil are infinite: Hinduism, so solid from a distance, is riven into sects and clans, which radiate and join, and change their names according to the aspect from which they are approached.'

Forster's social comedy works to provoke, among several different, sympathetically viewed groups, those ironic international and intra-national encounters that occur when one value-system meets another to produce confusion and muddle. But his other aim is to call up, by a poetic irradiation, the ironies lying within the forces of mystery and muddle in the constituted universe of nature itself. Here, too, are deceptions—above all the absence of Beauty, the traditional form for infinity, so that the discourse of Romanticism becomes negative under the hot sun, which is 'not the unattainable friend, either of men or birds or other suns, . . . not the eternal promise, the never-withdrawn suggestion that haunts our consciousness; . . . merely a creature, like the rest, and so debarred from glory.' Though India invites cosmic meanings, it also places both man and the infinite:

Trees of a poor quality bordered the road, indeed the whole scene was inferior and suggested that the countryside was too vast to admit of excellence. In vain did each item in it call out, 'Come, come.' There was not enough god to go round.

Not only does this stretch the enterprise evoked by the title to vast levels of inclusiveness; it means that Forster has to place the social and human aspect of his novel in a new way. We might amend Trilling and say that here the human plot of the novel is set in singular relation to the verbal plot, with its radiatingly expansive language.

The human plot of the book hinges on Adela Quested, who comes to India to marry, has doubts about her marriage when she finds what India has made of her fiancé, and tries herself to create a more reasonable relationship between British and Indians. She goes on an expedition, arranged out of friendship by an Indian, to the Marabar caves; in one of them she thinks she is attacked by him. She accuses him of attempted rape and, though at the trial she retracts this, the incident sows dissent and discord and exposes the political institutions of the country and the stress they put on human relationships. The plot—set largely in and around the city of Chandrapore, at a time unstated but clearly intended to be the 1920s—thus moves us out from the personal to the social world. This social world consists largely of certain racial and religious groups, each with its own customs and manners: the Anglo-Indians (to use the phrase of the day), the Hindus, the Moslems. The English, whom we see largely through the outside visitors, Adela and Mrs. Moore, are embodiments of their institutional duties. Mostly professional people, they have undergone a process of adaptation to their functions, which are, as Ronny says, 'to do justice and keep the peace.' Fielding apart, they have learned the usefulness of solidarity, conventions, rank, and standoffishness; their ethics are dutiful and serious; they have a strong sense of rational justice; are distrustful of mysticism and lethargy; and in general their deep Englishness is reinforced by their situation, while their range of relationships—the ties that bind them together, and enable Forster to thread his action from one to another—are based on the political and social roles they play.

The other group, the Indians, we see first largely through the eyes of Aziz; again of the professional class, linked to the British by their duties, to their own people by friendly and familial relationships, they are themselves divided by religion and caste, above all by the gap between Moslem and Hindu, a gap Forster carefully differentiates, showing their respective versions of India. But where both differ from the English is in their long and adaptive response to the confusions, which are also the mysteries, of their country, a response which obscures the firm lines of value which the British in their isolation can protect—and which permits lethargy, emotionalism, and mysticism.

Forster explores Indian custom and faith in great detail, noting their own patterns of classification, their own ways of making or not making social and moral distinctions, above all recognizing that Indians have adapted to a different physical environment by being comprehensive or passive, rather than orderly or rationalistic. He stands at the mean, which is the humane and classical mean, and densely gives us each world as it connects with and draws apart from the other. And what interests him is not only the relations between people—the novelist's normal subject—but also their separation. For in the novel's social scenes we are persistently conscious of those absent; indeed much of the conversation of the early part of the book is about those not present—the whites talking of the Indians, the Indians of the whites. The interest extends beyond the direct social boundaries of the novel into an enormous inclusiveness, spreading beyond the communities established for the sake of the action into a cast of thousands: nameless marginal characters who appear for a moment and are gone, like the punkah wallah, the voice out of the darkness at the club, the inhabitants of Chandrapore who seem made of 'mud moving'.

Out of this complex social world derives a complex moral world, in which the values of no one group are given total virtue. The English may have thrown the net of rationalism and 'civilization' over the country, but India's resistance to this—'The triumphant machine of civilization may suddenly hitch and be immobilized into a car of stone' —puts them in ironic relation to Indian reality; they scratch only the surface of its life, and theirs is a feeble invasion. On the other hand, the passive comprehensiveness of India is seen as itself a kind of social decay, debased as well as spiritual, leading to a potential neglect of man. The traditional repositories of Forsterian virtue—goodwill plus culture and intelligence—function only incompletely in this universe; and Forster's own liberal passion for social connection motivates a large section of the action, but does not contain its chief interest. Certainly, beyond the world of social organization is that world of 'the secret understanding of the heart' to which Aziz appeals; this is the world that is damaged when Ronny and Mrs. Moore discuss Aziz and she finds: 'Yes, it was all true, but how false as a summary of the man; the essential life of him had been slain.' Forster is, as usual, superb at creating that 'essential life' and showing what threatens it, and much of the book deals with its virtues and its triumphs. At one level the social world *is* redeemed by those who resist its classifications—by

Adela and Mrs. Moore, Fielding, Aziz, Godbole. Forster does not belittle their victories directly except in so far as he sees their comedy. But he does place beyond them a world of infinitude which is not, here, to be won through the personal; indeed, these acts of resistance, which provide the book's lineal structure, are usually marked by failure. Adela's is a conventional disaster; she makes the moral mistake of exposing the personal to the social. Fielding's is more complicated; he is an agent of liberal contact through goodwill plus culture and intelligence, but he, like Mrs. Moore, meets an echo:

'In the old eighteenth century, when cruelty and injustice raged, an invisible power repaired their ravages. Everything echoes now; there's no stopping the echo. The original sound may be harmless, but the echo is always evil.' This reflection about an echo lay at the verge of Fielding's mind. He could never develop it. It belonged to the universe that he had missed or rejected. And the mosque missed it too. Like himself, those shallow arcades provided but a limited asylum.

As for Mrs. Moore, who does touch it, she encounters another force still —the moral nihilism that comes when the boundaries are down. Her disaster dominates the novel, for it places even moral and mystical virtue within the sphere of contingency; it, too, is subject to spiritual anarchy. Beyond the world of the plot, the lineal world of consequences and relationships, there lies a second universe of fictional structure, which links spiritual events, and then a third, which in turn places these in history and appeals to the infinite recession of the universe beyond any human structure that seeks to comprehend it.

One way we see this is by noting that in this novel, as compared with the earlier ones, the world of men is clearly granted reduced powers. The universe of time and contingency is made smaller, by the nature that surrounds man, by the scale of the continent on which man's presence is a feeble invasion, by the sky which over-arches him and his works. It is a world of dwarfs and of dwarfed relationships, in which the familiar forces of romantic redemption in Forster's work—personal relationships as mirrors to infinity, a willingness to confront the un-seen—undertake their movements towards connection without the full support of the universe. The theme recurs, but Mrs. Moore expresses it most strongly in chapter 14, when she reflects on her situation and grows towards her state of spiritual nullity in the cave:

She felt increasingly (vision or nightmare?) that, though people are important, the relations between them are not, and that in particular too much fuss has been made over marriage; centuries of carnal embracement, yet man is no nearer to understanding man. And today she felt this with such force that it seemed itself a relationship, itself a person who was trying to take hold of her hand.

The negative withdrawal is, of course, an aspect of that 'twilight of the double vision in which so many elderly people are involved', and is not the the only meaning in the book. But it is dominant. It is by seeking its obverse that Adela compounds her basic moral error:

It was Adela's faith that the whole stream of events is important and interesting, and if she grew bored she blamed herself severely and compelled her lips to utter enthusiasms. ... She was particularly vexed now because she was both in India and engaged to be married, which double event should have made every instant sublime.

Human relationships are dwarfed not only by the scale of the historical and social world, which is potentially redeemable, but by the natural world, which is not.

Of course, intimations of transcendence are present throughout the novel. Structurally they run through the seasonal cycle, from decisive hot sun to the benedictive healing water at the end, from Mosque to Caves to Temple. By taking that order, Forster is able poetically to sustain the hope of a spiritual possibility, a prefiguring of the world beyond in the world below. The climax of this theme is Godbole's attempt at 'completeness, not reconstruction'. But what happens there is that divine revelation is shifted to the level of the comic sublime; Forster's rhetoric now puts what has been spiritually perplexing—the webs, nets, and prisons that divide spirit as well as society—back into the comic universe of muddle. The Mau festival is the celebration of the formlessness of the Indian multiverse, seen for a moment inclusively. The poetic realm of the novel, in which above all Mrs. Moore and Godbole have participated, and which has dominated the book's primary art, is reconciled with the muddle of the world of men, in an emotional cataract that momentarily repairs the divisions of the spiritual world (through Godbole's revelation) and the social world (through the festival itself). It satisfies much of the passion for inclusiveness that has been one thread in the novel, the desire that heaven should include all because India *is* all.

Godbole consulted the music-book, said a word to the drummer, who broke rhythm, made a thick little blur of sound, and produced a new rhythm. This was more exciting, the inner images it evoked more definite, and the singers' expressions became fatuous and languid. They loved all men, the whole universe, and scraps of their past, tiny splinters of details, emerged for a moment to melt into the universal warmth. Thus Godbole, though she was not important to him, remembered an old woman he had met in Chandrapore days. Chance brought her into his mind while it was in this heated state, he did not select her, she happened to occur among the throng of soliciting images, a tiny splinter, and he impelled her by his spiritual force to that place where completeness can be found. Completeness, not reconstruction. His senses grew thinner, he remembered a wasp seen he forgot where, perhaps on a stone. He loved the wasp equally, he impelled it likewise, he was imitating God. And the stone where the wasp clung—could he . . . no, he could not, he had been wrong to attempt the stone, logic and conscious effort had seduced, he came back to the strip of red carpet and discovered that he was dancing upon it.

Godbole's doctrine—'completeness, not reconstruction'—is, of course, a species of transcendence, a momentary vision of the whole, the invocation of a universe invested with spirit. It links up with the symbolist plot of the novel, its power as a radiant image, rather than with plot in the linear sense, with its world of 'and then . . . and then . . .' Threading its way through the novel, to an old woman and a wasp, it takes these 'soliciting images' and puts them in new association —not with all things, but with each other and with what else comes almost unbidden into the world of spirit. But the stone is left, and equally spirit may or may not invest the universe in any of its day-to-day affairs: 'Perhaps all these things! Perhaps none!' Things, in freeing themselves from their traditional associations, social and historical, form a new order, beyond dialogue, beyond human plot, in the realm where poetic figures function on their own order of consciousness. Yet here, too, irony is at work: mystery is sometimes muddle, completeness is sometimes the universe where 'everythings exists, nothing has value'. If history ultimately obstructs, and does not give us a final, rounded structure in terms of human events, if the horses, the earth, the clutter of human institutions say, 'No, not yet,' then like obstructions dwell in the realm of spirit and symbol, too: the sky says, 'No, not there.'

The linear social plot, then, has stretched a long way in search of a structure of its own that will provide coherence in the world, but if it finds one it is in the form of an oblique, doubtful, and ironic promise; personal relations only go so far to solve the muddle of history. As for the symbolist plot, it transcends but it does not redeem; it is there but 'neglects to come'. The power of the novel lies, of course, in the Whitmanesque ambition to include multitudes, to find eternity in some order in the given world. But is this ambition realized? Intimations of eternity may have their symbols in the world of men (in love and relationship) and in the world of nature (in the force of mystery that resides in things); the social and the natural worlds have in them touches that promise wholeness. But they do not of themselves have unity; they are themselves afflicted by the double vision which is all that man can bring to them, grounded as he is in history and hope at once. The world stretches infinitely about us, and there is infinity beyond us. But questions bring us only to the unyielding hostility of the soil and the unyielding ambiguity of the sky.

The universe, then, is less intimation than cipher; a mask rather than a revelation in the romantic sense. Does love meet with love? Do we receive but what we give? The answer is surely a paradox, the paradox that there are Platonic universals beyond, but that the glass is too dark to see them. Is there a light beyond the glass, or is it a mirror only to the self? The Platonic cave is even darker than Plato made it, for it introduces the echo, and so leaves us back in the world of men, which does not carry total meaning, is just a story of events. The Platonic romantic gesture of the match in the cave is the dominating ambiguity of the book—is the glimmer of radiance a promise, or is it only the self that the universe gives back in its endless solipsistic cycle?

There is little to see, and no eye to see it, until the visitor arrives for his five minutes, and strikes a match. Immediately another flame rises in the depths of the rock and moves towards the surface like an imprisoned spirit: the walls of the circular chamber have been most marvellously polished. The two flames approach and strive to unite, but cannot, because one of them breathes air, the other stone, A mirror inlaid with lovely colours divides the lovers, delicate stars of pink and grey interpose, exquisite nebulae, shadings fainter than the tail of a comet or the midday moon, all the evanescent life of the granite, only here visible. Fists and fingers thrust above the advancing soil—here at last is their skin, finer than any covering acquired by the animals, smoother than windless water, more voluptuous than love. The radiance increases, the flames touch one another, kiss, expire. The cave is dark again, like all the caves.

In the end, Forster seems to say both, to indicate both total unity, the oneness of the world and what lies behind it, and total multiplicity. He does so because comedy and poetry share the book between them in perpetual interplay, proliferating muddle, yet manifesting formal order. The human world may be unredeemable, but Forster venerates those who try to redeem it; it may be plurally incomprehensible, existence without value, but the values those who seek to comprehend it. Yet the world of wholeness and vision is, in a sense, too easy, and not enough; the material and human world must subsist first before it may have credit. The task of the full novel must therefore be undertaken not alone by the social novelist, and not alone by the symbolist one, as Virginia Woolf undertakes it. The result is, finally, a dualistic world, a world founded on contradictions at once potentially mystery and muddle. As Virginia Woolf—who shared Bloomsbury with him, but maintained her novel as a rather purer species—complained, Forster is a materialist novelist, very much aware of the powers of time, refusing to live life at the level of perpetual vision: for to him vision is rare and not always redemptive. So the human plot tells of life in time, and Forster awards enough meaning and tone and style to that to make it matter fully; the verbal plot tells of transcendence, of epiphany, through art, through suggestion, pattern, and leitmotif, the opening out of meanings, and Forster gives wholeness to that too, the wholeness which is the unity of art, but which is what Alan Friedman says the ending of the book is, 'a new and final opening outward left incomplete.'[1]

In fact Forster ends the book ironically appealing both to the transcendence through form and against it. In this novel of all his novels, he establishes with great fullness the elements of formal transcendence —through continuity by the image, or that musicality of composition, of sound in blocks, which in *Aspects of the Novel* he calls 'rhythm', and which stitches a book together from the inside—even as he substantiates, materially, the world of history and time. Art may reach out beyond the world of men, and be more than they; but this transcendence is far enough beyond the world not only to criticize it but be criticized by it. The symbol itself, being infinitely recessive, is subject to irony. This paradox of artistic transcendence is recurrent in modernism, where we repeatedly encounter the transcendental form—be it hard unitary image, epiphany, objective correlative—under pressure from the contingent and formless world of history. Hence the lapsed world of Joyce, where the epiphany seems to reveal how unredeemable

[1] Alan Friedman, *The Turn of the Novel: The Transition into Modern Fiction* (New York and London, 1966), 128.

the world of man is; or that of Fitzgerald, where the brute and material
economic process takes over the transcendental dream of stepping into
the timeless American pastoral; or that of Mann, where, potentially
more hopefully, history amends the deathly purity of art. Forster is
perhaps closest to Mann; and, as with *The Magic Mountain*, his classic
work qualifies art with history in wary suspicion, perhaps even with
a positive hope for the however dwarfed world of time.

It may be this last, and the forms he expresses it in, the forms of
social and moral comedy, that leave us with the lingering suspicion that
the world of community and society mean too much to Forster, for
him to be finally and fully the modernist novelist. But if that is the
price on which we gain his moral balance, his humanism, the book's
basis not only in artistry but in decency, then it seems a price patently
worth the paying, one that leaves *A Passage to India* still standing
among the classic novels—with *Women in Love* and *Lord Jim* and
Ulysses—of our century.

VII

Virginia Woolf and Ford Madox Ford:
Two Styles of Modernity

I

After James Joyce, whose *Ulysses*—with its plurality and parody of styles, its ironic juxtapositions of past and present, myth and realism, its use of stream-of-consciousness and other such 'spatial' modes—is the great classic in English of modernist perception, then Virginia Woolf's is probably the name we would next draw forth to show that English fiction after the First World War had a modernist phase. We have now come to take her as the imaginative contemporary of the great European and American modernists—Proust, Mann, Joyce, Faulkner— and as someone interested in the same kind of formal experiment, driven by the same kind of aesthetic aspiration. Her account of that aspiration, in her criticism and in the creative self-analysis of her *Writer's Diary*, has become a representative exploration of the modern artist's dilemmas and resources. We might name her thus with a certain caution, aware that Bloomsbury is not Montparnasse, that her sensibility can be private and shrill, that not all her books wear well, that her modern experience has a less extended social range than some of the other writers who embody modernism for us. Yet she is one of those writers who have disestablished something of the novel of the past and on those ruins built a new one, who visibly fought, on native grounds, the battle for new fictional modes arising from the challenges the novel had to face once James, Dostoevsky, Proust, and Joyce had written. In *Mimesis*, that brilliant study of European realism, Erich Auerbach hence takes her as the central representative of the arts of modernist 'realism' in fiction; and, if one interest of his chapter is what he makes of that seeming contradiction, another is the way *To the Lighthouse* becomes, under his critical illumination, the distillation of the most important experimental procedures and typologies: of the disappearance of the objective narrator, and indeed of objective reality as something generally valid and recognizable; of subjective consciousness serving to present a multiple impression of all that is perceived; of the contrast between 'interior' and 'exterior' time; of the presentation of interior life through a randomness 'neither restrained by a purpose nor directed by a specific subject of thought'; of the reduction of the exterior life through cutting away the direct significance of staple events in history or the deaths of characters.[1] After his statement, it must be granted that Virginia Woolf was seriously and deeply implicated in those extraordinary developments in the means and assumptions of the novel which go back to James but are then renegotiated in the second decade of the century, and that she does this, in some books, on a scale compelling among her great contemporaries, among whom we should include Lawrence, the breadth of whose experimentalism grows increasingly apparent.

One thing crucial to her importance is that she proposes a novel in which the devices of symbolist presentation become whole and entire, conditioning the total experience we read, and in which the characters live, the events occur. This is what Forster meant when he said she wrote by 'stretching out from her enchanted tree and snatching bits from the flux of daily life'; it is what makes his work look, by comparison, materialist, or unvisionary (part of the point of *A Passage to India* is that we cannot live in a perpetual state of vision). But Virginia Woolf's novels, even the historical ones, dissipate, with varying degrees of success, the world of environment, the world of the socially conditioned, the notion of a life enacted through social forms and historical time; her books—at any rate her central ones, where she is best—substitute a prevailing state of consciousness, into and through which the world is filtered.

The emergence of the 'insubstantized' novel—the novel which not only articulates its own means, but does this on the assumption that material is only authentic when it has been captured by the consciousness controlling those means—dates back to the 1890s, and to the presumption that, as William James had stressed in *Principles of Psychology*

[1] Erich Auerbach, *Mimesis: The Representation of Reality in Western Literature* (Princeton, N.J. and London, 1953).

(1890), reality was not an objective 'given' but was perceived subjectively through consciousness. That presumption gave us not only a disturbance in fiction but a phrase now taken into its description, for, arguing that the mind is not the mirror of matter but is active and has its own movement and structure, James proposed: 'In talking of it hereafter, let us call it the stream of thought, of consciousness, or of the subjective life.' In the work of his brother Henry, and in much subsequent writing, one can see the concept of interior time becoming of increased significance, 'consciousness' being interposed as the primary intermediary between world and man. As this became crucial for novelists, it resulted in a wide variety of tactics and logics, which in different forms moved into the modernist stock. One of the consequences was a psychological realism, an intensified impressionism, a novel of Paterian 'quickened, multiplied consciousness'. Another was a heightened concern with authorial consciousness as such, both as a form of apprehension or an artistic awareness and as a managing instrument, demanding enormous precision of presentation and point of view, increased formalism. These two kinds of novel—the psychological, and the experimental or fictive—both desubstantiated material reality, and they often tended to merge. This was especially true at the time when Freud was becoming known, Dostoevsky influential, Bergson important, when the claims of aesthetics to provide an overview of human, and especially modern, experience were being put forward with missionary energy, and when Bloomsbury was finding a secular religion in aligning the sensitivities of art and form and delicate human relationships. That means, in short, when Virginia Woolf was beginning writing; and her novel of vision is clearly of this double sort.

The notion of a composition spun entire from a presiding authorial consciousness whose own psychology was so attuned as to produce the symbolist metamorphosis, the epiphany of form, obviously underlies an extraordinary sequence of novels of sensibility, psychology, and high artistry that began appearing in the second decade of the century. In 1913 the first two volumes of Marcel Proust's eight-volume *À la recherche du temps perdu* came out; in 1915 there appeared the initial volume of Dorothy Richardson's twelve-volume novel called *Pilgrimage*, completed in 1938, as well as Lawrence's novel of the 'unstable ego' and the 'dark, potent secrets' inside men, *The Rainbow*, and Virginia Woolf's first book, *The Voyage Out*; the following year saw book publication of Joyce's *A Portrait of the Artist as a Young Man*. All could be seen as novels experimental at once in the psychological and the aesthetic realm.[1] In different ways, for different purposes, at different levels of absoluteness, the structure is secured from orders drawn from psychological—as opposed to historical or communal—time. In various ways form becomes coincident with consciousness; it soaks over the entire work, the plot being not some discernible separate story but the vision from which it is told, so that discreteness of character or traditional logic of story are overwhelmed. The centre of the fictional construct becomes some dominant consciousness artistically disposed— perhaps the subjective consciousness of a character, or the intermingling consciousness of several, or some vector of consciousness passing between character(s) and author. The crises and discoveries of the action are species of psychic growth or aesthetic awareness. Chronological time is weakened as consciousness, with its large memory-constituent, moves backwards and forwards, recollecting, selecting, synthesizing, working irrationally or subconsciously through oblique and random stimuli, often emancipating the mind not only from objective data but also from the dominance of a particular present: Erich Auerbach's elegant phrase for this last is 'symbolic omnitemporality'.

At its most spectacular, this kind of novel therefore yields an intermittent, flickering universe, in which life becomes stuff and the impulses of the mind towards registration, awareness, assimilation, order produce a new, and difficult, type of aesthetic structure, based on a new historiography of the mind. It was and remains decidedly modern, and can and does become a mannerism; still, the basis of the modernity lies in its power to assert authenticity, to show this not simply as a vague impressionism but an intimation of the inner bases of being. This sort of writing—because it dwells on the borders between things and awareness *of* things, between sensing and naming, between chaos and the mind's order—is often thought of as a form of anti-novel. Indeed much of its manner comes through to the contemporary *nouveau roman*, and it is useful to recall in considering Mrs. Woolf's writing the injunction given by John Sturrock to readers of that genre: these new novels must never, he says, be read as exercises in naïve realism or

[1] On this see Leon Edel, *The Psychological Novel 1900–1950* (New York and London, 1955), and Morris Beja, *Epiphany in the Modern Novel: Revelation as Art* (Seattle, Wash. and London, 1971).

naturalism, but as studied dramatizations of the creative process itself.[1]

Now to this broad and important modern development, Virginia Woolf is clearly a central contributor. Like many of her successors in new fiction, she was very much concerned in elaborating a new and commanding posture for the author; and, like them, she is a writer who not only patiently *embodies* a new aesthetic but is herself devotionally aesthetic, asserting the sovereignty of her own artistic sensibility and offering her art as a sequence of meanings and visions validated precisely *by* that sensibility. The sensibility itself was much shaped by a well-developed tribal body of assumptions about creative personal relationships and emotional states, and by the aesthetic upheaval that took place in Bloomsbury after the exhibition of Post-Impressionist paintings organized by Roger Fry in 1910 (a year Virginia Woolf regarded as the turning point into modern history). Bloomsbury was of course very modern, but also very intellectual, and with its distinct inheritances. One was social, the upper-middle-class Victorian intelligentsia from which it derived directly and against which it reacted, quite as directly; the other was aesthetic, a body of assumptions, evolving through from Pater and certain later philosophical inheritors, like G. E. Moore (who said in *Principia Ethica* (1903): 'By far the most valuable things we know or can imagine are certain states of consciousness, which may roughly be described as the pleasures of human intercourse and the enjoyment of beautiful objects'), to Roger Fry and Clive Bell—assumptions about the formal deliverances art may, through its 'significant form', give to us, and about the human importance of those deliverances. The point about Bloomsbury's radical aesthetics was not only that they were radical, but that they were very aesthetic: the prescription they satisfy is close to the spirit of a generation before, for whom certain essential states of sensitivity, synaesthesia, and social humanism were of the essence.

Virginia Woolf's novels—the first appeared in 1915, the eighth and last twenty-six years later, in 1941—show all the marks of ferment, especially if we look to the middle group of *Mrs. Dalloway* (1925), *To the Lighthouse* (1927), and *The Waves* (1931). They still remain startling, and in explaining them to us—as she did in her essays 'Mr. Bennett and Mrs. Brown' and 'Modern Fiction'—she gave them an historical justification. She speaks there for the new novelist, released

[1] John Sturrock, *The French New Novel: Claude Simon, Michel Butor, Alain Robbe-Grillet* (London, 1969).

from traditional views of time and identity, and stresses three aspects of the 'new' novel which, running together, make it technically so spectacular: the novel, by a withering away of old conventions and necessities, becomes formally more itself; it manifests a new mode of perception; and it also releases and reveals the 'real' spirit of life, life as we know it to be once intervening materiality is discarded. All three aspects come into the famous passage in 'Modern Fiction' where she represents the writer moving from the kingdom of necessity to the kingdom of light ('If a writer were a free man and not a slave, if he could write what he chose, not what he must, if he could base his work upon his own feeling and not upon convention, there would be no plot, no comedy, no tragedy, no love interest or catastrophe in the accepted sense, and perhaps not a single button sewn on as the Bond Street tailors would have it'), and then goes on to speak of life as 'a luminous halo, a semi-transparent envelope surrounding us from the beginning of consciousness to the end', such life being what the novelist must convey, with 'as little mixture of the alien and external as possible'.

This makes the novelist a realist of consciousness; and it needs noting that Mrs. Woolf means by consciousness something other than many of her contemporaries meant. For a number of these, from Joyce to Faulkner, the new novel of consciousness is there in part to reveal contingency, disorder, and historical stress, a world from which wholeness has gone; and their experimentalism, though it may have a joyous element, is also clearly witness to the strain of finding language, structure, order in a demythicizing age. In James, consciousness can be seen as the ordeal of fine minds in a specified social and historical environment, and in *The Ambassadors* it is a strongly apprehensive instrument for coping with an intensive, international range of experience. As we come nearer the present, the intimations of disorder increase. For Joyce consciousness in the novel has something to do with disorder, and something to do with aesthetic apprehension; by *Finnegans Wake* the 'stream of consciousness' has moved towards being a psychic current taking up from the substratum myths, images, and symbols, powers well below both the conscious and the aesthetically responsive ego. In Lawrence's very different version of the novel of consciousness, the task is to break down the stable ego in order to explore energies, vitalistic and deathly, that pass among individuals as an evolutionary flow in an apocalyptic time. In Faulkner the intimations of disorder are likewise strong; the 'flow' arises from an apprehension of temporal disorder and reaches to the point of seeing life as 'a tale told by an idiot'.[1] But Virginia Woolf's assumptions are away from *all* these things—because it was her point that consciousness was unconditioned, was poetic, was dominant. And this makes her a very lyrical modernist.

The phrase is something of a contradiction; and reading her we begin, in due course, to sense the contradiction. One of the things, I am suggesting, underlying modernist structure—which is to say modernist difficulty—is the need to witness to difficulties of ordering and shaping, a turning towards symbolism and a reaching away from worldly coherence, which is both manifested and then exposed as incomplete. And so the art of metamorphosis, the Daedalean voyage into the unknown, was itself bound to a paradox; it fled the contingency of an inchoate world, but its timelessness, its resultant symbol, is touched with disorientation, with the dangerous and deathly magic so profoundly explored by Thomas Mann. To account for modernism's spirit in fiction, we must look not only to the novel's move towards a psychological-symbolist mode, but to the awareness, in those pursuing it, of the contingency of the universe from which a modern form must escape, in order to *be* a form. In this light, Virginia Woolf's mode is, for all the disturbance we know underlay it, an oddly joyous one. Certainly she does afford, for that mode, an historical cause, the famous transformation of December 1910, when, she says, all human relations shifted and put traditional reality in question. But this is not the great apocalyptic lesion of much modernism, rather a transformation in the history of forms and consciousness, coincident with the Fry Post-Impressionist exhibition and the coming of the Georgian world. The transformation is not to contingency, chaos, loss, which other writers appeal to, but a complex of new impressions, a new aestheticism and joy. Human consciousness, especially *artistic* consciousness, could become more intuitive, feminine, poetic; art could fulfil itself by escaping its onerous convention about reality, and entering the realm of intui-

[1] In the course of a good discussion of distinctions here very lightly made, Alan Friedman (*The Turn of the Novel*, New York and London, 1966) remarks of the 'final unstable form' of some modern novelists: 'Perhaps I may suggest—playfully, but not on that account without seriousness—that we can usefully understand the art and the achievement of the three greatest masters of modern English fiction by recognizing that James writes a stream of conscience, Joyce a stream of consciousness, and Lawrence a stream of the unconscious' (p. 177).

tion, imaginative and instinctual patterns, heightened responses. The experimental novel of consciousness was thus explicitly a formal emancipation, a fiction in which neither the novelist nor the consciousness he creates as narrative texture is conditioned, socially or psychologically, is neither culture-bound nor archetypal. The novel of consciousness is like 'uncircumscribed' life, aesthetic apprehension being the way of grasping it; the problem of the luminous order outside time, the problem of symbolist transcendence (artistic metamorphosis, chaotic universe) is stilled or else simply commonplace. And so Virginia Woolf moved, in her central fiction, into the realm of consciousness without being in a strict sense a psychological novelist, without concerning herself with psychic reasons, drives, archetypes, or 'unconscious' myths. Consciousness was a species of free action; and her new novel is nearer to being a reverie of the ego than an emanation of the id.

So, in short, for Virginia Woolf consciousness is intuitive and poetic rather than subterranean or mythopoeic; and hence it is the creative energy of the self which makes its own subjective time, its Bergsonian *durée*, out of the connective tissue linking the immediate moment with the past. The flux has no marked social origin—in *Mrs. Dalloway* there is an inference that the city has to do with these fleeting and multiple impressions, but there is no such suggestion in *To the Lighthouse* or *The Waves*—and, with whatever Bloomsbury and Bergsonian additions, the essential sensibility harks back to the spirit of Pater's 'Conclusion' to *Studies in the History of the Renaissance* in 1873 ('While all melts under our feet, we may well grasp at any exquisite passion, or any contribution to knowledge that seems by a lifted horizon to set the spirit free for a moment, or any stirring of the senses, strange dyes, strange colours, and curious odours, or work of the artist's hands, or the face of one's friend'). This is why Virginia Woolf's novels impress us not for their realism, not even their psychological realism, but for their sensibility. Only relatively is she interested in the psychological continuum, or the individual identity. The novel of consciousness affords the opportunity of a lyrical impressionism, a fiction of intensified sensitivity and fine sensations; and is rendered usually through a sensitive supraconsciousness that works in association with the characters but which is the narrator's own, dominating and unifying the action. So, commonly in her novels, consciousness is permitted to shift not only temporally (backwards and forwards in time) and spatially (from this place to that) in the individual ego, but from character to character; while the characters often share a common focus in relation to an external symbol—like the lighthouse or the waves. Though the novelist remains in the same condition of immediate responsiveness as the characters, knowing little more than they, sharing their bewilderment and wonder, and though the events all remain essentially internal, the stream of consciousness is finally the emancipated associative flow of the novelist herself (who can function as an independent source of reflection in the absence of any character whatsoever, as in the 'Time Passes' interlude in *To the Lighthouse*).

Consciousness so does more than apprehend the flux and contingency of life, that 'incessant shower of innumerable atoms' the author speaks of in 'Modern Fiction'; it is also concerned with poetic intimations, moments of vision, 'little daily miracles, illuminations, matches struck unexpectedly in the dark' (*To the Lighthouse*), and trembles persistently on the brink of an authorial revelation. She can and does create the flux in its terrifying enormity—Septimus Smith in *Mrs. Dalloway*, dislocated by the war, accepts that 'it might be possible that the world itself is without meaning'; Eleanor at the end of *The Years* recognizes that the atoms that 'danced apart and massed themselves' might hardly compose an identity, 'what people called a life'—but the flux is also the context for a sensitive appreciation of the essences in things. Time, in her work, often tapers to a point and distils, in the direction of Mrs. Ramsay's intimation in *To the Lighthouse*:

there is a coherence in things; a stability; something, she meant, is immune from change, and shines out (she glanced at the window with its ripple of reflected lights) in the face of the flowing, the fleeting, the spectral, like a ruby; so that again tonight she had the feeling she had once today, of peace, of rest. Of such moments, she thought, the thing is made that endures.

This *is* symbolist, though Virginia Woolf sees these intimations, as her characters do, from within time, so that they are never absolute. Even so, the repeated hints of a pattern which traces its mystery in the universe, the repeated suggestion that the flux is potentially a world of broken forms mirroring true forms in a world beyond, is the basis of Mrs. Woolf's charged style of discourse. In *To the Lighthouse* and *The Waves*, her two most evidently symbolist novels, lighthouse and waves are really symbols *about* symbols; the lighthouse's brief pulses, the faint and evanescent patterns left by the waves, are both rhythmic and temporary, resonant and incomplete. They are recessive forms from a vaguely suggested world beyond, like the momentary glimpses we are given of things as essences, 'single, distinct':

It seemed now as if, touched by human penitence and all its toil, divine goodness had parted the curtain and displayed behind it, single, distinct, the hare erect; the wave falling; the boat rocking which, did we deserve them, should be ours always. But alas, divine goodness, twitching the cord, draws the curtain; it does not please him; he covers his treasures in a drench of hail, and so breaks them, so confuses them that it seems impossible that their calm should ever return or that we should ever compose from their fragments a perfect whole or read in the littered pieces the clear words of truth. For our penitence deserves a glimpse only; our toil respite only. (*To the Lighthouse*)

Hence her characters live between flux and pattern; and because the novels themselves are patterned and rhythmic she inevitably validates most of those characters who have an aesthetic and symbolist propensity of her own sort.

In so doing, she not only tends to poeticize modernism, but also to feminize and domesticate it. In *To the Lighthouse*, the male world is materialist, historicist, philosophical, public, a system of assessment and identity repudiated by the book, which celebrates the female world in which sensitivity, intuition, beauty, and domesticity unite. The men who 'negotiated treaties, ruled India, controlled finance' are excoriated and *protected* by sensibilities, notably Mrs. Ramsay's, attuned to higher matters, disdainful of the claims of history, abstract ideas, the materiality of things, all part of the 'fatal sterility' of the male. Because of this, the essential form of Virginia Woolf's novels, whatever the complexities of their pattern, is always finally that of the domestic novel of sensibility; and this limits the matter of consciousness with which she deals, too easily permits her states of 'rapture' and completeness. Her method, unlike that of Joyce or Forster, prescribes a large cutting away of much modern experience in the interests of keeping her fictional world intact.

To the Lighthouse is probably her best novel, but there is something unsolid and aloof about its achievement—as if its deliberated perfection of form cannot quite be substantiated through the materials of life with which the book must deal. Its two episodes, an evening and a morning ten years apart, split by an interlude which focuses those ten years of history into tiny parentheses, describe a world with Mrs. Ramsay in it and a world without her. Thematically, the book deals with a number of matters fundamental to Mrs. Woolf's works: the relation of male to female, intellect to intuition, the difference between the isolation of pure thought and the social and humane quality of living, like Mrs. Ramsay, 'in beauty'. Mrs. Ramsay, a reconciling and invigorating force, is a unified sensibility:

Mrs. Ramsay, who had been sitting loosely, folding her son in her arm, braced herself, and, half turning, seemed to raise herself with an effort, and at once to pour erect into the air a rain of energy, a column of spray, looking at the same time animated and alive as if all her energies were being fused into force, burning and illuminating (quietly though she sat taking up her stocking again), and into this delicious fecundity, this fountain and spray of life, the fatal sterility of the male plunged itself, like a beak of brass, barren and bare.

With her beauty and her 'capacity to surround and protect', with her 'raptures of successful creation', Mrs. Ramsay is very much the book's centre; but that centre is removed midway. There is perhaps something faintly punitive about the formal placing of her death—a certain feminine temperamentality, a saying of 'See how you can manage without me' unmistakeable in the tone. All the same, it is to the point that Mrs. Ramsay's 'rain of energy' may unify herself, even to a point her family, but does not unify life; that more ultimate question is what Virginia Woolf has in mind. Hence Mrs. Ramsay dies; the lighthouse acquires something of the character of an impersonal substitute. As such, of course, it is not equivalent; but the removal of the human centre throws the emphasis on other effects and other matters, matters of the 'phantom universe' that surrounds reality, so giving to the idea of unity not a humanistic but a mystical association. The novel decreates the historical world; it sacrifices the human one; what it reinstates is the world of sensitive awareness, a world close to art and fulfilled within the book by Lily Briscoe, who provides the frame to an almost unframeable experience, an experience itself a search for a pattern beyond the achieving.

Nonetheless it is distinctive to Virginia Woolf's method that the novelist of such intimations, the novelist who emphasizes both the contingency and its potential pattern ('Let us record the atoms as they fall upon the mind in the order in which they fall, let us trace the pattern, however disconnected and incoherent in appearance, which each sight or incident scores upon the consciousness'), is decidedly iconographic. Her attack on the externally desired coherence of things is telling; yet there is something too fine and fixed about the insights she must, against that exteriority, authenticate, make her own. The images of *To the Lighthouse*, as the passage quoted above perhaps shows well, are decorative, shaped, fine; they are complex metaphors which draw upon, though they never esemplastically realize, the iconography of poetic romanticism: trees, fountains, rain, waves. Such 'iconographic' moments run through the novel: Charles Tansley seeing Mrs. Ramsay's beauty plain, Lily Briscoe seeing human thought as a scrubbed kitchen table in a tree, Mr. Ramsay going to 'a spit of land which the sea is slowly eating away, and there to stand, like a desolate sea-bird, alone', facing the dark of human ignorance. The book is full of moments of gazing, of contemplation, of rapture; moments coming less out of the action than out of the emphasis of the writer. The characters, stopping to admire and venerate one another, and particularly to worship or recall Mrs. Ramsay's 'knowledge and wisdom', seem able to do so because little else can happen in their universe, because they inhabit a world in which this is a norm of human activity and relationship, its basic human obverse being the sense of loneliness and isolation. The world of the novel is scarcely penetrable from outside, by the real as opposed to the stylized contingencies of life. And as for the novel as a whole, that too is a total metaphor, shaped and fined, ending as it does with the last brush-stroke to Lily Briscoe's picture—in effect the signal for the total filling out of the composition. It ends *as* a composition, entire and of itself; while the flux may be the flux of consciousness, it moves inevitably towards a coherence, not of the human mind of the characters but of aesthetic composition. So pattern seems, finally, the pattern of art as artifice, and this limits the ultimate scale of Virginia Woolf's modernism. For all her registering of the evanescent, her work is on the one hand too crystalline and complete, on the other hand too dependent on her particular and personal sensibility, her self-conscious femininity, at times her quaintness and her whimsy, to be a guide for others. It is a peculiarly personal refinement of a tradition rather than the creation of a general style.

This, of course, does not limit her absorbing interest; but it does personalize it. Her sensitivity is infinitely rewarding; one re-reads her with pleasure. That should be enough—except that, precisely because of the rarity of the species, Virginia Woolf has not only become the great exemplar of the English experimental novel but, for a number of writers, an indicator of its limitations. Her own unease about her entire success in what she was doing, patent enough in *A Writer's Diary*, is evidence enough that in some ways this was a harsh sentence; while claiming to exemplify a new fiction, she had not thought to be the one and only proof of the pudding. But when writers of the thirties found the experimental novel bourgeois and private, and chose, as George Orwell had some sense of choosing, against it, it was largely Virginia Woolf they chose against, a fact that increased her guilt about what she was doing. And when in the 1950s, for different reasons, another generation of writers explicitly reacted against the experimental novel, it was not the novel of Proust they were reacting against (Snow and Cooper, for example, both greatly admired Proust) but the novel of Virginia Woolf and her few latter-day imitators. In fact her 'enchanted tree' was a special world of the modern, though the hidden order of its art is very much a form for our times; to appreciate and value it, it is best read for its distinctiveness and sheer personal sensitivity. What that may well mean, though, is that if an inheritance from modernism did pass into the postwar English novelist, it got there via other means.

2

By, perhaps, the example of Ford Madox Ford. The critics have always been rather more doubtful about Ford's reputation than Mrs. Woolf's, and with reason; his work, his sensibility, the shape and merit of his mind were all, so to speak, uneven. Yet he is one of those novelists who, perhaps out of an instinct for convenient derivation, saw and mastered modernism as a craft or technique; doing that, he made, one suspects, its manners and modes into a kind of modern realism which could be inherited as common stock by subsequent writers. This may seem to suggest something inauthentic about Ford as a writer; the accusation has indeed been made. But it is probably truer to see him as a pro-fessional writer sufficiently soaked in modernist assumptions as to regard them as imperatives of serious technique in fiction. Ford grew up with modernism, was bound up in its main events. In the 1890s he was close to Stephen Crane and Henry James and Joseph Conrad, when the argument was about Impressionism. He was still central, as the editor between 1908 and 1911 of *The English Review* (which first printed Lawrence and Wyndham Lewis), when Post-Impressionism shifted towards Imagism, Vorticism, and the search for an energetic centre. After the war he shifted to Paris and the expatriate climate where the epical dimension of modernism came in, when a decided war-weariness and cultural exhaustion invested the equation, when there was a fresh infusion of post-adjectival, post-causal style from Stein and Hemingway; here he edited the expatriate magazine *transatlantic review* which printed Stein, Joyce, and Hemingway.[1] His attentiveness to the places of the new probably brought out the best in him. In his very uneven career, *The Good Soldier* (1915) is a central advance: a tight psychological novel of sexual relationships energized by an extraordinary detachment, experientially and formally a very modern book. But the peak comes with the four novels composing *Parade's End* (1924–8), a work that grows right out of the epic phase of modernism. Focused on the war, it is neither existential (like Hemingway) nor a-causal or a-sequential, for Ford believed in history. In fact he clearly attempts to crystallize in it the whole era up to the twenties, in a socio-psychological sequence distilling both a period and an art authentically suited to its treatment. In just that way he did succeed in making fully potent the aesthetics of a tradition of modernist practice which had been in his armory for some time.

Ford knew his modernism; in many respects the assumptions and motives in his writing are of a piece with those of Virginia Woolf, Gertrude Stein, and the contemporaries or younger writers he saw around him and judged to be the devotees of his own passion: the application of maximum craft, of a new intensity of expression and of rendering, to the writing of fiction. But Ford was also reasonably close to a prevailing style and preoccupation of the Edwardian novel (there are certain marked resemblances between *Howards End* and the *Parade's End* sequence) and in other ways to the more realistic epic-historical vein of nineteenth-century fiction. The novelist he is closest to is Conrad, writing on whom he says many things that clearly apply to his own work. Ford's name for the kind of writing he valued was 'impressionism', a term he uses in rather a different way from Virginia Woolf. An experience is, as for Virginia Woolf, composed of 'various unordered pictures', and the artistic recreation of it demands not an evocation of a single stated reality observed by the writer and registered as a fact with the reader, but an impression (or as Ford would say a 'constatation') rendered by recognizing the shifting matter consciousness becomes aware of, when it experiences, when it recalls, when it tells. But for Ford this also involved the notion of the aloof or detached

---

[1] For this general climate see Mark Schorer, 'Some Relationships', in *The World We Imagine* (New York, 1968; London, 1969) and Arthur Mizener, *The Saddest Story: A Biography of Ford Madox Ford* (New York, 1970; London, 1972).

narrator, presenting the novel 'without passion', and with a guiding selectivity. To a considerable extent, this is consonant with Virginia Woolf's aesthetics, but there are marked variations.

They are variations that made Ford's fiction very much more available than Virginia Woolf's, and in a way more representative. For the point of Ford's technique was less that it should predetermine the experience dealt with by the novelist than that it should answer to it, enable it to exist. To Ford, the subject-matter of a novel was—he used a word of James's—an 'affair', presented by oblique techniques to the point of maximum intensification and effect. Behind that lies another of his aesthetic convictions—his belief that art's task is registration, and that that means registering the temper of the age. So *Parade's End* is panoramic, in a way Virginia Woolf's novels (even *The Years*) could never be. Ford sustains many of the interests of the nineteenth-century novel, in the public life, in the social web, in 'history'. The sequence is specifically involved in historical events and it takes its temper and forms its needs according to the telling of a history; the spots of time on which each chapter or section is focused usually bear some essential relation to a major historical moment, and the over-all theme is 'the world as it culminated in the war'. The techniques, then, are techniques for presenting large-scale dispositions of time, of characters, of moods and insights, of bringing the large and the small into relation—in the interests of giving not only a sense of psychological verisimilitude but social accuracy. Indeed *Parade's End* is an historical allegory with a psychological centre, a 'condition of England' work in which the centre of registration is an individual who, nonetheless, *enacts* history.

So Ford saw the sequence's central character, Christopher Tietjens, as the focal point of numerous forces, a man with a full awareness of history and society and capable of responding to these: 'I seemed to see him stand in some high places in France during the period of hostilities taking in not only what was visible but all the causes and all the motive powers of infinitely distant places.' Tietjens—the Yorkshire Tory, the representative of a line of feudal and ministerial inheritance, a man of 'clear Eighteenth-century mind', passionate and enduring, agonized and expressionless, a man living out an old code in all its contradictions to its last possible conclusion—is the focus of this historical world; he draws it together, and also suffers from it and for it. The whole novel sequence turns on his power to experience, survey, and suffer so many forces from so many sources—the result being, in fact, one of the most agonized and agonizing historical novels ever written. But to convey the fullness of experience around Tietjens, experience both detailed and incidental and vast and systematic, Ford has to create a complex realism, a sense of the fullness and complexity of life in history and time. This is the point of attention for his experimentalism—his experiments, his use of time-shift, of oblique narrative at ironic distance, of *progression d'effet* or intensification through sequence, are craft-devices rather than self-conscious art-devices. Ford held that a novelist should express his temperament but not, explicitly, his values or prejudgements; he should stand above and beyond while yielding as far as he could to the logic of his material. The result is that his own fiction at its best, as here, is a fiction of inexorable thoroughness, a vast and complex web of experience, persistently elaborated by every means Ford had at his disposal. His purpose is not to master his material, to bring it into a total metaphor or symbol as Virginia Woolf sought to do, but to handle it, as fully as possible. In that, he is closer to epic modernists like Proust or Joyce. On the other hand, he catches history just at the point before total disunity sets in, before art comes to seem the only possible means of giving any order to history at all. *Parade's End* indeed combines two aesthetics, one drawing on the epicality of nineteenth-century fiction, the other drawing on the crafts of modernism; and it therefore succeeds in carrying a public theme— that of dramatizing, in Ford's phrase, 'the public wants of a decade'— and a private theme—the psychological history of Christopher Tietjens —side by side. The novel is both a social and a psychological history, concerning both the world external to the individual and the individual's assimilation of event and process.

Ford is able to manage this because he takes as the centre of his 'affair' a character who can unite within himself the public and private lives, while at the same time living out this responsibility as an unbearable strain—so unbearable that Ford seems to suggest that this is the last time a man of this kind could even envision mastering the two realms of experience. Tietjens is a member of the 'governing classes', and is deeply conscious of his role in a caste, though as a Yorkshire feudalist he is also distanced from its values; he feels obliged to live by its codes and yet in certain details or through certain weaknesses to transgress them, and to carry experience from the past and the future into his response to the present. He is therefore both the explorer of the culture, a culture in radical change, and its scapegoat. Tietjens is in a very specific way the last of his line, the last Christian gentleman, the last just inheritor to his estates, the man hoping to take 'the last train to the old Heaven'. His is a sacrificial, even a suicidal, heroism; his chivalric notion of male and human nobility is threatened by social change, the transformations of war, and the shifting relationship between the sexes; three wars—social war, world war, sex war—are intricately related in the novel. He is a figure of romance caught at the point of historical extinction; after him there will be no more parades, no more glories, no more men who 'do not'. To some extent he is an absurd figure with a perverted creed. But he sees the contradictions in himself, as he lives through the code he believes in yet seeks to reach beyond it, as he masochistically sustains his own identity yet radically questions the society he lives in.

Certainly, in Ford's allegory of change, Tietjens's agony precedes the war; it is not the war that is the basic solvent of society, but rather the strains in the body politic and the minds of men which make war almost a necessary purgatory. The agony is there from the novel's beginning; it comes from the false, unhappy marriage Tietjens has contracted with his unfaithful wife, Sylvia. This 'chivalric' act—Sylvia, with whom he has not had relations, is apparently pregnant—inevitably throws the Tietjens heritage into doubt, but Tietjens sustains the chivalry by refusing to divorce her. Sylvia—one of the most frightening immoralists in all literature—is devoted to an endless assault on Tietjens's chivalry, attempting to bring him down to human scale. The same assault on the chivalric disposition—caught in a distilling symbol in the moment when General Campion's car hits the horse Tietjens is driving—is intensified as the action moves from the relatively secure world of 1912 to the world at war—a war of mismanagement, bureaucracy, politics, and red tape, where the forces threatening the hero are less the enemy than his own government, the leaders of his own army, and Sylvia, symbolically entrenched with the General's party in France. But the war turns the cycle and begins, in a dark and bleak way, to lead towards a new life for Tietjens. He collapses towards madness but then manages to cut himself off from his own past, to find a life beyond agony and purgation. This is all very explicitly a fable of an historical irony, a story of a change which is inevitably a disaster, for Tietjens's evolution is also a moment of historical lapse into a lesser world. The age of the aristocrat gives way to that of the bureaucrat, the chivalric to the mechanical, the age of values and convictions gives way to the world of valuelessness—but Tietjens has suffered enough for history and finally (like Guy Crouchback in Evelyn Waugh's *Sword of Honour*, the equivalent fable for the Second World War) he forgoes the epic pilgrimage and makes his settlement.

Tietjens's ironic position in history is supported by the irony of the novel itself. For Ford's technique of 'aloofness', derived from Flaubert, is not only an art of effective registration but a condition of moral and evaluative distance. However much the sequence may seem lovingly to evoke an old England in which a residue of eighteenth-century *mores* and values survives, Ford stands historically beyond all that, in a stance of detachment apparent from the opening words of *Some Do Not* . . . onward:

The two young men—they were of the English public official class—sat in the perfectly appointed railway carriage. The leather straps to the windows were of virgin newness; the mirrors beneath the new luggage racks immaculate as if they had reflected very little; the bulging upholstery in its luxuriant, regulated curves was scarlet and yellow in an intricate, minute dragon pattern, the design of a geometrician in Cologne. The compartment smelt faintly, hygienically of admirable varnish; the train ran as smoothly—Tietjens remembered thinking—as British gilt-edged securities. . . .

And the two young men, administrators of the world, are located in an historical distance and put at an artistic remove, as throughout the novel Ford registers both through his characters and beyond them. The whole novel, working as it does by a technique of chronological distillation which suddenly intensifies and makes symbolic particular foci of consciousness and particular points in time, develops, therefore, by presenting its characters in the light of a long, oblique vision—which is a way of withdrawing from an historical to a technical structure. Ford does of course attempt social history, but the gradual reduction of the novel towards the experience of individual consciousnesses parallels Tietjens's own withdrawal from the historical and social centre; all that can be left is a kind of authorial remoteness. For if, as Tietjens learns, modern history is not a form for action but a form for suffering, then the artist himself must withdraw from it. What is striking about the sequence is that it concerns itself with external as well as internal events so fully as to make manifest the conditions bringing about this kind of style. It has a real as opposed to an implied historical dimension; it can and does deal in event as well as artistic metaphor; but it leads the way towards a tactic of 'fictional indifference', a withdrawn irony, which is one of the hallmarks of much twenties writing. Ford's 'modernism' of technique is therefore an oblique or ironic species of realism, a way of dealing in history and event without direct celebration of it. And his detachment is not finally a withdrawal into the province of art but a separation from his hero through technique—the strategy of much post-modernist fictional art.

VIII

The Modern Comic Novel in the 1920s:
Lewis, Huxley, and Waugh

> The problem of architecture as I see it . . . is the problem of
> all art—the elimination of the human element from the con-
> sideration of form. . . . Man is never beautiful, he is never
> happy except when he becomes the channel for the distri-
> bution of mechanical forces.
>
> Professor Otto Silenus, in *Decline and Fall*

I

According to Ortega y Gasset, a distinctive feature of our modern art
has been its tendency towards dehumanization—its flight from both
humanism and middle-distance realism towards forms much more
distant, detached, and self-aware, from the representation of the
familiar and rounded human figure towards shape, perspective, or
context.[1] This process has partly been a great celebration of art itself, a
respect for the means of the making; Ortega remarks, indeed, that
perhaps a very humanized or 'naturalistic' art as in nineteenth-
century realism was not the norm but the aberration. Nonetheless, we
can, I think, fairly readily recognize that the process visible in art has,
dismayingly, its modern parallels in history and society—that the
withdrawal from a sympathetic portrait of the rounded human person
has something in common with the dehumanization of a modernizing
world. Nor, indeed, has that dehumanization been something outside
ourselves which art and humanism have fought to resist. It is a presence
close to the modern will and modern thought, of a piece with the

[1] José Ortega y Gasset, *The Dehumanization of Art and Other Writings on Art and
Culture* (Garden City, N.Y., 1956).

growing subscription to environmentalist, determinist, and historicist theories, which have tended to give man over to his circumstantial conditions, his place in larger plots. And it is also of a piece with many of our best democratic sentiments, so that the idea of the awesome separateness of the human personality has come, in an age of confrontations and violated privacies, to be regarded as an unwonted withdrawal.

The paradox that many of our theories of greater liberation are simultaneously theories of reduced freedom has its equivalents in the fortunes of the modern novel. There can be little doubt that one important impulse promoting modern fictional experiment is the desire to free the individual, or consciousness, from the iron grip of a linear plot, to give consciousness its due, to speak to the texture of reality as it comes to us in waves and impressions, to open out art into or even beyond form: 'and his heart was going like mad and yes I said yes I will Yes.' There are theories of irony which take that famous ending of *Ulysses* back into the book, as the ending of *Finnegans Wake* turns back to its beginning to form the perfect circle; still, the element of openness of form that Conrad discerned in Henry James's novels ('It is eminently satisfying, but it is not final') has a model here, and we can urge that it constitutes one of the recurrent preoccupations of modernism.[1] The freeing of the human agent from the confines of a plot-like grid, the relaxing of the power of the dominant novelist so that the characters have an existential right to assert themselves, are purposes that run through the 'new' novel, from *The Portrait of a Lady* to John Fowles's *The French Lieutenant's Woman*. But we may discern our paradox; the condition of a greater freedom is often a higher abstraction, a more conscious presence of the novelist, who may be less the plotter or story-teller than the exposed collector of impressions, but all the same is decidedly no less, and often vastly more, a figure in the making than his Victorian predecessor.

[1] Alan Friedman, in *The Turn of the Novel: The Transition to Modern Fiction* (New York and London, 1966), argues this case in a valuable form, suggesting that somewhere around the beginning of the century a new type of novel came into existence, an open rather than a 'closed' novel: 'The new flux of experience insisted on a new vision of existence: it stressed an ethical vision of continued expansion and virtually unrelieved openness in the experience of life' (15–16). This seems to me a just account of *one* development in the modern novel; the aim here is to indicate the significance of another, countervailing bias, towards certain forms of irony.

Moreover, that Victorian predecessor often displayed capacities for humanism far greater than many of the modernist writers, for whom the idea of free character was a realization but also a perplexity, as it was in Henry James; and sometimes a delusion.

I only care about what the woman *is*—what she IS—inhumanly, physiologically, materially—according to the use of the word: but for me, what she *is* as a phenomenon (or as representing some greater, inhuman will), instead of what she feels according to the human conception. That is where the futurists are stupid. Instead of looking for the new human phenomenon, they will only look for the phenomena of the science of physics to be found in human beings. They are crassly stupid. But if anyone would give them eyes, they would pull the right apples off the tree, for their stomachs are true in appetite.

Lawrence's famous letter to Edward Garnett, which has become our great *texte d'explication* for *The Rainbow* and *Women in Love*, and marks a transitional point in his career, challenges the idea of the well-formed character, and poses the notion of a new and less human basis for fictional personality, not so much as a perplexity but as a compulsory endeavour. The expansive structure is not an opening out for the individual humanist personality, but for an inhuman will, the self disintegrating in order to advance. In Virginia Woolf's *To the Lighthouse* it is something else again; a formal touch of the brush on a painting rounds out the human plot, and yet is it not curiously an *in*human plot, with the loving centre, Mrs. Ramsay, dead part way through the novel and a tactic of intensifying abstraction dominating the latter part of it, replacing person by form? And even in Forster, whom we praise as a humanist writer, there is a curious thrust away from the world of personal relationships and sensitivities; the imperfections or insufficiencies of equal human contacts suddenly fall under a long gaze, people look 'like dwarfs shaking hands', exhaustion or simple failure supersedes. And in Forster's ideal of 'pattern', the sudden 'opening out' of the work, this abstract vision has, not its defeat, but something like its formal equivalent.[1]

Ortega y Gasset spoke of modernist writing as an art of observed as opposed to lived reality—by which, as Joseph Frank has stressed, he meant to say that the modern artist has become less and less interested in representing the human form for its inner human expressiveness; it

---

[1] The equivalent in criticism is the 'new' view of character as a term in poetics in C. H. Rickword's two essays, 'A Note on Fiction', in *The Calendar of Modern Letters* in 1926.

can thence be distorted at will to meet the artistic necessities of the creator's vision.[1] Ortega also noted how important, in this proceeding, was the ironic mode; and the pervasive presence of irony in our modern art has been noted by many of its critics. One is Northrop Frye, who historicizes the situation into something like an over-all period style; his famous anatomy contains a typology of literary modes, concluding with the comic and the ironic—to which, he then proposes, art comes closer as it comes towards the present day. The basis of these modes is that we observe men in situations where they are less competent than we are; from a securer human position we look down upon them.[2] This proposition has in it just enough truth to be useful as well as elegant; there *is* a remarkable presence both of irony and comedy in modern writing, and in a number of writers a fascinating collocation of the two, so that when we think of modern comedy we are likely to think of something different from, and decidedly bleaker than, much of the comedy of the past. For in the past comedy, though decidedly concerned with the creation of artifice, with the making, by an amusing narrator, of a world of special conditions and laws, has also often been concerned to humanize, to invoke geniality and benevolence. This capacity of comedy to generate identification and sympathy is the basis of our relationship with some of the great comic heroes, like Quixote, Walter Shandy, or Mr. Pickwick, despite the fact that they occupy strange and extravagant worlds: in some comic novels the worlds, too, partake of a humane realism, a central balance that destroys extremes and gives the centre its due, as is the case in Jane Austen or E. M. Forster. But this has not, on the whole, been the main spirit of modern comedy, though there are writers who work in this mode, from Forster to Kingsley Amis. A good deal of modern comic writing, though, has been concerned with a vastly more distanced and decidedly cooler view of man and his situation, and has done a good deal more to adjust the human agent to the absurdity of the universe than to turn that absurd universe into a very possible place for man to live.

In this, it has been much closer to a tradition—of which we have presences in the past, in Sterne, or Swift, or Gogol—which has explored, or fantasized about, the grotesque nature, and the strangeness and

[1] Joseph Frank, 'The Dehumanization of Art', in *The Widening Gyre: Crisis and Mastery in Modern Literature* (Bloomington, Ind. and London, 1968).

[2] Northrop Frye, *Anatomy of Criticism* (Princeton, N.J., 1957).

inhumanity, of a supposedly human world, and has drawn on modes of authorial indifference or satirical venom to enforce a decidedly bleak image. The comedy of human exposure and absurdity, where the object of contemplation is not man's normal and familiar social existence but his uneasy place and posture in a cruel and contingent universe, has come to seem increasingly close to us; and this vision of arbitrariness has vastly more to do with Sterne, with his world of random association and inconsequentiality where the comic voice functions as a refuge or stay of laughter, or Swift, where the barren, irrational world of men has no human salvation whatsoever, than with Jane Austen or Forster. Comedy, then, appears to have become a very possible language for addressing a sense we have of ourselves in a world such as ours—a world of change and chaos, transitory experience, divided nature and confused hope; above all, a world in which the processes of social modernization have created that instability of identity and society, those possibilities of disfiguration and deception, which are habitual parts of a comic universe. This chaotic, Dionysian type of the comic, which has long been recognized as a part of the species, but which has usually existed within structures which are restorative, which contain its force and reassert a final order, and especially its potential for abstracting or dehumanizing a supposedly human world, have been central to contemporary comic writing. And in this form it has been much a part of other experiments in abstraction or detachment which are part of the stylistic character of modern art.

In the modern English novel, the 1920s seems the distilling period of this potential; it is a curiously splendid era of comic fiction. Wyndham Lewis, a central participant and the most aesthetically articulate figure, indeed conceived of satire as *the* stylistic form of modern art, which he expected to be an art of 'polished and resistant surfaces'. The theory depends on a presumption about the dominance of the mechanical in the modern age, and the separation of the rational from the emotional which produces disjointedness or, precisely, mechanism in the human agent; this leads explicitly to the need for an external view of the human figure. Certainly the 1920s does see a remarkable revival or reinvention of comic forms in fiction, as if they offered an ideal means for coping with a postwar world in which disorder seems notably prevalent, value historically extracted, chaos come again, as a direct result of the war and its disorientations and dehumanizations. The three writers who seem to me most fully and variously to embody the range of these comic possibilities are Lewis himself, Aldous Huxley, and Evelyn Waugh; I believe their forms of writing, their habits and manners, have more to do with the modern forms than we have often understood. What particularly they have in common is the possession of a post of observation on a world that has been strangely modernized, so that it is contingent and aberrant, and the human figures in it strangely shaped or distorted, prompted with purely mechanical vitalities or lassitudes. Each of these three writers, too, is concerned with the making of style in society; all, in their posture as novelists, are devotees of highly sophisticated worlds, in which characters are very conscious of their historical milieu and their responsibility to the instant, seeking to embody an image of a decidedly contemporary man. This concern with the prevailing social, moral, and emotional performance, the current fashions, habits, and manners, is a certain sort of style-making; and it decidedly conditions the *literary* style of each of these three writers.

Here, then, are three comic novelists interested in their times as the satirist is, moving into their material with an abstracted involvement which leads them into the exploration of values which they do not as such espouse, and the conditions and social determinants which produce these values or humours. The result is not just simply a gift for grasping at the detail of the fashionable life-styles and distilling it in successful images and vignettes, though this they do, by touching a *Gesellschaft*, modernized society at some of its most exposed points— the metropolitan smart set, style-hungry bohemia. It is also the formation of a style of address; it is their particular means of authorial displacement, their strange presence but also their strange disappearance as narrators, their representation of illogicality, finally their cool withdrawal, that is compelling. All are very commanding creators; in an age in which the omniscient narrator is frequently a threatened figure, they are almost overassertive in the role. This gives them a hard style which is in part a willed—perhaps simply a reasonable—refusal entirely to go along with the new barbarism or vitalism that seems to offer a way out for some of their characters, and some of their contemporaries. The refusal to be sympathetic is a refusal to be psychologically immersed; it is an old satirical mode in a new balance. The balance itself does have a decided extravagance, and a comic place for the narrator too—though one sometimes insecurely held, like Waugh's

Mr. Pinfold, within a disguise that from time to time can collapse. The resulting comedy is decidedly not compassionate, and makes no attempt to reinstate forms of social or moral virtue or humanism. It is compelled by its own sense of contingency and absurdity, transliterating human experience into a world of conditioned farce. The farce, for each writer, is a different one, presented with different degrees of involvement and urgency. Nonetheless these fictional worlds— distorted, oblique, abundantly rich in indifference, mechanism, generational struggle, and insecure identity, and so leading to a state of affairs in which all quests are suspect, all virtues unestablishable—are sufficiently like the prevailing world outside to be more than amusing. All questions of innate propensity towards comedy in their creators apart, there are times that merit or generate comedy and times that don't; here are three writers who show us the relevance between the species and their age.

2

Of the three, it is of course Wyndham Lewis who is closest to classic modernism; this makes him especially instructive, because he does explicitly indicate the debt of his type of comedy to some of our most influential modern aesthetic theories. From *Tarr* (written either just before or during the war and published in 1918) onward, Lewis's writings turn on a very distinctive and idiosyncratic mannerism and a basic disposition towards outrage that has its roots simultaneously in his own quirkiness and in his attempt to identify a significant anti-romantic aesthetic for the times. Lewis was a movement man. After a spell of painting in Munich and Paris, he returned to London in 1909 to be drawn into writing and the new ferments in the coterie groups that had formed round *The English Review* and the Omega Workshops, and were culling from Cubism and Post-Impressionism theories of new perspectivism and new energy-devices in art. He moved, with Pound, through the aesthetics of hardness and generative juxtapositioning towards Vorticism, with its celebration of machine-like forms and the energetic node or centre. Just before the outbreak of war he started *Blast*, a magazine and manifesto which was in certain respects an anglicization of Marinetti's Futurist manifestos (though Lewis had his strong dissents from Futurism). After the war he conducted a very independent career, simultaneously promoting and attacking *avant-garde* radicalism —but above all the prevailing vitalism, recognizing that the wild immersions of the new forms of subconscious and unconscious writing, obsessed with inner flux and time-flow, were in fact theories of self-mechanization. This drove his literary manner, always acerbic, towards emphasis on an objective, depersonalized art and towards an increasing polemical and satirical harshness—the Enemy stance from which he scowled at a clownish age, which had seemed to promise an art of rational will and individuality and instead was sacrificing to the romantic and the communitarian spirit. The comic mode, as a way of distilling a perspective on his age by 'outward' means, means that permitted observation rather than involvement, had always been important to him; the impulse grew increasingly abstract and theoretical, and hence moved in the direction of satirical apologues, those great works of fantasy, extraordinarily architected and designed, powerful mixtures of aesthetic grotesquerie and argumentative bile, that dominate the later phase of his writing.

What, though, is very clear is that Lewis saw the basis of a modernized poetic as lying in the comic forms. This partly arises as a view of man, or of the representation of man as a figure in fiction. Lewis's theory is of a piece with that of Waugh's Professor Silenus, that very modern architect attempting to replace the old humane King's Thursday with a new composition, and facing 'the problem of all art—the elimination of the human element from the consideration of form. . . .' Lewis, like Silenus, has a sense of humanistic representation as being a problem in formal composition; he also has a conviction of man's *modern* ridiculousness, as he slides from will to feeling, shifts from civilization to barbarism, converts himself into a 'wild body'. (They share the mixture of machine and Dionysus: Silenus is the leader of Nietzsche's comic rout in *The Birth of Tragedy*.) This of itself provokes comedy; that man in the twentieth century should not be barbarianized but should will his own barbarism, welcome his own reification, subordinate himself to the unconscious or the mass, was itself the distilling basis for contemporary farce. But what generally provokes it is the need for an art of objectivism. Lewis's comments on the comic in *The Wild Body* (1927) are decidedly Bergsonian, except he goes further: 'The root of the Comic is to be sought in the sensations resulting from the observations of a *thing* behaving like a person. But from that point of view all men are necessarily comic; for they are all *things*, or physical bodies, behaving as persons.'[1] Bergson's view

[1] Lewis expresses the bulk of his argument about satire in *Men Without Art* (1934).

of comedy, in *Le Rire* (1900), is very important to comedy in the 1920s, if only because a lot of the other things that Bergson had been saying, above all about creative evolution, were important then too; a significant point about Lewis is that he does engage with Bergson directly, being strongly at odds with his celebration of subconscious process and subjectivized time. Bergson holds that laughter occurs when the *élan vital* of man is absent or deliberately arrested, producing anaesthesia of the heart in the observer. But Lewis, suspecting the *élan vital* to start with, extends the argument and universalizes comedy as the means of dealing with man's self-evident depersonalization.

The results are paradoxical; they also involve deep-seated questions of Lewis's odd success and failure as a writer. The forces at work in his fiction seem in the end to drive in contrary directions. The vision is tragic; the form is macabre-comic. The art is one of deliberate mechanization, shaped by a theory of impersonal rendering and of the analogy between modern art and the machine-forms and structures of the city of modern life; yet the satirical object is a thrust against mechanism and especially the dehumanization of romanticism or immersion in the barbarian group will. Indifference thus assaults indifference; abstraction assaults the wrongs of abstraction. The result is in fact an energetic and vigorous thrust of art conspicuously spending itself in splendid inconsistencies. In *Tarr*, for example, Lewis, among other activities, represents the figure of Kreisler, a comic machine-man operated by a spasmodic romanticism. The application of one formalism to its opposite has extraordinary effects in local comedy; the figure is modernly funny. But Lewis suggests that it is precisely in the state of romantic intensity that man is most mechanized, and that only through art and intellect can he escape from his indulgent predicament. In the prologue, he describes Tarr's function in the book as to 'exalt life into a Comedy, when otherwise it is, to his mind, a tawdry zone of half-art, or a silly Tragedy'; the elevation of the comic purpose, and its alliance with art and intellect, is thus clear. But comedy is also a milieu in which absurdity and riotousness can be tolerated, and excused; lacking a centralized norm in the book we read it without close identification. That impersonality is doubtless part of the intended effect, but it also means that Lewis has difficulty in sustaining any direct satirical thrusts he is making.

What is true is that Lewis acquires the means for operating superbly between a Bergsonian comic indifference and a very explicit comic disgust. In *Tarr*, which is in the end a formally quite extraordinary work of art *and* an energetic polemic at the expense of pre-war Parisian bohemia; in *The Childermass* (1928), an abstract epical comedy of ideas set on an arid steppe on the threshold of heaven (later extended into the *Human Age* sequence of the 1950s); in *The Apes of God* (1930), a social comedy of ideas directed against English Bloomsbury-bohemia in the twenties—in his work of the twenties, then, he maps out a satirical intention that is in part immersed in the changing age, and is in part remote from it. He explicitly rejects 'fiction from the inside' (the interiorized novel of Joyce or Stein) on the grounds that it intrinsically romanticizes, and comments: 'The *external* approach to things (relying on the evidence of the *eye* rather than of the more emotional organs of sense) can make "the grotesque" a healthy and attractive companion. . . . Dogmatically, then, I am for the Great Without, for the method of *external* approach.' In many ways his is, strangely, a decidedly psychological fiction; but it is psychology rendered comic by withdrawal and by the techniques of grotesquerie. Hence Lewis's distinctive prose constantly jogs from within to without, with the drift of the comic *reductio* always working towards a sense of mechanism, as in the exemplary modernisms of *Tarr*:

Tarr possessed no deft hand or economy of force: his muscles rose unnecessarily on his arm to lift a wine-glass to his lips: he had no social machinery at all at his disposal and was compelled to get along as well as he could with the cumbrous one of the intellect. With this he danced about it is true: but it was full of sinister piston-rods, organ-like shapes, heavy drills. . . .

In *The Childermass*, where the satirical intention is intensified, this goes away often from the specific occasions of a realized comedy towards satire of ideas, or apologue. But the balance returns in *The Apes of God*, a grand vision of the twenties, where Lewis balances comic detachment and satiric disgust. Focusing on mock-bohemia and the artistic amateur, the 'general rabble that collects under the equivocal banner of ART' (these are the Apes who are, in Lewis's vision, bringing art in society to its end by confusing it with life), he can be much more explicit about the social and structural sources of the mechanism and the romanticism he attacks. England is a culture 'dead as mutton', trapped in the 'insanitary trough' between the wars, its social and intellectual and artistic decline going hand in hand. Lewis gets good comedy out of this, as in a superb passage on the General Strike, but also a savage satire that fully enjoys its disgust. The kind of vigour, and its modernist classical mode, is usefully seen in this passage, describing the aged Lady Fredigonde Follett, as obvious symbol for the whole culture, rising from her chair:

The unsteady solid rose a few inches, like the levitation of a narwhal. Seconded by alpenstock and body-servant (holding her humble breath), the escaping half began to move out from the deep vent. It abstracted itself slowly. Something imperfectly animate had cast off from a portion of its self. It was departing, with a grim paralytic toddle, elsewhere. The socket of the enormous chair yawned just short of her hindparts. It was a sort of shell that had been, according to some natural law, suddenly vacated by its animal. But this occupant, who never went far, moved from trough to trough—another everywhere stood hollow and ready throughout the compartments of its elaborate mental dwelling.

Lewis may be capable of this kind of dehumanizing comic force, and of the intelligence needed to hold such episodes as part of a coherent vision, but he can also at times become quirky, quaint, and shrill. Still, his contribution to modern comedy and satire is immense, and shows the links between the comic and the later development of modernism. Like Eliot and Pound, Lewis maps a general social transition of mores and values and tests this against the arts as a species of intelligence and purity. But because art is seen as *in* society, his attention turns to that society, as Pound's does in *Hugh Selwyn Mauberley*, fully and elaborately, and his species of technique so becomes an important register of his age. In his work, the new style both expresses the needs of modernity and seeks to control certain aspects of it: it aims to open out new energies while deploring many of those that *are* released. If this is classicism, it is a very modernized form of it, a radical classicism that generates a vast amount of novelty in the very process of asking questions about the value of novelty. Lewis's narratorial position is in fact filled with an extraordinary violence; the Enemy thrusts out, needing extra energy in a time when every object that satire might react to is already touched with a sense of its own absurdity. In Lewis's writings, the human world has become farcical, a centre of sickness; it is dangerous to thought and dangerous to art. Both continuity and salvation for art therefore lie in a violent indifference, and in the extremities of satire. Indeed, for Lewis, satire constitutes the only possible modern form, the one channel by which the creative energies of man can continue to live.

3

Some of these same issues are obviously at work in the fiction of Aldous Huxley, particularly in his four key novels of the twenties— *Chrome Yellow* (1921), *Antic Hay* (1923), *Those Barren Leaves* (1925) and *Point Counter Point* (1928)—which represent an entire phase of his work. Like Lewis, Huxley is a very intelligent and self-analytical writer with an enormous native talent for satire; also like Lewis, he is extremely concerned for the fate of art and intelligence in a world whose props and stays seem threatened from outside art and thought and also from within them. Like Lewis, too, Huxley is obsessively concerned, as is his character Gumbril Senior, in *Antic Hay*, with the problem of the 'wretched human scale' which limits thought and action and holds the body to itself; and this unease is of course a familiar basis for satire. The difference is that Huxley ends up focusing most of his satire at the point of balance where humanism and aspiration, body and soul, split. His work is comedy of ideas in a universe thus dichotomized between intellect and passion; what, though, is clear is that he recognizes that he himself is one of the order of persons he is satirizing —the new artist-intellectuals—and this induces narrative unease and even guilt, though it is of course essential to the sense of compelling honesty in his books. But it is also evident that his work arises in a very specific social milieu and the unease has a decided historical location. These novels of the twenties are very much *about* the twenties; Huxley writes them about and for a world in which his own sources in culture and art are insecure. The world is in a bewildering disorder; intelligence and reason alone cannot save it, but stand, with several of his heroes, bewildered before barbarism and passion.

Frequently the books start with the brilliant cultured surface of the intellectual and social smart set; then, of course, they penetrate beneath to the boredoms, discomforts, and animal passions that stir there. Though the novels occasionally seem narrow in locale—Huxley often uses the device of the English or Italian country-house party familiar in the novel of ideas from Peacock onwards—his world is in fact essentially urban and sophisticated, with a collapsing aristocracy and a traditional middle-class intelligentsia somewhere in the background manifesting their withdrawal or their half-extinction. At the centre, usually, are a group of new semi-bohemian but upper-middle-class artists, writers, intellectuals, living in a 'pointless landscape' and usually conducting incomplete or ineffective, but decidedly modern, sexual liaisons. Indeed, in this world modernity is a frequent spur to action or to the desire for action. The cast is usually large enough for Huxley to follow out a multiplicity of stories, sometimes supplemented by stories within stories that recall the past. And most of these illuminate the fact that his characters are men of an idea, attempting to make passion cohere within reason, and usually not succeeding. Two basic types recur: the sensitives who, while sympathetically presented, usually fail, and the arrogantly insensitive who frequently succeed, in those areas of love and self-fulfilment with which most of the actions are concerned. As a result, Huxley's novels are largely novels of inaction, for his scrupulous, devastating analysis usually produces in the central characters a masochistic withdrawal from action. At the same time, the novels turn on the emptying out of the centre from any dream, hope, or institution, and hence have an apparent air of cynicism, a suggestion of universal failure.

But what is so very Huxleyan about these books is that the author's own cynicism and detachment are very much part of the matter for analysis. The embarrassment of the novelist's feeling that his own ideas and assumptions are themselves a sterile or incomplete view of life comes out most clearly in *Point Counter Point*, where the writing of novels of ideas becomes part of the theme, and where the character of Philip Quarles is the novelist's self-surrogate. But this element runs through all the twenties novels, starting in *Chrome Yellow* with the figure of Dennis, the sensitive writer conscious of the loss of a real infinite to feed upon:

'I make up a little story about beauty and pretend that it has something to do with truth and goodness. I have to say that art is the process by which one constructs the divine reality out of chaos. Pleasure is one of the mystical roads to union with the infinite—the ecstacies of drinking, dancing, love-making. As for women, I am perpetually assuring myself that they're the broad highway to divinity. And to think I'm only just beginning to see through the silliness of the whole thing!'

Behind the lost divinity, though, lies a world of inevitable chaos if also of inevitable freedom from ideals. The mind is left to its own convulsions—to intellectual hobby-horses, a sense of cultural loss, a vague hope of aristocratic withdrawal or of a new élite's emerging—while the body is left to the basic human satisfactions or to pullulating animalism. As part of the supersession of art and intellect, the novel ends with Dennis driving off to the station in a hearse, while over all its action lies the vague promise of apocalyptic last days, caught in the figure of the iron Mr. Bodiham. Huxley plays the consequent ironies both ways, showing the follies of idealism and the vices of animalism.

As the twenties progress, and as Huxley shifts his scene more directly into the world of the urban intelligentsia, the mood of disillusion gets more clearly stated, the sense of what Lawrence found in *Point Counter Point*, a theme of the 'slow suicide of inertia', increases, and a vision of man as the Freudian hypocrite, a creature of self-delusion farcically posturing in the role of a sublime and civilized being while really seeking to fulfil simple and often gratuitous passions, grows. But for Huxley the modern is a species of evolution as well as a matter for excellent comedy and farce, and so his world of parties, free love, adulteries, revolutionary and reactionary passions, and the boredom of 'disillusion after disillusion' is an intense experiencing of the times. The cultural and moral passions both expose and are exposed by the new freeing of repressions, the new sorts of men and women, the new freedom, but also the new anarchy of the post-Freudian as well as the postwar universe. The artist, here, is deeply implicated in the modern not only as an art form but as an enveloping experience. 'Living modernly's living quickly,' says Lucy Tantamount in *Point Counter Point*. 'You can't cart a wagonload of ideals and romanticisms about with you these days.' Huxley's fictional world is one in which this may produce a sense of yearning loss, but one in which the view is taken for granted. If the consequence is that intelligent man is left in a comic predicament, in an historical void, Huxley sees that as inescapable—such is the contemporary historical acceleration. The result is hardly cynicism but a complex blend of involvement and disgust. He is satirically savage, but not satirically secure; his novels are a continuous, tentative intellectual inquiry into new forces as well as a display of ironic detachment. Indeed, the desperation and absurdity of the characters is not at a total distance; it touches the novelist as well.

4

Indifference is an important clue to modern comedy; but it comes in many forms. Lewis actually threatens his by a push towards violence, which makes him belligerently satirical; Huxley threatens his by undercutting his fictional structure and showing his own complicity in its dilemmas, which makes him ironical. But Evelyn Waugh stands apparently utterly poised and composed in the midst of a comic and absurd modern world, and that makes him a very pure—and I think a very splendid—comic writer. The position conceals him; he seems a very disingenuous narrator, without great complexity of theme or technique. Technical questions have in fact roused his distrust; he has always represented his work as an elegant enterprise in language, external to him, made to please others: 'I regard writing', he told his *Paris Review* interviewer, 'not as an investigation of character, but as an exercise in the use of language, and with this I am obsessed. I have no technical psychological interest. It is drama, speech, and events that interest me.'[1] Among other things, this is a piece of self-protective poise; but it does link with certain central features of his work—his indifference, his distance from his characters, what A. E. Dyson calls the 'absence of compassion' that is central to his method. The coolness and even heartlessness of his manner—as in his classic way of disposing, in those famous few short sentences in *Decline and Fall*, of Little Lord Tangent, here today and gone tomorrow—have to some commentators seemed of a piece with lack of substance in his work; in his book on the twenties, *The Vanishing Hero* (1956), Sean O'Faolain sums him up as a writer of 'purely brainless genius, which he has amplified by the possession or development of enormous technical skill'. In fact though Waugh may be the least intellectual of these three writers, he is stylistically the most successful, the surest inhabitant of the comic mode.

His achievement is a complete style, a modern comic form. It is one that functions partly as a disguise for him, a means for not expressing opinion; but it stands securely as itself and it releases a high creativity, letting Waugh portray buoyantly and richly the operations of a modern world to which he grants no direct significance or credit. The style is dependent on his traditionalism, but is itself remorselessly modern. The critics who dwell on that traditionalism miss the point.[2] Traditionalism—that past elegantly embodied in his aristocratic pastoral of great houses, chestnut-tree drives, craftsmanship, hierarchy,

[1] (Julian Jebb), 'Evelyn Waugh: An Interview', in *Writers at Work: Third Series* (New York and London, 1967).

[2] A good example of this emphasis in Waugh criticism is 'Donat O'Donnell' (Conor Cruise O'Brien), *Maria Cross: Imaginative Patterns in a Group of Modern Catholic Writers* (London, 1953), where the novels are taken as very literal fables; 'O'Donnell' sees that Waugh deals with man's exile in the world, but is outraged into finding his perceptions 'childish' and politically abhorrent.

culture—establishes the ideal of civilization, order, and permanence; but Waugh's comic act is to violate it with modernity. The novelist of instability, beyond such humanism, he depends on the *memento mori*, the macabre intrusion, the bleak reminder of the folly of seeking fulfilment inside time or history; the posture consorts elegantly with a modernizing history which, to his comic eye, is devoted to the same riotous and brutal reminder. The tradition of social comedy he belongs to is not Fielding's but Gogol's: society is an unstable, extraordinary fiction in a wilderness of space; and we embody it as caricature, strangely, absurdly—as his own surrogate, Gilbert Pinfold, does in acting the part of 'eccentric don and testy colonel' until that is all his friends and critics see. Waugh's version of history is of a disintegrating proceeding, a movement from greater to lesser, civilization to chaos; but that releases Dionysian comedy and a self-ironizing but poised narrative posture.

Indeed one reason why he seems so pure a comic writer is that—like his hero in *Decline and Fall*, Paul Pennyfeather, who accepts all outrage as it comes and is inert—he takes a disingenuous stance. He is not satirical in Lewis's way; when you reach back into the presence of the novelist he seems not indignant but composed. He is not a dialectical comedian of ideas in Huxley's way; his work yields ideas only dramatically. Instead the narrator stands at the centre of his comedy, omniscient yet evasively neutral, surrounded by outrage and absurdity; the world around is conveyed as an impression, a moving collage without psychological depth, flickering, quickly rendered, given largely through dialogue, short scenes, rapid transitions of place, and a wide range of characters whose inner lives rarely detain us. This economical technique Waugh seems to have got partly from the cinema and partly from Ronald Firbank, another important figure in this stylistic phase. Waugh wrote very appreciatively of Firbank, noting especially the way in which he balanced subject and form so that effect could be given without cause: 'a brief visual image flashes out to illumine and explain the flickering succession of spoken words,' so affording an art that alternates 'the wildest extravagances and the most austere economy', and which lets the writer be 'objective'. In fact it permits a narrator whose moral absence can have decided comic potential in and for itself—a potential realized vastly more by Waugh than by Firbank.

Waugh indeed conducts that moral absence superbly, even managing

it for satirical purposes[1]—which he can do because the world of comic
invention, though a figment operating according to its own laws, still
has significant relationship with the contemporary world, and because
he engages in much local parody of the familiar. But basically what
Waugh gives in his early books is a world utterly unteleological, without serious purpose or moral evolution, in which people are without
substantial identity or psychology and in which coherent motives or
aims are impossible—for the universe is contingent and operates
according to whim, chance, or fortune. It is comic according to a
familiar principle: effects represented without causes are funny. Waugh
also exploits the Bergsonian principle of the momentary elimination
of humanity, the reification of the human object, the mechanical
encrusted on to the living; indeed he makes a form of it. The comic
consumer consents in the depersonalization and victimization of human
figures in his plots because they are part of a continuous world of
anarchy and aberration, beyond moral law. In such a world the desire
to maintain stability and identity becomes farcical; institutions are
constantly becoming displaced or disoriented; systematic unreason
prevails and alternative laws operate. Much of this—the dissolution of
the person, the absurdity of identity, the substitution for human substantiality of duplicities, disguises, exchanges of role, sudden shifts of
situation—is basic to the comic stock. Waugh, though, distils a new
and compelling importance from it, a very modern one: that is why he
delights and appals us as he does. His books are very much comic *fictions*,
each making a coherent absurd world with its own laws; but each
of these worlds makes reference to the prevailing one, and exposes it,
by means of an entirely comprehensible vision of barbarism and
disintegration. The realization of comic wholeness has its distinct
historical location; it belongs to the times and has its roots in them.

In the early books Waugh uses the historical reference obliquely;
as his career develops, however, he has no trouble in uniting closely the
free-standing comic world and the world of historical experience and
event (*Brideshead Revisited* (1945) is actually a 'condition of England'
novel of a recognizable type, with much endeavour to cover recent
history, and the *Men at Arms* trilogy (1952–61) is a classic exercise in

[1] James F. Carens, *The Satiric Art of Evelyn Waugh* (Seattle, Wash. and London,
1966); there is another useful account from a not dissimilar perspective in Stephen
Jay Greenblatt, *Three Modern Satirists: Waugh, Huxley, Orwell* (New Haven,
Conn., 1965).

rendering historical hopes absurd by comedy). The comic throughout is the form for treating a world in which Waugh takes enormous, delighted curiosity but no moral pleasure whatsoever; that is why the notion of him as pre-eminently a traditional writer is false, since it suggests only the basis of how he arrives at his contrasts and vision, not the basis of his invention or, above all, its form. The critic's task is to define the peculiar relationship in Waugh between the comic world, which he enjoys, and the historical world, which he sees in decline, the Marxist process operating in it according to Gresham's Law—the supersession of the older classes and consciousness by the newer is not a movement towards value or reality, and bad history drives out good. You can call this a conservative fiction, though as a way of talking of the ongoing movement of the century it is as apt a fictional historio-graphy as the more consoling, self-justifying variant. The assumption is that to suppose the world has an ongoing, secular significance and that history creates a meaningful plot is absurd; hence plot itself is degenerate, except when, as in *Brideshead*, the thread is twitched and the divine Plotter may be thought to intercede. David Lodge calls this Waugh's myth of decline, but rightly adds: 'When culture is seen as a process of continual decline, nothing is invulnerable to irony. The modern is ridiculed by contrast with the traditional, but attempts to maintain or restore the traditional in the face of change are also seen as ridiculous; and in any case the traditional usually turns out to be in some way false or compromised.'[1] If Waugh calls up glimpses of an alternative pastoral world, itself often in the form of a delusion, behind the dehumanized and barbaric world of his mock-present, he does so to mock a larger delusion: that we are capable of living in a humane or proportioned world, a world of significances. Typically those of his characters who try to act so are his innocents; and they are pulled firmly back into the barbaric universe of comedy, the world of the modern acids, and the free-running energies that compel it. Waugh's comedy is a rescinding of significant plot, and this puts him in close relation with the modern absurd novel.

This is the broad vision; of course, as is very possible in comedy, it shifts from book to book. In the early ones, as in Huxley's, the representation of that barbaric and modernizing world is his main subject-matter. In *Decline and Fall* (1928), *Vile Bodies* (1930), *Black*

[1] David Lodge, *Evelyn Waugh* (Columbia Essays on Modern Writers) (NewYork and London, 1971), 9–10.

Mischief (1932), and *A Handful of Dust* (1934) Waugh draws for his
motifs on a variety of popular jazz age themes and situations, for his
subject-matter on spectacular detail from the immediate present, the
gossip column, the motor race, the sense of cultural impermanence, of
cynicism and world-weariness, of style-hunger. His Metroland—
which is his Wessex or Yoknapatawpha County—is a *Waste Land*
world of pleasure and parties and style lightly covering anguish and
unease, of Bright Young Things being agonizingly bright and con-
suming fashion and trend for the press's and their own dissatisfaction.
Waugh consciously catches at some of the main themes running
through the period: he conveys the obsession with acceleration and
pace, the division of body and spirit, the cloaking of unease by urban
chic, the lure of the city as a sophisticated melting pot, the insolent,
strained clowning in the semi-aristocratic milieu in which most of his
early fiction is set. The resemblance to Huxley is considerable; the
prime difference is that Waugh keeps all this inside the comic frame,
so that his own complicity and judgement is out of evidence. That, in
turn, gives him a style that is very inventively and excitingly related to
the sort of world he perceives. 'Faster, faster,' says Agatha Runcible
in *Vile Bodies*; his fiction is one of very rapid pace, moving the characters rapidly and illustratively along an absurd, busy plot, treated with
a cool, firm, very external approach. It is of course a style much in
tune with Bergson, the anti-psychological emphasis of Wyndham
Lewis, the Freudian account of wit as a principle of economy, the
entire modernist doctrine of impersonality, objectified emotion,
'classicism'. In short, like the work of his own Professor Silenus,
attempting to deal in architecture with the 'antiquated mischief'
called man, with his 'vile becoming', remote from the being of
nature and the whatness of the machine, Waugh's style is perfectly
of a piece with the modernizing twenties he so faithfully explores.
And his work runs with the prevailing barbarism and vitalism, the
Dionysian pleasure, while retaining the pose of reason and the detachment of an author capable of standing apart from the arbitrary farce
of the universe.

The differences among some of his early novels show a number of
fascinating variants on the relationship between the barbarism of the
comic universe and the barbarism of the world. His first novel, *Decline
and Fall*—aptly subtitled 'An Illustrated Novelette'—is, for all its
modern form, close to certain traditional comic modes. As in *Tom*

Jones, there is a self-sustaining, discrete comic universe, with its own laws and probabilities, its own distinctive justice and injustice, its notion of comic fortune. The story begins when the central character, Paul Pennyfeather, is sent down from his Oxford college, in conditions of complete unfairness. An *ingenu* hero, Candide-like, innocent and passive, Paul readily accepts this enforced entry into an aristocratic, irrational looking-glass land of strange misfortune and fortune. Waugh comments on this when halfway through the novel he says Paul has become a shadow; Paul is allowed briefly to return to 'reality' and

materialize into the solid figure of an intelligent, well-educated, well-conducted young man, a man who could be trusted to use his vote at a general election with discretion and proper detachment, whose opinion on a ballet or a critical essay was rather better than most people's ... This was the Paul Pennyfeather who had been developing in the placid years which preceded this story. In fact, the whole of this book is really an account of the mysterious disappearance of Paul Pennyfeather. ...

Because Paul must discard his nature to enter this comic universe, it has the special status of a fiction—an alternative world where characters disappear and reappear improbably in new situations, die and are re-born; where chance and fortune operate mysteriously, breaking apparently obdurate barriers; where comic roguery, illusion, and the manipulation of identity abound. The main characters who generate its action are versions of the picaresque type. So Captain Grimes, protected by an old school tie, a bigamist and sponger who apparently dies in the course of the action, only to be reborn, is, we are told, a Life Force. He leads the action in the direction of the Honourable Mrs. Beste-Chetwynde—'a very wealthy woman, South American'— into whose hands Paul enters by spending 'a very modern night of love', and so passes into a world quite beyond the grasp of his innocence, both because it is amoral and because it is very modern. Paul first encounters it by going to the ancient country seat of the Pastmaster family, King's Thursday, formerly a Tudor mansion which Margot Beste-Chetwynde proves to have torn down and replaced. The modernizing architect is Professor Silenus, who speaks for the de-humanized novelties in which Margot and her 'dynamic' metropolitan group live. The cycle of luck appears to rise when Paul goes to the altar to marry Margot; but the ceremony is interrupted and he goes to prison instead, taking the blame for Margot's white-slaving enterprises. He sees a certain unfairness in the situation, yet a certain logic: it does not make sense to think of Margot in prison. In fact he discovers the injustice and amorality on which this dynamic world is built, and also that he has not the powers of survival that fit him for the modern fray, those comic and anarchic powers that Margot, Grimes, and Silenus possess. The book ends by elegantly completing the circle. Paul sacrifices his identity in order to get out of prison, for he has to pretend his death; reborn, with another name, he concludes the book just as he had begun it, a student of divinity at an Oxford college. To him everything has happened, and nothing; he resumes his place in a world outside the central comic milieu, recognizing only that the 'still, small voice of conscience' totally unfits him for the modern—or the comic—world, makes him 'static' rather than 'dynamic', a poor actor on the big wheel at Luna Park to which Professor Silenus compares modern life.

'But the whole point about the wheel is that you needn't get on it at all, if you don't want to.' Such is Silenus's judgement; such the one lesson Paul takes away with him. But with Waugh's next novel, *Vile Bodies*, this option is foreclosed. There is no existence to be presumed outside the farcical, fictional universe; the worlds of comedy and of history wholly overlap. The urban milieu is now a complete metaphor, the dominant setting one in which all hopes, values, traditions, institutional forms of permanence are closed away in the past. Despite his name, Adam, the central character, is no innocent; and he is not a victim but a survivor, though in a completely shifting world. It is a world undergoing some extraordinary acceleration, the world of Agatha Runcible's 'faster, faster', with its mad motor-races, endless parties ('those vile bodies'), brief affairs and flimsy marriages. There is no permanence and no identity; religion is a farce, politics a ridiculous activity. Indeed underlying the story is a vision of economic collapse and disorder and of political chaos, giving a world of the last days where the drive is towards herd-suicide, and the only energies are demonic. The apocalyptic theme, so patently present in Lewis and Huxley too, is distilled by a specific end of ends: the book concludes on a war between unspecified parties on the biggest battlefield in the history of the world. This surrealistic intrusion of an invented history is consonant with the mood of the whole book, which uses a flickering and filmic technique to catch a succession of manners and moments out of the decade. Waugh shows the acceleration as an unstoppable process; the characters may yearn for stability, and feel that things cannot go on like this any longer, but there is nothing to go back to. The 'radical instability of the world-order' is not itself subjected to direct analysis; for the purposes of the book economic and political chaos is a condition rather than an issue. Nor is there any inward analysis of the anguish of the characters, only external forms for it, nor any direct sympathetic attachment to any of them, despite the conditions of their lives or their deaths. The absence of a moral or psychological level of existence is not now a result of entering a special shadow world, but the basic premise of the relationships arranged between novelist and matter. Waugh thus shares the twenties preoccupation with the idea of a barbarism underlying the crust of the moral and the civilized world; but, though he sees much that is comic in the barbarism, he does not see anything that is *redemptive* in it (other writers, including Lawrence, did). That, indeed, is the point of his next book, *Black Mischief*, which is a very explicit indication of the basis on which, once the notion of civilization and morals which adds dignity to our human affairs is withdrawn, barbarism and comedy are simultaneously generated.

Waugh is a novelist of these absences; as God is to an unredeemed world, so is Waugh the novelist to his characters and their universe. In his next book, *A Handful of Dust*, he does represent the consequential agony in his central character, Tony Last, to whom we attend more closely—he is a figure taken beyond stereotype, credited with hopes and purposes and values. This is potentially tragic, but nonetheless the comic mode persists in its entirety, and Tony is taken from his happy marriage and home into the Amazonian forest and a mock-death by a sequence of disasters which are again simultaneous triumphs of barbarism and comedy. Waugh attributes no blame or guilt; it is all 'nobody's fault'; if he implies it, that is a deduction made by the reader as a result of taking the narrator's indifference with scepticism. This pattern is to recur in some of the later books; the degree of 'humanization' of the characters increases, and occasionally Waugh's sympathetic attachments become apparent; but then he builds up new compensating mechanisms, so that those who accrue sympathy become figures innocent, isolated, and ripe for disaster, the disaster being represented by the spirit of comic anarchy that runs through all things. Each book is, in these terms, its own universe; but comedy persists, because it can live with barbarism, and provide all the logic that is necessary. Thus comedy's demonic and picaresque elements provide a type for the prevailing universe, and the neutral method, as in modern black humour, becomes the ideal tactic for giving fictional pleasure along with a vision of cultural chaos and human absurdity. It comes out, in Waugh, as a superb basis for structure, comedy replacing an explicit satirical assault or an inward analysis and therefore having the elegance of a pure aesthetic posture.

5

The method of what Wyndham Lewis calls 'the Great Without' has not always seemed important in our modern art. This is partly because there has been a strong tendency for writers, and critics, to see the dominant modern novel as the novel of inner consciousness, the novel of assimilated impressions and awarenesses. 'For the moderns "that", the point of interest, lies very likely in the dark places of psychology. At once, therefore, the accent falls differently; ... at once a different outline of form becomes necessary, difficult for us to grasp, incomprehensible to our predecessors,' said Virginia Woolf in her essay on 'Modern Fiction'. By contrast those ironic forms which involve long and hard distance between the writer and his human material have often provoked concern in proportion as the tactical indifference of the novelist, his withdrawal from the work in order that it may subsist as a self-governing whole, becomes a species of moral withdrawal. It is the emergence of this kind of irony that has disturbed some of the critics of Conrad's *The Secret Agent* (1907), a novel which has no hero, no plot, no real location to which value can be attached, and which moves within the circular, raw, grotesque world of its own anarchy.[1] Yet irony, even at this extreme, has formed a central strand in the evolution of modernism, which abounds in prototypical figures of chaos and disorder and figures for meaninglessness or void. In the

[1] Another aspect of this distrust has to do with the dominant presence of a narrator who diminishes his characters by means of what has been called 'neutral omniscient narration'. This matter has been very usefully discussed by Norman Friedman, 'Point of View in Fiction: The Development of a Critical Concept', *PMLA*, LXX (December 1955), 1160–84, who notes that criticism has tended to emphasize the fact that in modern fiction the assertive author has disappeared. But this view—argued in Joseph Warren Beach, *The Twentieth Century Novel: Studies in Technique* (New York and London, 1932)—can hardly be extended to include some recent developments in fiction discussed later in this book.

twenties especially this seems to come forward as the basis of an aesthetic posture. The sense of the contingent nature of contemporary action, the feeling of a loss of logic running through society and history, the notion of a 'gap in the continuity of consciousness', to take a phrase from another central work of the period, Lawrence's *Lady Chatterley's Lover* (1928), produces a sense of authorial displacement. The result is a species of comedy that turns neither on compassion or, in any direct sense, nostalgia, but on the immediate field of action seen by a distanced, confident narrator as a conditioned farce. The consequent aesthetic form is the making of a fictional world that is distorted and oblique, irrationally ordered and operated, in which metaphors of apocalypse, indifference, mechanism, and circularity predominate. A self-conscious modernity of content transacts with a self-conscious modernity of form, a parallel hardness and economy. 'Ours is a tragic age, so we refuse to take it tragically. The cataclysm has happened, we are among the ruins, we start to build up new little habitats, to have new little hopes': so begins *Lady Chatterley's Lover*. But if we do not take it tragically, we can take it comically; such, it seems, is the presumption of this significant group of styles.

PART FOUR

THE NOVEL TODAY

IX

The Postwar English Novel

I

One of the striking things about most of the critical discussion on the postwar novel, in England and elsewhere, is an element of curious unease; it seems to arise from the assumption that the novel of our time has already been written, in the early years of the century, and in the manner of modernism. Two themes are prevalent in this criticism, the first being the notion that The Novel Is Dead—a conviction that has been asserted in various forms throughout our century, but has acquired special applicability to the contemporary novel. Once the assertion was disappointedly applied to Mann, Proust, and Joyce, who wrote novels of formal strain and artistic extremity, un-novels, anti-novels. Now those novels represent the forceful energy and possibility of the form, stand *for* the modern novel; it is what has followed since—or, rather, has *not* followed—that brings out the funerary note in criticism. The second prevalent notion is that the novel is not dead but fled; it is alive and well and living in America. It is the English novel only that bears the marks of exhaustion, of provincialism, of 'reaction against experiment', a reversion to an outworn materiality or a traditional realism in a time of significant generic evolution. By contrast, in the United States the spirit of modern experiment in fiction survives, large aspiration persists, vigour of invention, plenitude of technique, and spirited aesthetic curiosity sustain the species as an art form. In these assumptions we have an interesting antithesis, and a view of it: a contrast between realism and experiment, and a proposal that realism is a feature of moribundity and is English, and experiment a feature of growth and is American. Both critical themes draw on this view, and so—as I shall try to show—are less contradictory than they appear.

It is worth reminding ourselves at the outset that we live in an age of criticism, an age when interesting literature is no sooner written than taught and examined, an age, moreover, when the fictions of critics, who plot and order the large-scale developments of the novel, have considerable power, not least over novelists themselves. 'Crictions', one critic has nicely called these critical fictions;[1] and as enabling instruments, helping us the better to understand and grasp the powers in the novel, they have decided uses. But they also shape and presumably sometimes dishearten those who write the novels; and their prior existence as lore clearly affects literary practice and literary reputations —so that, we must confess, it is often when a writer's preoccupations begin to consort with the like ones of an influential critic that he secures serious notice. Critics and writers can interfuse; they can also diverge. Elegant critical plots, theories of the nature of literature, arise and describe, or prescribe, a history of a form in such a way as to demote entire areas of expression and literary experience into marginal activities.[2] Today, in criticism as in literature, we are given to apocalyptic accounts of affairs, to theories of crisis in language and technique; the result is to lend great vigour to the view that the current novel has a special onus on it, that there is a special threat to it. Hence the assumption, in theories of the curious death of the novel and its potency for rebirth, that the sort of liberal realism to which the postwar English novel has had a particular attachment—hence, we are told, its provincialism—has collapsed, both ideologically and technically. I shall shortly be arguing that this asssumption is misleadingly narrow; much contemporary English fiction has just not been like that. But my question here is how such a view of the character and duties of the modern novel ever arises.

[1] Jonathan Raban, 'Criction', *London Magazine*, x, 2 (May 1970), 89–94.

[2] One central shift of this kind has been a recent move away from the well-established presumption that the novel was characteristically a socio-moral form, concerned with manners and social life, with appearance and reality in culture, and the critical assumptions and terms that went with this view (powerfully stated by Lionel Trilling in 'Manners, Morals, and the Novel', *The Liberal Imagination*, 1950). A familiar deviation from this mode was the symbolist, allegorical, or metaphysical mode called 'romance'. Today a traditional posture of novelists and critics in the past has been reversed, and the standards of the 'romance' novel have become normalized, so that the social form of the novel has come to seem, to many critics, eventless and unsatisfying, and its distinctive humanism hard to address with an appropriate critical language and sensitivity.

Reading the current critics, it would appear that there have been two Deaths of the Novel: the first around the turn of the century, the second in or around 1941, with the deaths of Virginia Woolf and James Joyce and the second collapse of European bourgeois society. For these two Deaths several sound historical—or historicist—reasons can be adduced. The novel was the great liberal bourgeois form, the 'burgher epic';[1] but that social order and its world-view are gone or in discredit. It depended on a shared communal language, through which shareable experiences and interpretations of the world, structures of value and perceptions about reality could be mediated, interchanged without comment; the language has lapsed. That language gave 'realism', but the notion of a substantive reality has gone, both because it was a perceptual conspiracy in too few hands, and because it set a false membrane between perceiver and perception which the novel had to violate, this being one of art's main means of growth and negotiation. It depended on a notion of character no longer effective or true, an idea of the rounded, individuated, private self, a recognizable being who could be identified with and who humanized the world he entered; this personalization of the universe is at odds with our view of man.[2] It developed through 'plot', significant chronological-causal sequences in personal or general history, in the lives of people and the progress of time and society; the feeling of inherent growth in the clock of man and history has gone, and so has the emblematic significance of a story or plot, which has now come to seem either a grid forcibly imposed upon the familiar anarchy of experience, or an elegant artistic falsity. In the course of the century, all these constituents of the novel have come into question. The modernist novel, near the beginning, showed us that: and held the form in suspense at the point of ultimate exhaustion. But now modernism as a stylistic phase is ended, leaving the writer with nothing to go forward from, and

[1] According to the formulation of George Steiner, in *Language and Silence* (1967), the novel was the form in which 'the dreams and nightmares of the mercantile ethic, of middle class privacy, and of the monetary-sexual conflicts and delights of industrial society have their monument'. It is clear from Steiner's more recent writings that he regards this phase as past.

[2] As John Bayley puts it (*The Characters of Love*, 1960), in noting that the liberal ideal of character has lost decidedly in credit: 'For a writer to show delight in character would seem today rather naïve, an old-fashioned response left over from the days of Dickens and Surtees. The literary personality has gone down in the world.'

nothing to go back to. This is the new Death of the Novel: not until we get a new reality will we have a new novel—unless, of course, the mode or medium itself proves to be the wrong form of expression. And now that modernism is so highly esteemed, this has come to seem the irreversible situation of the century; so that to move against it is to move back.

And indeed, as if in fulfilment of the plot, there were plentiful signs in the western literatures that the novel after World War II was ailing: the enormous void in German fiction; the philosophical unease and the humanistic absences of the French *nouveau roman*, criction in its own right; the retreating selfhood and anguished, self-exposed forms of American fiction, in which it seemed that to enter on describing American life was to enter landscapes of modern exposure. Existential Plight, Loss of Self, Crisis of the Word, disturbance of matter and mode, seemed widespread and indicated surely post-modernist and post-mortem twitch, a literature minimalizing itself and manifesting its own disorder. So fiction seemed; and then it was noticed that the British had adopted a peculiarly nasty subterfuge, and were writing novels as if there was no predicament at all. Their writers, the critics claimed, were refusing experiment, the strains and pains of form and perception; they were reinstating materialist and liberal realism, avoiding the meaning of Beckett, Joyce, Virginia Woolf, and reaching to Wells, Bennett, and even back to Henry Fielding. They restored an anciently liberal and humane universe; they celebrated their own provincialism. This could have been exciting news, suggesting that history, both real and fictional, was better than everyone said; better, that there were historical lacunae, that there was an appeal against the beast. In fact, though, what gained currency was the notion that the English novel, not knowing about the Death of the Novel, was dead in the lowest and dullest of senses: it was simply uninteresting.

This view, for both good and bad reasons, has now won considerable currency. The bad reasons are patent; the theories themselves, as applied to the postwar novel, depend on an *a priori* interpretation of the historical situation, projecting a sense of the developing tradition from a simplified view of what is historically authentic. The good ones are those which observe the difficulties the novelists of the postwar generation have had in defining themselves against the weight of a tradition of which, indeed, modernism had become a part; the major postwar writers were slow to emerge, and some minor talents took on

excessive value. The striking thing is that, now that a highly varied
and not at all depressing scene exists, something like that same assessment persists, and in the same historicized form. In his influential, able
survey *A Reader's Guide to the Contemporary English Novel*, written in the
late 1950s, Frederick Karl made a judgement comprehensible at the
time but decidedly too widespread since: from around 1930 on, he
held, the English novel tended to become 'restrictive rather than
extensive, to bring back traditional character and plot rather than to
seek the inexpressible; in brief, to return to a more self-contained
matter while retaining, however, many of the technical developments
of the major moderns. The contemporary novel is clearly no longer
"modern".'[1]

   This distinction was also used in Stephen Spender's *The Struggle of
the Modern* (1963), though now spread back over the century; Spender
saw twentieth-century writing split between two prime traditions, the
'modern' (technically advanced, concerned with the world as a
fragment cut off from the whole, despairing, formalist) and the
'contemporary' (technically routine, a partisan action in the modern
world, potentially progressive and realist). The great historical phase of
the 'modern' was past; and so, it seemed, the 'contemporaries' reigned.
The evidence for this was discernible in the fifties, among some
writers: those in reaction against Bloomsbury, those reacting, as
Kingsley Amis did in *I Like It Here* (1958), against both romanticism
and modernism in favour of a comic empiricism, those like William
Cooper, who remarked, in a famous essay: 'We meant to write a
different kind of novel from that of the thirties and we saw that the
Thirties Novel, the Experimental Novel, had got to be brushed out of
the way before we could get a proper hearing.'[2] A particular kind of
angry 'social realism' seemed to have grown dominant in English
fiction; and on this the largest part of criticism of the contemporary
English novel has concentrated. The argument still persists, even
though it seems fairly evident now that most of the writers developing
in the fifties were not alone social realists. In more up-to-date form it

[1] Frederick R. Karl, *A Reader's Guide to the Contemporary English Novel* (New
York, 1959; London, 1963), 4. Nearly all the book-length discussion of postwar
English fiction has looked, limitedly, at social-realist writers centrally: see Rubin
Rabinovitz, *The Reaction Against Experiment in the English Novel: 1950–1960*
(1967) and James Gindin, *Postwar British Fiction: New Accents and Attitudes* (1962).
[2] William Cooper, 'Reflections on Some Aspects of the Experimental Novel',
International Literary Annual, No. 2 (London, 1959).

has been brought back by Bernard Bergonzi in *The Situation of the Novel* (1970), where he argues that the English novel is 'no longer novel', has reached aesthetic standstill, in that many varied kinds of work appear, but all relate back to previous conventions and presumptions about fiction, and so lack the sense of expansion and growth he judges to be inherent in the novel form, and its prime characteristic from the eighteenth century on. The English, he says, 'including the most talented among them, seem to have settled for the predictable pleasures of generic fiction': they have forgone the stylistic dynamism needed for the onward thrust of the novel form.

Bergonzi's argument differs somewhat from earlier versions, however, in that he distinguishes between 'liberal' and 'totalitarian' forms of the novel, and sees the second superseding the first. The change in the novel is associated with the decline of liberalism in western culture; the novel has traditionally had an association with liberalism and a concern for character, people and their freedom of action in a probable world, but in the modernist experiment we had 'the first imaginative reponses to a changing world view which involves the death of liberalism', and with that view the most vital modern fiction has consorted. The English novel has not: hence it has not spoken to the universally anguished, depersonalized condition of modern man, and his harsh relations with modern reality; the rebellion of its heroes has not been a true rebellion, a search for new values; the tendency of fiction has been to reach back to the past, both in subject-matter (as in the nostalgic *romans fleuves* of Anthony Powell, Evelyn Waugh, C.P. Snow, the fiction of Angus Wilson) and in techniques and the assumptions implicit in them as a mode of organizing relationships and perceptions. The English novelist has reached back towards the humanization of art, that consonance between the individual and the circumstantial social web that textures nineteenth-century English fiction, and gives special value to the notion of 'character' and that 'contingency' and 'opacity' of persons of which Iris Murdoch speaks in her essays.[1] By

[1] In a later essay I suggest that Miss Murdoch's view of character is much more complex than this – and involves a sharp intellectual distinction between, in her terminology, the Ordinary Language Man of linguistic empiricism, who surrenders to convention, and the Totalitarian Man of existentialism, who surrenders to neurosis. In her sense of the term a character appears to be an agent capable of acknowledging the contingency around him; it does not mean a self-subsistent person. Thus some of Miss Murdoch's agents *become* 'characters' in the course of her novels.

contrast, the most vivid modern fiction has been alive with hostility to such principles: so the comic apocalyptic dimensions of much American fiction, the dehumanized, *chosiste* world of the *nouveau roman*. In refusing to accede to the idea that reality has become apocalyptic and incredible, and the independent self unprotectable, English writers have tended to evade new fictional possibilities. They have manifested the 'ideology of being English', which is the feeling of somehow being specially immured against history. That, given the sort of thing that nowadays passes for history, this might be a desirable state of affairs, that a literature capable of maintaining the values of humanism might have profound worth for us, Bergonzi clearly recognizes. In this sense his book appears to embody a paradox, the things which draw his formal appreciation being the things that appal him most morally. But the argument is very solidly presented, it raises a recognizable disquiet we are likely to share, and it has at heart a real issue. Ortega, speaking of the 'dehumanization of art', saw this at once as crisis and a purely formal evolution: 'first, things are painted; then sensations; finally ideas.' Formal evolutions are not necessarily a truth about history; they may be an inward finding of art. But Bergonzi—contemplating such writers as Heller and Pynchon and Robbe-Grillet, but also Burroughs and Mailer and Genet—senses more: the presence of forms concerned with penetrating the human surface or façade not in a formal but almost a psychopathological sense. There is that art, and we know it; and that could be where the novel, as part of some general disturbance of consciousness, is going, feels forced to go, to yield up that curious, almost impenetrable, authenticity of style, mode, and internal relationship that we sense to be in order for us, to be ours. In short, Bergonzi utters a suspicion not uncommon, that contemporary English fiction is somehow not in tune with the stylistic act of the times.

I am not sure that, in an age as stylistically plural and eclectic as ours, we shall ever easily know what a modern stylistic authenticity feels like; but I do believe that the thesis that the English novel has, since the war, taken a separate and self-isolating path is itself becoming a mystifying falsity. The presumption that apocalypticism and surrealism, which are American and French and also modern, contrast with realism which is English and very unmodern, compounds a number of confusions. There are sharp temperamental differences between contemporary English novels and contemporary American and French ones, but it is much to the point that these differences began to be defined precisely at the time when the view that the American novel, far from being a pale reflection of English modes, had its own distinct line and preoccupations, was historically of the tradition of romance rather than the novel, and was more symbolist in style, more metaphysical in disposition, more gothic in mode, was gaining currency. In short, the definitions we get of the importance and character of novels tend to be linked with broader critical preoccupations. But supposing that realism, liberal or otherwise, is not necessarily an antithesis to experiment, nor a self-evidently unspeculative mode, but is perfectly capable of being seen *as* experiment? Suppose that the conspicuous consumption within the text of its own means is not the only evidence of technical self-awareness? Suppose realism is in any case not the only form postwar English fiction has taken, and that criticism, in selecting and defining what the postwar English 'tradition' has been like, has opted for a very narrow portrait?

In his recent book *The Novelist at the Crossroads* (1971) David Lodge suggests at least a move in this direction. He accepts that the postwar novel in England has had a marked disposition towards realism, and he calls that an 'aesthetics of compromise', identifying it with the novel's median centre, its grounding between history (the world of discrete facts) and romance and allegory (species of formalism and fabulation). But in recent developments he sees a move away from that centre:

Realistic novels continue to be written . . . but the pressure of scepticism on the aesthetic and epistemological premises of literary realism is now so intense that many novelists, instead of marching confidently ahead [on the realistic road] are at least considering the two routes that branch off in opposite directions from the crossroads. One of these routes leads to the non-fiction novel, and the other to what [Robert] Scholes calls 'fabulation'.

(In fact the two paths, if they seem to lead out from realism in opposite directions, have strange ways of drawing together further on, bringing fact into the universe of fictions, fictions into that of fact.) If this is true, it is surely an international phenomenon, as Lodge's examples, ranging from Julian Mitchell to Norman Mailer, show. But it appears to me that, in a similarly international conspectus, these signs were already evident in the 1950s, and have much to do with the general postwar temper in the novel. Moreover, the introversion that Lodge is concerned with is itself a kind of critical development that surely might help us recognize the fictional complexities of median realism itself.

At the risk, then, of adding yet another criction to an already large pile, I want to propose that the categories as we have them are in need of further complication. For one thing, the idea of realism as a formally uncomplex species of fiction is undergoing, now, considerable disturbance, and rightly; we can see that in the developing discussion of nineteenth-century fiction. For another, the notion of the English 'tradition' as somehow separate and distinct is also proving uneasy. And at the present time it seems to me to close off many essential recognitions about the similarity between developments in fiction in England, Europe, and the United States. There are notable resemblances in the way in which western novelists in the postwar period have attempted to mediate between realistic, or documentary, and introverted fictional modes; this is hardly surprising, for it has been a persistent feature of the entire evolution of the novel. The terms necessarily shift, 'reality' being not a stabilized phenomenon, any more than 'fiction' is. These resemblances seem to me of compelling importance because they amount to a broad re-experiencing of the context and nature of fiction in the postwar world. In other words, I propose that there has been, with whatever local variations in intensity, whatever fascinating distinctiveness of emphasis in different national traditions, a decided similarity in the situations, the aesthetics, the practice of postwar western novelists. This has elicited a number of recurrent and common preoccupations, among them being a response to the problem of the contemporary novelist's relationship to the modernist art of the century—which both dominates current writing and threatens to limit it—and to the creative traditions of realism and naturalism which have persisted in their importance for twentieth-century writing. This double claim has been felt in a time of large-scale cultural and political change, which means too large-scale change in consciousness. In short, I think one can sense in the postwar period a new literary milieu and a new set of preoccupations, emerging, as David Lodge suggests, as we pass from the cultural and political climate of the first two decades after the war to something else. Neither milieu nor preoccupations seem startlingly novel in their basic elements; both, I think, involve a change of emphasis with regard to the felt possibilities of the novel form. In that general enterprise I think the important English novelists have been significant participants; and like writers in other countries they have had their own ways of relating effectively their sense of a traditional past for their form and their awareness of the pressing obligations put upon that form by the times in which and through which they live.

2

In most of the western literatures, the World War of 1939-45 seems to mark a watershed; and in the novel this coincides with the emergence of a new group of writers, with new problems, in a period of great social solvency, great human exposure, great cultural restructuring. There can be little doubt that the Second World War and the long uneasy peace after it represent a transition out of modernism's environment. This is true not only of English fiction. By this time the major modernist figures—James, Conrad, Proust, Mann, Lawrence, Virginia Woolf, Kafka, Faulkner—were, if still living, near the end of their life's work. A new kind of life, a welfare state, cold war, modern miracle, lonely crowd world, was starting to emerge in a climate of changed global power; the spirit of high formalism was hard to maintain in the presence of a changed experience and new political orders. The moods of post-modernism began to crystallize: 'Periods end when we are not looking . . . ', said Cyril Connolly in the August 1941 issue of *Horizon*. 'The last two years have been a turning point; an epidemic of dying has ended many movements.' By the issue for December 1947 he was complaining that 'such a thing as *avant-garde* has ceased to exist', and it was more than a parochial judgement: the same assertion could be heard in Europe and America. The war represented a break for most of the European fictional traditions, and the American; and the newly emerging writers, belonging to a generation that found the works of modernism not great cultural shocks but required reading for class, were very much aware of change, of educational boom and meritocratic expansion, in which their own fortunes were implicated. The social order was becoming increasingly inchoate; and mass society itself seemed, as Irving Howe said, to make modernism, with its sense of the violated yet still eternal values of culture, its privatization of art, less viable. In the different national literatures there were considerable signs of pluralism, of the age of No Style that Al Alvarez saw as the postwar temper. But one feature of this was a turning away from symbolist and formalist separation, as well as from a traditional humanistic moralism, a turning which led to some complex explorations of the relationship between the world of form and the world of history. That process in fact tended to bring realism and experiment oddly close together, giving us, among other things, a realism almost surrealist because it so much distrusted the constituents of reality, and a formalism that was obsessively concerned with documentation. In brief, there was a considerable blurring of old categories, and, slowly emerging, a new debate about the status of fiction, as well as a fresh and lively phase in literature.

In England there was a marked reaction against what had gone before, not only against modernism but Bloomsbury and a particular literary and cultural milieu which had decided class associations. The writers who came early to notice after the war tended, in their reaction to this, to seem un-*avant-garde*, indeed anti-*avant-garde*. The strong tendency I have noted in criticism to see this as a resurgence of social realism, and to regard that, in turn, as the dominant mode and manner of postwar English fiction, was always a simplification: to propose what is a no more than slightly better one, we might suggest that postwar English fiction divides into two main streams. There is the realistic, 'contemporary' manner, especially influential in the 1950s, heavily concerned with making over into fiction the new social alterations and viewpoints of postwar Britain, often from a lower-middle-class or working-class perspective: the significant names include Amis, Wain, Sillitoe, Braine, David Storey. There is the more 'visionary' and 'fantastic' manner, too: Beckett, Malcolm Lowry, Durrell, Iris Murdoch, William Golding, Muriel Spark fit better here, some of them, of course, inheritors of certain experimental modes and assumptions of the 1930s and 1940s. But clearly the alignment is extraordinarily irregular, and this is because a number of writers in the first group belong, at least for some of their work, in the second, and vice versa. Still, we can say that in the early 1950s a group of novels appeared and set a tone or climate, will represent the 'Fifties' novel in the way that a certain sort of social-protest fiction stands for the 'Thirties'. The works in question would include William Cooper's *Scenes from Provincial Life* (1950), Angus Wilson's *Hemlock and After* (1951), John Wain's *Hurry On Down* (1953), Kingsley Amis's *Lucky Jim* (1954), Iris Murdoch's *Under the Net* (1954), John Braine's *Room at the Top* (1957), Alan Sillitoe's *Saturday Night and Sunday Morning* (1958), and David Storey's *This Sporting Life* (1960). A few other writers (say Thomas Hinde, Peter Towry, Keith Waterhouse, Stan Barstow, even Malcolm Bradbury) can be associated with the tendency, but on inspection it proves quite plural; nearly all these books were first novels by new writers. Around this time there also appeared a good number of novels with vastly more *avant-garde* credentials: Malcolm Lowry's *Under the Volcano* (1947), Philip Toynbee's *Tea With Mrs. Goodman* (1947) and *The Garden to the Sea* (1954), the central trilogy of Beckett's work: *Molloy* (1951), *Malone Dies* (1952), *The Unnamable* (1953), Durrell's *Alexandria Quartet: Justine* (1957), *Balthazar* (1958), *Mountolive* (1959), *Clea* (1960). Most of these were not first novels; some came from older writers whose styles were formed before the war; a number were from expatriates. Between the groups are unmistakable contrasts, different locales and rationales for the fictional act. Thus, where the more experimental writers wrote from an *avant-garde* place and from a posture inviting high inquiry into formal means, and sustained their force and authenticity on that basis, the others were apt to employ a more commonplace rhetoric, to live with a known language rather than make one.

Beyond these there are a number of recognizably important novels and novelists—Golding, whose *Lord of the Flies* appeared in 1954, Nigel Dennis (*Cards of Identity*, 1955), Muriel Spark (*Memento Mori*, 1959), B. S. Johnson (*Travelling People*, 1963), Doris Lessing (*The Habit of Loving*, 1957)—who fit somehow between the sets. In these writers there is characteristically a mythical, religious, or comic grotesque bias, a disposition towards a romance-like form for the novel, or else an element of fantastic vigour thrusting towards, but not finally at this stage sustaining authority from, the experimental spirit. You might think of this as the middle ground between the two modes; but what then is notable is how many of the writers already cited come, at various points in their careers, to occupy it. Once past those first novels of the fifties a number of these figures moved in precisely this direction: David Storey, for example, whose *Radcliffe* (1963) is a total remaking of the detailed world of his earlier fiction into a metaphysical landscape, a technical species resembling a collaboration between Emily Brontë and R. D. Laing. Iris Murdoch is now incomprehensible in terms of the critical discourse into which she was first placed. The same is true of Angus Wilson, whose career is an extraordinary development: *Hemlock and After*, his first novel, is in form a liberal fiction, but the recognition of the 'dual nature of all human action', which disables its hero, Bernard Sands, who loses confidence in the civilized surface of life, is the basis of the complexity of Wilson's later work. And as a result his fiction moves towards that compelling tradition of comic grotesquerie which in fact has come to invest much of our writing, the modern mode of absurdity and also of fictional self-parody which is so clear in the writing of Muriel Spark or Anthony Burgess. One has only, indeed, to inspect a sufficient range of works and careers to see that in various forms mythic, symbolist, and grotesque styles of writing, which might be thought of as non-realist styles, have been constant in postwar English fiction; in this it consorts with much happening abroad. And that is true too of much of the indwelling speculation attached to these matters, which in many cases surfaces and takes the form of expressed technical preoccupation. Both these tendencies have increased in later years, but they have long been there.[1]

As for that technical speculation—which is usually assumed, if a little too easily, to be in abeyance in realist fiction—this has become increasingly explicit and increasingly focused. When a particular aesthetic preoccupation arises in literature, when mannerism occurs, it may do so for a wide variety of reasons: like phenomena have different pressures and promptings behind them, and they are given different justifications. In the past we have been inclined to see this as a movement away from realistic modes of presentation, and that indeed has been occurring. But in some areas, as David Lodge pointed out, there has been a decided intensification of the realistic mode on the interests of making it articulate and systematic. In some writers, elaborations of technique—B. S. Johnson's hole in the page, or his novel in a box to be shuffled—are aimed at the reinforcement of truth, the assertion of exposure to familiar contingencies, and involve a heightened autobiographical statement (thus *The Unfortunates,* Johnson's novel in a box, is a multiform portrait of a *real* person). In Doris Lessing's *The Golden Notebook* (1962) the problem is the mode of approach to the true story; in other writers, like Alan Burns, the mode is a collage of history. In Angus Wilson's *No Laughing Matter* (1967), the released imagination of the novelist gives history a parody element, by treating events in pastiche modes: in David Lodge's *The British Museum Is Falling Down* (1965), the parody mode is of the essence, but is a mimetically justified device to expose and explore the literariness of the central character and his problems of self-definition. In Iris Mur-

[1] For a detailed and specific survey of these developments, see my chapter 'The Novel' in *The Twentieth-Century Mind,* vol. III: *1945–1965,* ed. C. B. Cox and A. E. Dyson (London, 1972), which also contains an extended bibliography of the critical books I have here been reflecting on.

doch, who has said more than anyone about the modern problems of the novelist, there are problems of language which are problems having to do with contingency and form, problems that apply to the agents in the fiction, and problems that apply to the performing novelist herself. In John Fowles's *The Magus* (1966) and *The French Lieutenant's Woman* (1969) these are problems about the status of a fiction and the possibility of making a meaningful myth; the coercive nature of fictional story is particularly attended to, and the question of whether there can be a free plot, a plot that opens up the universe to the characters, arises. In Muriel Spark, on the other hand, purity of composition is of a piece with something like an alternative decision, the decision that contingency must of necessity be interfused with necessity if the world of the commonplace is to be revealed in its deceptive trickery; this leads to something like the pose of the satirist, but also to the idea that everything a novelist does is very exposed and very exemplary.

These are the matters looked at in more detail in the essays that follow, to which the present essay is a locational introduction. But I would take it that that conviction I have elicited from Miss Spark, that novels are exposed and are exemplary, is something we have to read back into all of them; it has its implication for realist writing too. When the novelist serves as his own critic, as novelists increasingly are apt to do in these last years, then that helps criticism. But he also helps himself, helps himself to clarify means which, in a particular age of style, seem to become present and available simply as means in the novel, and then require a convincing articulation. The postwar era has been an era of changed means, or so I would suppose. And that has generated a period of new realisms, new passions for the grotesque, new commitments to the subjective, new disquiets about the writer's omniscience or his wisdom. These are comments on the times and they arise from the times, not through an historical imperative, but as an aspect of the task of achieving a felt and significant fiction in particular circumstances. The enterprise of articulating means, of clarifying and ordering, of testing implications, is of a piece with the other, more diachronic activity which we think of as realistic. As for the scene as a whole, I find it decidedly exciting; the varied reasons for finding it so will, I trust, appear more substantially in the following pieces.

X

Malcolm Lowry as Modernist

I

When the postwar English novel comes under fire for failing to continue with the traditions, ambitions, and artistic pretensions of the modernist movement, and for lapsing into literary quietism, there are a few names we can produce to refute the charge. The most obvious are Samuel Beckett, Lawrence Durrell, and Malcolm Lowry, writers, clearly, of different qualities and commitments, but all obsessively concerned with an experimental and cosmopolitan view of art. There may be contextual reasons why such experimentalism and cosmopolitanism have had strange fortunes in postwar English writing (just as there are reasons for supposing that a climate is evolving in which in different forms they are emerging again). But that itself makes the case of those writers who have represented and extended the tendency into this era of very great interest. These three writers do have certain features in common; all, like many of the leading modernists, expatriated themselves and subjected themselves to an international range of influence, all take technical expertise and ostentation as an epistemological imperative in art, and all stake a large part of their artistic effort on procuring the right conditions, economic and contextual, for maintaining an ethos of artistic dedication. And of course all of them, though they made their substantial reputations after the war, began writing and publishing before it, and undoubtedly take some of their attitudes, colouring, and artistic assumptions from the climate of the 1930s, when the internationalist and experimental aspects of modernism survived with greater force and had a direct continuity with the great modernists of the previous two or three decades.

In the contemporary climate, writers of this kind produce clear difficulties of assessment. Though, on the one hand, we have become less confident that theirs is the *essential* tradition of modern fiction, we are nonetheless sometimes inclined to take their commitment, their dedication, and the scale of their pretensions as of themselves criteria of literary worth, though of course these can be as factitious as any other aspect of a writer's work. Then again, it is possible in Lowry's case, and probably in Durrell's too, to suppose that the modernist air was not a fully assured possession, was a commitment that divided his power or else stood in excess of what those powers could achieve. An inspection of the *Selected Letters of Malcolm Lowry* (1967), an anguished and engaging compilation of the greatest fascination for anyone interested in the contours of modern creativity, further exposes and extends this problem, which had been growing more and more apparent in Lowry's later work. That collection makes it that much clearer that his work was conceived of as a life-dedication, the dedication of a man of great intelligence and critical instinct attempting a full and responsible achievement. It also makes even clearer what one might also suspect from the work, which we still have only incompletely (plenty of manuscript remains to be released)—that that life-dedication proceeded according to the evolution of a nurtured creative instinct that was always working to place and shape an abundance of material which constantly challenged its producer. One of Lowry's favourite phrases in these letters is 'design-governing postures'—those techniques, often borrowed from others, which compose a wealth of matter already in a sense achieved, but which place and make resonant that matter. At the same time there are numerous uneasy signs of a creative direction never fully achieved, a bewilderment about the potential public meanings of his own type of creativity, a sense, not uncommon in modern writing, that what has been written is not of itself complete, or rightly acquired. Part of this may well be due to Lowry's unhappy dealings with publishers. But the problem strikes deep into his very creativity, and comes out (as it also does in Dylan Thomas) as a principle of vacillation between an extreme artistic ambition and the sense of never having achieved a proper subject-matter to serve it. Like Thomas, Lowry was a middle-class provincial boy for whom the dedication to art brought a species of suffering, and this suffering becomes a staple of the writing; if one presses personal passions and myths hard enough art will emerge, but as a kind of testimony to one's seriousness. So Lowry can say, in a letter to his Random House editor about *October*

Ferry to Gabriola, a book still somewhat clumsily personal in its un-finished, posthumously published form: 'the bloody agony of the writer writing it is so patently extreme that it creates a kind of power in itself that, together with the humour and what lyricism it may possess, takes your mind off the faults of the story itself. . . .'

Of course this sort of appeal is not worthless; there are kinds of writing—for instance the poems of Hart Crane—where the sense of what literary effort can't achieve *is* so patently achieved that we recognize worth and distinction. But such writing is more obviously romantic than modernist; and that is also very true of Lowry. Though certain modernist features seem essential to his work, his posture in relation to them is oddly oblique, incomplete. One can follow this out, for instance, in the pattern of his expatriation, which for most modern-ists was a movement to culture capitals, the new urban contexts of art and the centre of new movements and fashions in literary thought. Beckett and Durrell, for example, expatriated themselves via well-forged cosmopolitan links—Beckett to *avant-garde* Paris, Durrell to that and also to Mediterranean life and writing. But Lowry made only the most tentative links with established literary scenes and contexts (in Cambridge, Paris, and New York) and rather expatriated himself away from artistic centres, and to the idea of exile and voyage itself. When, after spending time in Spain, Mexico, and the States, he did settle for fourteen years, it was characteristically in a cabin with almost no facilities built, under pioneer's rights, on the foreshore at Dollarton, British Columbia, inconveniently over the U.S.-Canadian border and virtually inaccessible at times through the mails (a fact which added to the persistent confusions with which his life was bedevilled). He was equally uneasy about identifying his art or purposes with any particular literary centre or literary tendency. He was apt, in the later period, to regard himself as an American or a Canadian writer—but casually and very much, it would seem, in the mood of his hero in 'Elephant and Colosseum', in *Hear Us O Lord From Heaven Thy Dwelling Place* (1961) —a Manx author living in America because 'the people who believed in him were all Americans, and even here in Europe—once more came that inexplicable childish pang, yet so deeply he couldn't believe its cause was mean or unworthy—he'd received no word from the heart.'

And typically Lowry liked to stress the lonely nature of his genius, his general separateness from influence, even his ignorance. In a letter to Jacques Barzun, who had written a review of *Under the Volcano* attacking it as 'an anthology held together by earnestness', he complained: 'Having lived in the wilderness for nearly a decade, unable to buy even any intelligent American magazines (they were all banned here [Canada], in case you didn't know, until quite recently) and completely out of touch, I have had no way of knowing what styles were in fashion and what out, and didn't much care.' Obviously, as the stories in *Hear Us O Lord*. . . make evident, he was widely read and had assimilated a good deal from many twentieth-century moderns; there is clear influence from Joyce (after a Joycean punning bout he speaks, in a story and also in his letters, of being 'Joyced with his own petard'), from Thomas Wolfe, from D. H. Lawrence, from Scott Fitzgerald (whose *Tender Is the Night* he adapted as a reputedly brilliant scenario, never made into a film). But a more obvious debt is to the Romantic poets, particularly those associated with voyage and/or suffering. And his two great modern literary heroes were characteristically oblique ones— Conrad Aiken and the Norwegian writer Nordahl Grieg, both novelists of voyage to whom *he* voyaged in youth, shipping on freighters to the States and Norway in order to meet them. All the voyage and journal material of the (posthumously published) collection *Hear Us O Lord*. . . is bound together in a complex structure of literary allusion, founded on a wide range of reading from Prescott to Baudelaire, Marx to Wolfe, and some of it is clearly excessively literary; even so, there is a secure truth in Lowry's claim that (so he paraphrased his admired Melville) a cargo ship was his real Yale and Harvard. To a considerable extent, then, he was the romantic autodidact, and this element is sharply there in the work.

So it is that there lies, behind the experimental and modernist spirit, a deep vein of romanticism. The signals of modernism are evident enough; the texture of deep literary allusiveness, the commitment to formal experiment, the quality of strain and anguish which itself, as Stephen Spender stresses in a useful introduction to the 1965 reprint of *Under the Volcano*, links Lowry with the other central modernists in his concern with the 'modern breakdown of values'. Yet, as Spender says, Lowry's view of life is individualistic in a way in which those of the leading moderns are not, since through them a consciousness that is ultimately historic and even collective speaks.[1] But Lowry's

---

[1] Spender quotes a revealing passage from Sigbjørn Wilderness's journal in 'Through the Panama' (in *Hear Us O Lord* . . .): 'I am capable of conceiving a writer today, even intrinsically a first-rate writer, who *simply cannot understand*,

work is primarily *self*-projection, and the surrounding world tends to be solipsistically merged into that of the hero. Lowry's essential assumptions about art thus tend to be purist romantic ones, art seen as imaginative voyage and representative suffering, all this in the cause of a final transcendence, the fulfilment of a paradisial opportunity. It is against this that he introduces, modernly, a sense of tragedy; his primary themes are then the despoliation of the world by man, and the tragic condition of the serious spirit in the modern world. His heroes move through landscapes of destruction and waste, landscapes of hell in which symbolic ruination abounds, seeking the restitution of the paradisial garden. To some extent, as in Fitzgerald's work, the tragic derives from a sense of necessary identification with that world, a need to know its nature; and in Fitzgerald this view is supported by a superb cultural and historical awareness. But in Lowry the tendency is rather towards an auto-destruction in excess of what conditions it; at the same time, the imagined world of his books approves the nobility of that destruction. He tended to associate this scaled-up romantic dream of the self with creativity, which he saw as the principle by which we compose our lives. In the later work, I think, he sees the difficulty, and the stories in *Hear Us O Lord. . .* are marked by situations in which fiction, or the created romantic view of the self, is violated by reality; or else romanticism is dissipated by a critique of it, as in 'Through the Panama', where the need for talent to be uncritical of itself is played off against the need for criticism, and a notion of equilibrium emerges: 'And yet there has never been a time in history when there was a greater necessity for the preservation of that seemingly most cold-blooded of all states, equilibrium, a greater necessity indeed for sobriety (how I hate it!).' The confession is surely crucial, and at the heart of Lowry's artistic difficulties throughout his whole *œuvre*. In consequence, Lowry's 'large' romantic heroes, both in battle with the universe and striving to attune themselves to what is transcendental in it, are at once somewhat overly regarded *personae* for Lowry himself, and the subjects of the author's own criticism and even his uncertainty. The result is an achievement that has a fascinating development, an achievement at once magnificent and incomplete.

---

and never has been able to understand, what his fellow writers are driving at, and have been driving at, and who has always been too shy to ask.'

2

Lowry was born in 1909 in Birkenhead of upper-middle-class background, his father a Liverpool cotton broker, his maternal grandfather a Norwegian sea captain. He was educated fairly conventionally but after leaving The Leys School he shipped on a freighter out of Liverpool bound for the Far East, and this experience forms the basis for his autobiographical first novel *Ultramarine*, published after several years of revision in 1933 and then further revised by Lowry and reprinted in a new version posthumously in 1963. In many respects *Ultramarine* is a typical novel of the 1930s. The hero, a young man of nineteen named Dana Hilliot, of British-Norwegian parentage, signs on as a crew member for an Asian voyage of a ship called in the revised version the *Oedipus Tyrannus* (this is the ship that Hugh sails on briefly in *Under the Volcano*), with a British-Norwegian crew. Hilliot, a middle-class boy cut off from his fellow sailors by his background and his romantic sexual prudishness, seeks the acceptance of the crew and finds it when he finally stands up to and comes into community with the man who has taunted him most. To this extent the mood is familiar; the romantic instinct towards search and fulfilment can only be satisfied by achieving fraternity with his fellow men—the sea invites the romantic search, but only acceptance by the men in the forecastle can provide the field of redemption. But Hilliot's wandering, harbourless, dispossessed characteristics and confused nationality are something that he shares with the ship itself, and his 'wild self-dedication' is part metaphysical, a desire not only to prove himself to others but to achieve a delight beyond despair. He is obsessed by his 'incapacity to position things and see them in their places', and a good deal of the action is in fact concerned with his severance from his father and the need to find his substitute; as Hilliot says, in a magnificent drunken speech, seeing something of the weakness of this, 'I assume the guilt of a mother, or of a father, or of a heredity, imagine it completely, to be able on the one hand to give an adequate explanation of my more inexplicable actions, and on the other in order to be clothed in a dark, blood-stained dignity. Some of these points are raised, and you may have read for yourself, in my much maligned and certainly dangerous and misleading work, *Hamlet*. . . .' But it is after he has been accepted by Andy, in a fatherly role, that the chaos and disunion of the ship's machinery, seen as a vision of hell, falls into place—pitiless regularity, interdependence. Sexual love and desire become a romanticized 'sublimated all-embracing love for mankind' but, more than that, a romantic identification with the universe is achieved: 'Then at last again to be outward bound, always outward, to be fighting always for the dreamt-of harbour, when the sea thunders on board in a cataract...' The gesture is not much more 'than a gesture, but it *is* a romantic one, and it is specifically intended to place what otherwise might be read as a simple political message; what the sea finally gives is not social fraternity but imaginative voyage.

If *Ultramarine* is fairly directly autobiographical, *Under the Volcano* (1947) is so in much more complicated ways. Beginning as an auto-biographical novella, its incrementation (the published version is effectively Lowry's fourth) came about very much through events subsequent to its inception—the breakdown of Lowry's first marriage to Jan Gabrial in late 1937 when they were in Mexico, his subsequent drunks, and his experiences with the Mexican police, who arrested him and apparently thought him a spy. Yet the imaginary future that the Consul, Geoffrey Firmin, projects for himself with Yvonne in the letter in chapter 1 is clearly that Lowry led with his *second* wife, Margerie Bonner, at Dollarton. The book also in time came to be placed as part of a trilogy, the Inferno part; with *Lunar Caustic* (post-humous, 1963) as the Purgatorio and *In Ballast to the White Sea*, lost when his house burned down, as the Paradiso. Malcolm Lowry's two excellent if abstractly elaborate, and certainly not totally reliable, glosses on the novel in the *Selected Letters*—one to Jonathan Cape, who had proposed cuts in it; another to Derek Pethick who was giving a radio talk on it—make it clear that he saw the mythology of the novel as indeed infernal, the world of the ruined paradisial garden, which is hence coherent with Firmin's own auto-damnation. Firmin therefore has no alternative but destruction, since the given universe in which he moves is either destroyed or destructive itself. He is bound to the Day of the Dead—a much less contingent symbol than Bloomsday, at once more assertive and more literary. The destructive cycle is both an historical situation, specifically related by Lowry to the war, and an ultimate human situation; Lowry says the novel is concerned with the forces in man which cause him to be terrified of himself, with guilt, remorse, and doom. But what this means is that Firmin's inability to act for his own benefit is a given of this universe. Fellowship therefore lies only in common guilt and common suffering. His search can *only* lead to ruination and damnation; he is doomed from the start because he is a wild spirit. Having thrown up his post, broken with his wife, and acquired advanced dipsomania (Lowry calls this 'the abuse of magical powers'), he can only seek his own destruction heroically. When the possibility of the redemption he desires comes with the return of his wife, he can only, in his state of alcoholic possession, reject it. So he quarrels with his wife, runs into the middle of a dark wood to an all-night cantina, and there meets a group of violent vigilantes—and, encouraging their suspicions about him, accepting their provocations, he brings about his own death in the *barranca*: 'Nor was this summit a summit exactly: it had no substance, no firm base.' At the same time the imagined world of the novel can approve his nobility; for Firmin, 'a Faustian gent', is after all the shattered prince, his wife the broken princess, and he ends the novel clearly as an aristocrat of suffering, a Byronic romantic.

Under the Volcano is Lowry's most consistent work, a coherent imaginative unity handled throughout in a romantic mode; there can be little doubt of its magnificence. At the same time we can see why Lowry must have been uneasy about being totally committed to it, both because it emphasizes a 'diabolic' rather than creative view of the world, and because of its lonely self-dramatization. In a sense the work that follows, notably the collection *Hear Us O Lord. . .* , is a gloss upon it. In the Dollarton period Lowry recast his whole writing plan, conceiving of a sequence of six or seven books, to be called *The Voyage That Never Ends; Under the Volcano* was to be in the sequence, but as a work of the imagination, and the character Sigbjørn Wilderness, the writer who appears in *Hear Us O Lord. . .* , the sequence's central figure. *Lunar Caustic* returns into the canon, but so do other works including the novel *October Ferry to Gabriola* (posthumously published in 1971). It is apparent that these books must have been intended to exist in extremely complex relation to one another. For instance the story 'Through the Panama', in *Hear Us O Lord. . .* , is represented as 'From the Journal of Sigbjørn Wilderness' but refers to a novel Wilderness has written called *Through the Valley of the Shadow of Death*—which is in fact *Under the Volcano*. (Lowry justifies the imaginative necessity for this in a letter; an autobiographical *alter ego*, Wilderness must have been capable of this sort of act of moral courage.) One clear function of this complex mode of presentation is that of distancing Lowry's various versions of himself. In fact *Hear Us O*

Lord. . . , abounds in new versions; many of his characters are writers with distinctively similar histories, English, Manx, or Scandinavian in background. Moreover a persistent theme is the violation of fiction by reality, so that 'Elephant and Colosseum' has to do with a writer's discovery of literary dishonesty and false rendering, and the multiplying of his *alter ego* figures is not only a means of multiplying his own experience of life and the variety of interpretations he is capable of applying to it, but apparently serves also to soften the romantic core and enable a fuller *persona* to emerge. But the questions raised here must be for an author almost intolerable, in much the same way as they must become intolerable for J. D. Salinger, divided between the ironies of the art-life relationship and a prophetic role. Both writers, in fact, seem to come to the point where modernism—the ironies of the art-life relationship—and romanticism—prophecy and autobiography and the spiritual sense—diverge, leaving a presiding irony. Insofar as the divergence is the crucial dilemma of modern art, Lowry's path to it is of endless interest. If, on the way, he left one limited but coherent work, his *Catcher in the Rye*, so to speak, then we can be imaginatively gratified by, as well as fascinated with, the effort. And as for the whole open-ended, self-questioning construct which is his *œuvre*, that too has its obsessive pull as a mythological fund accrued at great cost and in its insufficiency totally challenging.

3

If the *Selected Letters* disappoint, they do so by not revealing enough about the quest.[1] But clearly the crucial thread present in the volume is that of the slow elaboration of Lowry's almost mystical notion of creativity. This doesn't emerge as a systematic philosophy, rather as an obsession cropping up in a number of the most illuminating letters (the one to Cape; another drawing a friend's attention to Ortega y Gasset's philosophy; another describing the plot of the lost novel *In Ballast to the White Sea* to an admirer, David Markson, writing on Lowry's work). Crudely extrapolated, it might be sketched something like this: creativity is an instinct for ordering natural to man, and it manifests

---

[1] It would have been easy, by better editing, a stronger selection from the earlier period, fuller biographical bridging, an improved index, and a record of Lowry's completed manuscripts, to make this the basic biographical record, at least until an accurate biography appears to dissipate the cloud of errors surrounding Lowry's career and intentions.

itself as a kind of evolutionary force, transcending the reality of nature and giving meaning and mythology to existence. In this sense life follows art. But because this is so, the most revealing aspects of art are those dimensions of it which make explicit the laws and orders that make a writer a writer, and cause him to modify life and create personages. Lowry's own sense of this order was never, as I have said, fully achieved; but it inevitably brought his writing in complex relation to his own biography . . . in which one of the essential biographical facts was that he was a writer. In this way Lowry's heroes are not only figures for himself—and often writers, for his purpose in art is to convey the experience of men of consciousness and conscience—but also are incrementally associated with his previous *personae* and his previous writing. Not only, then, does *Ultramarine* weave itself into *Under the Volcano*, through the in some ways ironic link of the *Oedipus Tyrannus*; so the existence of *Under the Volcano* must be made a biographical or historical fact in the life of Sigbjørn Wilderness, so that the retreat of past imaginings into history can enable the growth of consciousness, the evolutionary instinct. This complex interweaving, this incremental method of creation, is associated with the idea of the writer as the agent of unconscious powers—he must suspect, like Sigbjørn Wilderness, that he is not a writer so much as being written.

In this sense the writer must place himself, by right action, in accordance with some mystical Law of Series, some pattern of creative coincidence that will lead him to redemption. If the Consul of *Under the Volcano* has aligned himself with a law of series that leads to damnation (a view which explains the 'sympathetic' nature of the universe through which he moves), then the hero of *In Ballast to the White Sea* was conceived of as doing the reverse, and 'in effect', says Lowry in his summary of it, 'both the life of the imagination and life itself has been saved by A's having listened finally to the promptings of his own spirit, and acted upon those promptings. . . .' This is not only a force of life, but a creative operation of the soul, a capacity for identification with a transcendental. Dana Hilliot had found this through fraternity and voyage; Geoffrey Firmin makes a destructive identification; but the hope of a romantic affirmation seems always to have been strong in Lowry's mind. Firmin, towards the end of *Under the Volcano*, becomes aware of a sense of love as a transcendent principle and an upward movement, through which things have greater distinctiveness and separateness—so 'had he desired it, or willed it, the very material world, illusory though that was, might have been a confederate, pointing the wise way.' In terms of the logic of literary structures, the superstitious notion of creative coincidence has of course very great meaning. But Lowry wished also to see it as a moral force, the supernatural world informing the material. In fact it can never of itself turn into a total world view, only provide a posture for one. So Lowry's problem finally lay in capturing the notion of creativity as a genuine coherence; and for this to happen it had to be fully revealed to him and manifested, rather than written about.

But the divergence between a literary and a human transcendental seems finally to have divided him, both as a man and a writer. The romantic dream remains a dream, and creativity comes to mean questions, new starts and new obstructions. Yet of itself the effort— the effort at once to live and to write by an overwhelming principle of creativity—is superb and fascinating. And it is founded on a deeper kind of creative capacity, the capacity, so evident in *Under the Volcano*, to create a dense and living web of experience, which can give that effort a literary meaning.

XI

William Cooper and the 1950s:
Scenes from Provincial Life

I

Scenes from Provincial Life came out in 1950, apparently the first novel of a writer who in fact proved to have published fiction before under his own name, H. S. Hoff. It won good reviews and then increasingly it began to exert an influence on a number of writers rather younger than its author, who was born in 1910. 'Seminal is not a word I am fond of,' wrote one of them, John Braine. 'Nevertheless I am forced to use it. This book was for me—and I suspect many others—a seminal influence.' Now, looked at from today's standpoint, it seems to belong to the fifties as exactly as a certain kind of tweed sports jacket. In saying that, I have no intention of limiting it, of suggesting that it counted then but not now or that its only importance was as an influence. Anyone who reads it for the first time today will find it fresh, alive, and finely done. But this other importance of the novel has grown rather clearer; *Scenes from Provincial Life* has a lot to do with a stylistic turn that happened about the time the book came out, and perhaps even *because* the book came out, a turn which affected the fortunes of the postwar English novel and made them rather different from those of contemporary American or French fiction. It was a modest revolution (like all the revolutions of the 1950s in England), but it was quietly considerable and significant. The novel's qualities are not perhaps what one would ordinarily expect in a 'radical' book. It is a fairly simple (but artfully simple) lyrical novel set in the English provinces, self-conscious about the ordinariness of the life it deals with and the particular limitations and innocence of the main characters, caught in their twenties and their teens and in that sharp state of emotional intensity that belongs to the hunt for partners. The book doesn't even have the 1950s as its subject—it is set, in fact, on the other, 1930s side of that considerable cultural divide that was formed by the war. And the writers you might be led to think of as you read it are possibly H. G. Wells or, going further back and in a rather different direction, Turgenev. All this hardly sounds like a testament to modernity; but if it is true that a good part of the literary style and temper of the 1950s was set by this book, and then by this *sort* of book, there may be good grounds for supposing that what it stands for was a movement towards fictional expansion and survival.

The progress of the novel has usually depended on an oscillation between two parts of its powers and its nature. Novels tend to lie, to use Iris Murdoch's distinction, somewhere between the 'journalistic' and the 'crystalline'; which is to say that they can participate in the contingent and particular realities of the world as they are known and shared *as* realities, or they can explore art as a specialized knowledge, being concerned with the mode of existence of words, languages, structures, fictions. *Scenes from Provincial Life* is not of course an artless novel, but it is the novel in its empirical form. It could and did stand for an important swing away from the stylistic backlog of modernism, or what William Cooper calls the 'Art Novel': a swing towards an art of reason, an art of lived-out and recognizable values and predicaments, an art, even, of the social places we associate with ordinariness—the provinces, the lower middle classes, the world of growing up and getting on. Virginia Woolf once suggested that modernism had set the writer free, led him from the kingdom of necessity to the kingdom of light, by allowing him to dispense with traditional plot and character, traditional detailing and chronology, the need to tell a story or report material reality. But such freedom, as we can see from the deep sense of predicament that marks the great works of modernism, was of course itself conditioned. In any case, the revolt against the Victorian 'reality' and the Victorian conception of the artist produced a new convention, and a new socially specialized locale for art in the cosmopolitan and *avant-garde* intelligentsia. By the postwar period the root conditions of modernism were more or less exhausted in English society, and the cultural dominance of Bloomsbury was certainly coming to an end; it was hard for the new generation of English writers to take up the modernist mode for the exploration of their culture. Cooper later placed himself in the context of an explicit revolt against the 'Thirties' novel in its mannerist and experimental guise, and against the French *anti-roman*. Art, he said in an essay of 1959,[1] depended not on a series of attacks on the powers and place of the human mind, but an assertion of mind. It needed not a *reductio ad absurdum* of experience, but experience itself as it is given. It needed not the intense specialization of the artist in his own universe, but the sharing of the extant universe with others. (Or that, at least, is what I read him as saying, since it is an argument that influenced me very considerably, just as his novel influenced me: not only in what I wrote, but in my very belief that I could, on the basis simply of intelligently being, become a writer.)

So what came out of the novel and its climate—it is a simple truth that criticism has a way of forgetting—is that we do not need to abide by the climate of modernism, since it is not historically inevitable. I would not say, as William Cooper sometimes seems to say, that modernism does not count; and I would certainly deplore an evident slackening of scale that became part of the climate brought about by feelings of this sort. But we should also remember that this sort of statement is a statement on behalf of the humanist powers of art and their connection with life. It is an assertion that we live life above all in the realm of the given; that to find ourselves alienated from society or absurdly placed among things is an intellectual or technical abstraction as much as a recognizable truth, and it can be a limitation on our way of knowing ourselves or our world. It looks now as if we are moving into another phase of ideology and alienation theory, of grand resentment about the given realities and their meanness; and no doubt, if the novel still counts at all, it will seek to show that. But *Scenes from Provincial Life* has no such resentment about the given world, and it believes too in the active powers of the living mind and the consonance between that and the making of art. There is no assumption that the truth about man is that he is alienated, that realities are an enormous deceit, that the artist has no words left that are uncorrupted. Rather it is a book about how dense, substantial, and complex life is, taken on its ordinary terms; and about how a writer can take fictional life from such things; and how even if the provinces are not cosmopolis and the

---

[1] 'Reflections on Some Aspects of the Experimental Novel', in *International Literary Annual*, No. 2 (London, 1959).

place of high and abstract art they still have a culture which can itself lead to art. It is not all a writer today might say, but it is enough.

2

What is this provincial life from which the scenes of the novel are thrown up? It is the life of a largish provincial town left deliberately unnamed ('I will not describe our clock-tower in detail, because I feel that if you were able to identify our town my novel would lose some of its universal air'). If Cooper says that with mild self-irony, he also says it to make his town a representative instance of the familiar social web in which men live, amid composed institutions (pubs and the grammar school, parks and cafés, the marketplace and the clock-tower) and equally composed if sometimes strange customs (like the Sunday afternoon visits of Mr. Chinnock, 'regular as clockwork', to the land-lady's niece). The story is firmly set in its place, or one ought to say its culture; and amid a particular stratum of its life, its intelligent if not quite intellectual young people. If they do not quite belong, in the sense that they are somewhat shockingly advanced, if they seem to have yearnings that take them outside and beyond, if their roles don't always quite fit ('What *can* I behave like?' wonders Joe Lunn, the narrator, when told he doesn't behave like a schoolmaster), then that is provincial life too. They are schoolmasters and accountants and commercial artists who are also writers and poets and painters, but although they may be more ambitious in their aims and their feelings than others this does not separate them dreadfully off from their world. Joe is cautious about the proprieties and the bohemianism of all the group is of the most modest kind; even Myrtle's gramophone-record-playing sessions and her late nights are, by his sense of fitness, going a little too far. But of course the point is that they feel their place as well as their detachment from their place. And because of that, even though the action really concentrates on four figures only, it gives us a full sense of the community that surrounds and feeds them. Throughout the novel they talk of leaving it, to go to America under the fear that Hitler's aggression in Europe will end with a totalitarian state in England: 'Though we were three very different men, we had in common a strong element of the rootless and the unconforming, especially the unconforming. We had not the slightest doubt that were some form of authoritarian regime to come to our country we should sooner or later end up in a concentration camp.' But one senses, of course, that they won't leave, for it is the web of relationships, these meeting-places and events and the things that go with them, that stay real in the novel. The impending dislocation is an unreality. The dangers of 1939 count, of course, and they do finally *become* real; but that is beyond the end of the story.

But that isn't to say that the characters are passive, unintelligent, or unaware of what is happening. The narrator and his friends are all lively-minded people who are seeking to make sense of their passions, their ambitions, their environment. They have a strong sense of their slightly excessive pretensions; that is particularly true of Joe Lunn, and is part of his tone as the recollecting narrator. They enjoy bold emotional manœuvres but they usually end up with an unwonted feeling of tenderness, responsibility, or concern. They are not grand masters or moralists of personal relations, but they do know how to give them their due, to care sufficiently about others while caring sufficiently about themselves. The relationship between Joe and his mistress Myrtle, with Myrtle shifting beyond passion to marital ambitions and Joe wriggling to be free for ends not clear even to him, is conducted with a certain moral toughness on Joe's part but also with a precise moral delicacy. That, indeed, is one element that keeps it alive for so long; another is the human inconsistency by which feeling in any case countermands logical decisions, and which sets up those contrary pulls for permanence and impermanence which are central to the lyrical mood of the novel. Joe is half the ironist about these matters, and half the man of feeling:

> It was a light evening, and I could see from a long way off that she was in a state of abysmal depression. She had begun to look sadder and sadder during the last days. I suppose I was unfeeling and detached; I thought of it as her 'I'll-never-smile-again' expression. Really, she overdid it. I felt genuinely upset and, such was the weakness of my nature, faintly irritated by remorse. I kissed her warmly on the cheek.

If this sort of alternation of emotion is so very recognizable, it is because Joe is comically independent of the situation and also inevitably drawn, by 'something like instinct', as he says, to the power of the person, the place, and the feeling. The tone is a mixture of lyricism and comedy, which means that we are not asked very explicitly to judge matters of moral quality and characteristic; in any case, Joe can claim the privileges of the narrator to be independent from that sort of judgement. But we do recognize, in what Joe does and feels and the way he tells the story, the presence of a real intelligence which includes, among other virtues, the capacity to know oneself as absurd or ridiculous or obstinate and yet forced to act according to certain decencies. As Joe says, that becomes the more important if one believes one *isn't* a good man. All the characters show this kind of inconsistency, and it is very much what makes for that ebb and flow of life and feeling out of which the book is made. But my point is that it is the sense of living in a society and in the context of the values of a culture that has an existence in place and time that makes this so much alive.

We can see, of course, what this culture is; its roots are basically domestic and practical, and it thrives through a kind of middle-class and unromantic good sense. It supposes that people are relatively comprehensible and relatively rational, and that you can know sufficient about them to share feelings and values and make relationships. But then there are elements of the unknowable and the strange, which are personal and are as much there in oneself as in others. So relationships have a kind of mysterious rhythm to them; and one acts in the middle of them with a certain intelligent degree of comprehension of one's lovers and friends, and another element of incomprehension, a sense of the 'unknowable' that is 'something like instinct'. In Cooper's manner there is a rather stylized quality about the conversations, something tangential in them as each character follows out his own expression of the self's needs; but of course this is not the Pinteresque convention that really nobody can communicate with anyone else, that we all live in totally subjective systems of reality. It is really only in a fictional world that is both public and private that you can have a genuine sense of the morality of actions and relationships; and that Cooper gives us, the moral life of the ordinary world. For though Joe is an artist, and expresses his obstinacy sometimes as a matter of artistic need, it is out of that ordinary stuff that he makes his choices and finds his feelings. His strains, and those of the other characters, come from life and not from art; and art comes later, as the act of recollection, the turning of experiences offered and created as thoroughly authentic into 'material', 'delightful and disastrous, warm, painful and farcical. I reach for a clean new notebook. I pick up my pen.'

The book is made of this sort of illuminated and worked life. It is indeed *scenes* from provincial life—moments of meeting and parting, episodes of friendly conversation, love-making, love-talking—but a sequence of scenes distilled into an emotional whole. The action consists basically of a succession of episodes in the lives of the four central characters, caught up with many surrounding ones, and it covers the spring and summer of 1939. A good deal is kept out of the telling to make the distillation exact. Before the action begins, the two essential relationships—the affair between Joe, the schoolmaster narrator, and Myrtle, the commercial artist, and that between his friend Tom and *his* boyfriend and protégé Steve—have already begun. After it ends, in the coda of the last chapter, comes the roll-call of marriages and the record of war experiences. The threats of Hitler and marriage hang over the basic sequence—that phase of human life before marriage which does work out as a pattern of scenes and crises, imperfect understandings and regrets, strong feelings and cautious fears —and help us to see that the phase of life must by the very nature of love and history come to an end. The ebb and flow of feelings comes to contain—as Joe says of Myrtle's feelings—'too much ebb and not enough flow', and it moves, through its small world of constant meetings and a few basic locales, gradually towards final dissolution:

The end. And I knew with certainty she was there at last. I did not know the reason. I supposed that something I had said or done during the last few days must have been the last straw. I do not even know now what it was, and if I did I should not believe in it as she did. To most of us the movements of the soul are so mysterious that we seize upon events to make them explicable.

The theme *could* have led to a tragic mood of betrayed hope in passion that affects many nineteenth-century novels, but of course that is not the tone. For the novel is very much a comic novel, a comedy of authenticity; Joe's late and not entirely final discovery about Myrtle— '. . . I can only say that to the very depths of my soul I was fed up with her'—has that touch of truth that fiction only catches in rare moments. This is the authenticity of its culture *and* of its modernness, and it is what helps us to feel that the book is a book of its time.

Critics lately have tended to characterize this kind of fiction as sociological realism; but Cooper's book makes a much fuller use of the languages and tones of its culture than that phrase usually suggests. For it is much more than a report; it is a lyrical and comic evocation that is very carefully made. We can see this in the position and character of the narrator, Joe, himself; and the kind of comedies and ironies he plays over his story. He stands in a position beyond it, a position more advanced in time and in a bigger world. And so he can see the elements of innocence and absurdity in the story he tells: 'We were completely serious about it [the state of the world], and we became even more serious even as our actions became more absurd.' The provinces and the past intertwine as a recollected place and let him, too, be a little ridiculous; but his absurdity, and that of Tom, with his dubious insights into human conduct, Myrtle, with her red setter and her gun, and Steve, with his contradictory responses to the role of protégé, is part of the common fortune. For Joe as narrator does finally belong to this world, and so he is neither emotionally nor technically patronizing. His own lack of feeling, his absolute refusal to marry Myrtle—these things are the spring of most of the events—are his own foible and also his human right, part of his intelligent ridiculousness. The irony is therefore not complex and the tone is comically generous, the tone of a human openness that condemns very little, observes a great deal, and carries a wide range of feelings. Joe is the lyricist of the novel and the man who also sees life-history as a stuff to write about; his independent obstinacy is a convincing part of his total psychology as a man who also happens by nature to be a writer. The art he makes, the book he writes, is as much a product of this sort of life and place as the experience he feels. Life is a sequence of scenes and felt moments, something that derives from what exists in the given world to experience, to know, and feel; and novels are the products of one's own life-history, the product of all one's delights and disasters ('I think of all the novels I can make out of them—ah, novels, novels, Art, Art, pounds sterling!'). Joe's are not the modernist ironies of artistic distance, but they are those of character which somehow become those of an artistic position. So Joe not only makes a world as a writer must (as when he chooses not to emphasize politics for reasons of literary necessity: 'For some reason or other political sentiment does not seem to be a suitable subject for literary art'), and he does not only judge that world as a writer must; he also finds one in life. You can be an artist because you have intelligently seen, known, and can shape the experiences of the ordinary world.

3

It was no new discovery, of course. The book's newness lay in the particular kind of ordinary life, the particular culture, it found; and in the way it brought that alive as a vision, a pattern of motives, meanings, and significance, a way of living in the present. This has a lot to do with the way many writers in the 1950s did find means of bringing a sense of cultural observation and moral analysis of their changing society into relation with a new, an idiosyncratic, and very often a comic viewpoint upon it. If, over that period, the viewpoints and judgements of a provincially 'irreverent' (to use a favourite reviewer's word of the period) fictional attitude became vigorous enough to constitute a rich literary perspective, then clearly a great deal of credit is due to William Cooper. One has, perhaps, to remember how little this particular class and viewpoint has been presented in the fiction of the previous two decades to feel how important this opening out was; but it would not have been important had there not been writers who could manage the task with the kind of perfect lucidity William Cooper brought to it. *Scenes from Provincial Life* was in fact much more accomplished than many of its successors. It brings its language (usually) and its perspective (always) so thoroughly alive that it has a survival-value profoundly in excess of any sociological interest in it that might also hold us. If, too, it helped to keep alive the social and moral tradition of the English novel vigorous, in a phase where the direction of the form itself seemed uncertain, that was good fortune; its real and final interest is the pleasure we can still take in it.

XII

C.P. Snow's Bleak Landscape

I

C. P. Snow is one of those novelists whom one feels one can't do without; and yet there are times when, disturbed again before his books, one wonders why. The critics have not, on the whole, been very kind to him, and it is not hard to see why he should come in for a good deal of critical assault. He has made his peculiar mixture of the reasonable, neo-scientific, positivistic literary imagination into a kind of test case, a radical opposite to literary despair; and precisely because he has done that his weaknesses have a kind of emblematic significance. One weakness in particular is disturbing, not only because it tends to get worse from book to book, but because it has importance for the metaphoric status he has acquired: it is the tendency imaginatively to let things slide, to leave unsaid and even worse unfelt, to gesture at the events of the book without dramatizing, shaping, feeling into, making human. It is matched by a want of imagination of another kind, by a deliberate narrowing of the human scale—as if life has all its order in relation to the particular worlds one happens to live in now, and to no other life, and can be summed up on that evidence; as if the world ages as one ages, significantly sympathizes with oneself, can be amended by oneself, and as if all the important places of human action and feeling are the places one frequents, the places within a convenient taxi ride or train journey; as if, finally, the liberal reasonableness represented by the author and his fictional surrogate, Lewis Eliot, can cope with the bulk of human experience, and faces only one imponderable obstacle, that of death. But against that impression of Snow there is much to set, though setting it requires something like personal testimony. For there are few contemporary writers who have managed, as Snow has, to give us the dense feel of contemporary social experience, and in so doing to make it a matter of history, few who have identified our basic realities, recognitions, moral dilemmas and landscapes, and then drawn these into the order of time, of changing national and local event, of shifting temper and feel. His work recreates recognizable experience almost as an act of memory, not the significant, vividly recreative yet aesthetic Proustian memory to which he has himself drawn a comparison, but a much more public, communal, shared type of memory. He appeals, not as Proust does, to the surprise of psychological truth, but to the more muted shock of having set before one the detail of a known or very knowable world.

All this sounds like an inconsistent response; for surely if the imagination is not there it is not. But it is there, in a curious low-keyed way, a way occasionally illuminated, powerfully, by a sudden register of passion, passion not only sexual but moral and intellectual. Snow invites the inconsistency, because the reality he gives us is so ready and familiar, to him and to us, that we can scant it, and as we read we are probably all too ready to want to go beyond it, to see more than he seems to see. Eliot, as his narrator, seems not to get beyond it; and though Eliot is not Snow it seems an attribute of the author as well, a part of his prevailing ordinariness. Yet the novelist of ordinariness, when he has power, has an important place in the culture. The power is likely to reside in the presence of a genuine and a moral intelligence, an intelligence that ends up not only with its own weaknesses, but by seeing its own weaknesses. The cycle from hope to desperation, from cultural intoxication to a selfish involvement with one's own mortality, is Eliot's special cycle, and it is a very human one. In that cycle, Eliot has implicated modern history, so that his life is in a very real sense a worldly life; and now that the plot has been completed, and the *Strangers and Brothers* sequence has come to its end, we can look at the whole and see how deep those connections, between Eliot's own growth and then his weakening, and the growth and weakening of a certain view of the world, even a growth and weakening of the world, have been made. We can read that world along with Eliot, and we can also, because we know his weaknesses, read it against him. The range of any life, in relation to that of the world, is a matter of life and death; our time and its time are bound together. What Snow has done is to establish a convincing loose relationship between the career of Lewis Eliot and history, between the changes of self and the changes of time;

he has given it authority, yet left it curiously imprecise. The open structure of that eleven-volume *roman fleuve*, in the writing since 1940, kept loose and accessible to events yet to come, with a past completed but a present always on the edge of the future, has been the great enabling device of it all up to now; it is this that has maintained the imprecision. Now Snow has closed the sequence; and in closing it he has made it into a complete, though hardly a compact, aesthetic object. It looks different, and the moral problems can't be so easily left open; we are more inclined to judge, though it is perhaps characteristic that Snow has concluded the sequence by compounding the paradox, the paradox of his own inequalities.

2

The eleventh and final volume in the sequence is called *Last Things*; last things it is indeed. The entire sequence has made its bid—and whatever the qualifications it has to be taken as a serious one, an act of high ambition—to be regarded as one of the great documentary and recapitulative works of a century itself not easily susceptible to documentation, a chaotic century of multiple expression disposed to challenge the reality of realistic interpretations. The edifice is a large one if only because it does comport so well with modern history, touching on many central moments; as such it is as difficult to conclude authoritatively as it is to create. *Romans fleuves* do not need to stop; if they do that, as I have said, embodies an oddity. What Snow conceived was a narrative that was open to the things of time, to the changes of fortune in personal life and modern history. The early volumes, which dealt with periods well prior to the time of writing, have an appropriate sense of confidence and completeness. But as the sequence extends, as events come closer to the present, and as the forces in human life begin to extend beyond the life of the man who presents them, a certain touch of despair enters. In part, there is a proper terror about mortality itself; faith in the world does not assuage the coming loss of self. But we live in a time when it is hard to identify the proper boundaries of self, for we are defined socially and ideologically and psychologically according to historicist theories. We do not, indeed, live alone, even if we die alone. And so there is another terror at stake, which is about history, about the loss and dispossession of meaning in that, about the way it may defeat us. Snow's open-ended world was a hopeful world, demanding from the man of hope and science in the early novels and the man of affairs in the later ones a ceaseless attention and moral energy. In the aesthetic rightness of all this we had acquiesced. In ending the sequence, that sense of rightness has to be rescinded, and one of the strange merits of *Last Things* is that it does achieve that striking change of direction, if by somewhat odd means. In the course of *Last Things*, Lewis Eliot makes a struggling renunciation of political office, of 'the world'; he has made them before in earlier books, and it has been part of a certain moral banality in him that he has never made them properly, as if we knew that the world's plot needs an Eliot to untie it with reconciling efficiency. But this time a sort of finality, an obituary sentiment, suffuses the entire novel. For here we have a world that does *not* seem to need an Eliot, a world in which a generation comes to an end and with it an entire set of possibilities and affections; the end of it all is, appropriately enough, a roll-call of the dead.

Finality, the closing of the open doors, in fact dominates *Last Things*, and it is in this larger mood rather than in local detail that one senses Snow's novelistic authority. The big world of the earlier novels is seen shrivelling. Whether we took it *as* the world or not, we had to recognize it; it contained a large movement tracked through twentieth-century history and society, the movement of a meritocratic class towards power and responsibility, the movement of a certain kind of decent, optimistic, rational, mediating mind towards pre-eminence in the affairs of men. The mediation had its authority and its proper compulsions, but it constituted an odd version of modern heroism when one measured it against the literary witness, though not the witness of one's own social and political world. Eliot had a way of calling it 'the world', as if that was the only world there was; but it was other than the self, into which a retirement was possible, and in many ways lighter than it. That world is still present in *Last Things*, but it is less than ever *all* the world. Snow asserts its continuing presence and its power, but we can sense, in the less than completely articulated gestures that he makes towards recognizing the new movements and motive powers in the generation of radicals and sons, much larger strangers, that he has come to doubt its rightness, its controllability, its suscept-ibility to moral amendment by any intelligence of Lewis's kind. It might be said that this makes such intelligence look oddly valuable, and Lewis's withdrawal that much starker. For of course in the earlier novels that world, that model of society as a good committee, has

always been threatened; it has been threatened by self-seeking, possessiveness, the struggle of sexes and generations, the weakness of men.
Now, though, it is threatened by another kind of history; and it is not
only the novel but that world that seems, in the obituary mood of the
book, to be coming to its end.

Last Things, then, is an ending, a rescinding, in history as well as in
individuals; but of course it is above all an end to the voice, or the pen,
of the narrator who comprehended this world and acted ubiquitously
in it. Born, fictionally, in 1914, just before the age of nine, in an English
provincial town left deliberately unnamed; former solicitor's clerk,
barrister, scientific administrator, fellow of a Cambridge college,
committee man, higher civil servant, universal mediator; husband first
to Sheila and then to Margaret, brother to Martin, father to David,
Lewis (later Sir Lewis) Eliot has ceased to be in the one place where he
had ultimate power, which was on the page. Authorial mortality has
claimed him, though he lives on into the wordless future and survives
his own last page of print, This though, he only just succeeds in doing.
Midway through the novel, he suffers a three-and-a-half minute
cardiac arrest during an eye operation. He sees and reports his own
death; it is as severe a threat to narration as a realistic fiction can offer,
but he comes through. And where another kind of writer of greater
metaphysical pretensions might have given us an ambiguous limbo for
the last pages, Snow gives us an epic of ungracious survival. Eliot
achieves the end of the book—and writes down, rather than is included
in, the last obituary roll-call—with all the bitter irascibility against the
human condition, and even against the individuals who shore him up,
that old age can bring to bear. It is not an elegant survival. But in the
bleakly rationalistic and agnostic world he has inhabited from the start
of these fictional things it is, of course, precisely survival which is
crucial. Of the four last things—death, judgement, heaven, and hell—
he is convinced only by the first, which for him means biological non-
existence. By the end of the sequence death has undone George Passant,
Francis Getliffe, Austin Davidson, and a few more; hospitals and sick-
beds dominate this final book, with the healthy young drifting away
into a stranger and less responsible world. The triumph of *Last Things*
is, simply, Lewis Eliot's presence at the end of it, a muted enough
triumph, but one that means that there is a tomorrow not only for
the race, the society, the family, but for him too: 'That night would be
a happy one. This wasn't the end.' It is a bleak nihilism that we are

brought to, a startling reduction; still, it is something that comes logically out of the entire sequence.

It does so, of course, because Eliot's particular kind of rationalism has always been much obsessed by death. We usually think of Snow as basically a social and a documentary novelist, and so in part he is. Like Fitzgerald, who took the world of the rich as the place where, for better or worse, men act on the front edge of history, Snow took the world of power and gave it meaning as a line of force and morals running through the society. In his novels, social mobility, the emergence of the bright young man, is a metaphor for the mobility of the human race; he is a fairly exact heir of Wells and the evolutionary writers of the turn of the century who could make plots out of the belief that the emergence of a new class was a manifestation both of the life-force and a redeeming kind of knowledge, the special knowledge in question being that socially emergent and hence radical doctrine, science, a doctrine of responsibility and problem-solving redemption. Lewis Eliot carries this temper, and it is because of this that his emergence from lower-class provincialism into the world of universities, law, and government could be taken, of itself, as a working of history, a generalized manifestation of man. But Snow's universe has always been one in which the general moral and biological movement which he catches, first in *The Search* and then in the eleven-volume sequence, has also been at odds with the position of the individual, for whatever his part in the general human affair he has always been left to seek his personal validity, his emotional poise, his human assuagement, in tragic isolation. And his arrogant, powerful women, his self-seeking men, his politicians and dons and scientists, his fervent radicals, are the embodiments of a life force often dangerously untempered by reason, the power to be fair, or compromise. They perform frenziedly and fall back into lonely *angst*. In the New Men there is always the Old Adam, and it is a world of strange hauntings and disorders lying outside the firelight rooms of reason where Lewis so often sits. Snow has said of his Lewis Eliot that he begins by observing the human emotions in others, and later finds them in himself; the human emotions are typically those that lie outside order and pull in the direction of desperation. Thus it is that all the depredations on sweet reason, all the tragedies of solitude, all the loneliness of deathbeds which have their place right through the *Strangers and Brothers* world and are embodied in that paradoxical title have a way of coming home to roost in the narrator himself; and it is precisely in these later books—in *The Time of Hope*, yes, but also in *The Sleep of Reason* and *Last Things*—that we can see them doing so. Snow has laid out this movement from observation to involvement in several dimensions, several spheres of life; he has also usually made it a contingent observation, a persistent contrast, rather than an offered conclusion. Nonetheless beyond the world of reason and modest moral decency there has always lain a bleaker world. Snow's famous 'We die alone', not a fresh but an often re-iterated insight, has on occasion sounded like sententious or unearned wisdom; one might say of *Last Things* not only that this is its rubric but that the novel has helped make the perception felt, given it at last a certain conclusiveness.

We may protest that it is precisely this conclusiveness that tells against it, that the framing cycle of hope turned to despair, spring to winter, good history to bad is so familiar, so classical, that it contains none of the surprise of art. Even here the spirit is bland, or the words drain away the feeling. There is indeed something of this, and yet the disquiet at the centre seems imaginatively to invigorate a lot of the matter of the sequence. In its world, there are two main actions. The first is the action of the socio-historical web, in which families and localities, past customs and present meanings, are the substantial, lived-out places of the culture and of human life. Snow's sense of family and place, of the momentousness of these things, and of their continuing energy even after one has left them behind, as Eliot was always about to do, is powerful and remarkable, a striking effort of literary coloni-zation—which is one reason why he so interested a number of novelists in the 1950s. What in fact seems to lie behind Snow's fascination with these things is not simply the function of memory, nor only the desire for cultural distillation; he finds in this dense contingency forces of reason and growth at work, and in some of the later novels about the good family at the top he saw a rational social development, man using those decencies, those gifts of morally filling out his place, to make a reasonable society which was a fair embodiment of experience. History would move and times would change; generation would grow in new form out of generation; but this was the natural evolution of life, like sons leaving mothers and striking out into the feel of their own world. It was humane evolution, and it simply needed the right kind of administration. Snow's model for that becomes something like that of the good committee, where man adjusts to the new business thrown up by the evolutionary cycle, and above all the momentous changes of science itself. The college meeting or the parliamentary committee is a characteristic focus of his literary action, and whatever the separate passions at work in it, it is morally decisive. Of course between the thesis and the antithesis falls the Eliot, who comes out of the novels as an odd and morally disconcerting mixture of the good committee man and the struggling moral agent. There is the family of man moving densely through history, then; but there is another motion in the world, which belongs to the self. For, outside the meeting, man is left prey to Tolstoyan fears about his own place in that history. It demands a certain resignation; and hence the dimensions of despair, the plots of tragic compromise, the sense of things snuffed out, that also shape his world. These are the plots that lead to the fable of isolation, and are in turn apt to set in motion fears of another history, one in which liberal decency does not serve, in which the committee fails to agree, in which something much bleaker triumphs not only in the individual life but in the universe at large and the family of England in particular.

3

The sense of a world in which liberal reason might not prevail, in which the public and communal effort itself ends in nihilism, becomes an increasing power towards the end of the sequence; the obvious text for it all is *The Sleep of Reason*. The book is a kind of comeuppance for George Passant's cry, in the volume originally entitled *Strangers and Brothers* and now, as if to underline an emphasis, renamed *George Passant:* 'I should also like to add that people get on best when they're given freedom—particularly freedom from their damned homes, and their damned parents, and their damned lives.' The hope is the modern hope that presides at the beginning of the entire sequence; Snow calls up, in a line of historical places, this moment of setting free from possessiveness, the moment of liberal optimism. The moment in fact comes back at the end of *Last Things*, when David, Lewis Eliot's own son, casts forth from his parents much as Lewis had back in *Time of Hope*. But into the situation an irony has intruded, and Snow takes the irony out of history, from a moment in the culture that compels fear, serves as the emblem of an indulged and horrifying freedom. The moment is the Moors Murder trial, which Snow only lightly fictionalizes. And here the whole rationalistic and humanitarian enterprise embodied in the sequence touches its most dangerous point and an appropriate centre of contemporary disquiet, the fear that the drift to liberation and authenticity may not be a drift to more and better self but in fact the expression of some of the most obscene aspects of human nature. The dilemma arises, of course, not because liberal reason has failed, but because it has succeeded. Snow is excellent at getting at this sort of crux, and it is what gives a centre of significance to his entire sequence. But it is utterly appropriate to his methods that it arises in the context of many contingencies, in the rush and bustle of family difficulties and committee duties, and that as a result the crux fades back into cultural and personal life. This of course is as life is; and it is perfectly justifiable that Snow, having sounded his note, should let it wait to accrue further meanings for the reader when he reads the sequence as a whole. Yet the problem typically directs attention to the odd role of Lewis in all this, and especially to his final lack of authority as a moral performer. Once again he seems to end up as he always has, as that somehow less than adequate twentieth-century figure the rushed committee man, mediating neatly between irreconcilables, between reason and destruction, life and death, coming up with a compromise that will satisfy both parties in the interests of reaching the end of the agenda.

The nihilism of the good committee man, his isolation and despair, is, when set against Dostoevsky's, neither eminent nor wildly engaging; but one has to testify to its quiet compulsion. Lewis Eliot's flaw is in many respects the flaw of the sequence. One must, of course, read with a due sense of the distance between the narrator and the author; but the distance is not a long one at the technical level. Eliot's inadequacies are in many respects self-confessed, and at the end he achieves an unusual kind of self-recognition, for that irascibility against the human condition that dominates *Last Things* is also a compelling irascibility against part at least of himself, an awareness that he has not been much of a man, that his loving and giving have been muted and wanting, and that he has made a decent but not a very vivid and living self. These are precisely the things we might say about him and his role in the sequence. The difficulty is that we have to turn it to the writing itself and what *it* has not achieved. Moving on its own account, these understandings (and this is not the first time we have had them) remind us of the times when Eliot might, as narrator as well as as agent, have moved us more. They remind us too that Eliot, for all we have seen of his emotional life, has never touched certain psychological inner centres, has in some ways lived the public life in order *not* to live the private, has conducted a complicated transaction between affairs in the business and in the emotional sense in which his gift for compromise has, once again, obscured certain seemingly essential issues. Contingency is Snow's gift; it is also his weakness. Even in this last book, those essential questions that surround the last things, the great eschatological questions, tend to drift, to slide away into time. They are a sort of ultimate evocation of Snowland, that bleak landscape of tragic isolation beyond and outside the world of affairs and power where the self passes from day to day in the inadequate, unsatisfied solitude of simple biological existence. But what is bleaker still is that the history, the civilization, which is the stay against that inner emptiness suddenly loses substance; the moving culture of men's lives as a place of feeling and value, the family past potentially regainable, the province and the home, the committee and the club, these social families are also defeated by a formless time. The circle is rounded off with the fading of the hope that let that dense, substantiated fictional world of the early novels take on such compelling power, the power of being a culture co-existent in time and in fiction. For a writer who, it is often said, has no gift to move us, it is a terrible story.

XIII

The Fiction of Pastiche: The Comic Mode of Angus Wilson

There was nothing for it, Gladys thought, but to make them laugh. After all, she'd suggested the mirrors, so she couldn't let them spoil the afternoon. But when she saw herself she was too disconcerted at first to speak. 'Look,' Sukey cried, 'Gladys is upside down.' And so it proved – at the top of the glass, white boots in reverse; at the base, a plump face grown red with surprise. They all at last could laugh. To keep the fun going Gladys stood on her head on the shiny, linoleum floor . . . .

Angus Wilson, *No Laughing Matter*

I

The number of postwar English writers whom we can regard as major, as of long-term importance and representativeness, is clearly no more than a handful; still, Angus Wilson is obviously one. To many people he stands as the most developed and impressive novel-writer of his generation, the generation after Virginia Woolf, Evelyn Waugh, Graham Greene, Anthony Powell: a writer who carries an enormous substance in and behind his work, who has produced some of our bulkiest, socially most solid novels, who has expanded extraordinarily from the witty, economical brilliance of his malicious early stories into a fiction of extended historical and human scope—*Anglo-Saxon Attitudes* (1956), *Late Call* (1964), *No Laughing Matter* (1967). He has brought alive the possibility of a substantial, compassionate fiction, a realistic writing of moral evolution and growth; he has humanistically reactivated the tradition of the past, so that to read him is to feel the force of what nineteenth-century novelists as various as Jane Austen and Dostoevsky might pass on to a contemporary author; he has lived a significant, central cultural life as an observer and a critic, existed seriously for us as, in the broadest sense, a modern man of letters. That said, we must add that his reputation, though very high in credit, is very mixed in basis; the admiration in which he is held is based on judgements remarkably varied. Moreover, nearly every critic who has written on him seriously has felt an ambiguity, of emphasis and perspective, in his writings. Wilson himself has encouraged them in doing so, pointing, for instance, to the 'fierce sadism and a compensating gentleness' which leads to a simultaneous love and hate in his view of his characters,[1] to his sense of the dual nature of all action, at once rational and self-satisfying, and his awareness of the strange autobiographical illusions and obsessions that are involved in all writing.

What is more, there is something elusive about his gifts—a way of driving home his points unsteadily, or not sustaining the compelling substance of a theme—which seems mixed with this, *and* with the ambiguous status he has always attached to writing as such. In his confessional book *The Wild Garden, Or Speaking of Writing* (1963), he remarks on his early discovery that one purpose of story-telling was to exert charm, and win success, often by spurious means; in his *Writers at Work* interview, he speaks of the importance of recognizing that fiction is trickery: 'All fiction for me is a kind of magic and trickery— a confidence trick, trying to make people believe something is true that isn't. And the novelist in particular is trying to convince the reader that he is seeing society as a whole.' Knowledge of literature as counterfeit is a recurrent theme in modern writing; in Wilson's case, the understanding cuts deep into the speech and words of his characters, giving them something of that self-mimicking quality which is a typical attribute of tenure in his universe. But it also reaches back into the writer and implicates him. It promotes the admirable pastiche qualities of *No Laughing Matter*, but also those strange positional insecurities that keep on arising as the relationship between Wilson's narrative posture and his characters keeps proving oblique and surprising. Those who have seen his work as a realistic fiction of social range and moral maturity have always this side of his work to come to terms with; it is the biggest problem his writing poses. Of course he is that

[1] Angus Wilson, 'The Novelist and the Narrator', *English Studies Today* (Second Series) (Bern, Switzerland, 1961), 43–50.

sort of writer: he offers himself as a moral power; there *is* in his work a singular moral maturity and perceptiveness. But to overlook the elements of self-doubt and self-mockery would be to miss something quite as essential, and quite as creatively significant, having to do with an uncertainty towards, or a qualification of, that fiction of adult social seriousness he so much admires.

The area in which this is best elucidated is, I think, that of comedy; and Wilson's comedy is of a decidedly elusive and protean kind. *Hemlock and After*, his first novel, a brilliant work of liberal moral analysis, explores a novelist, Bernard Sands, who has developed from *enfant terrible* to moral scourge. 'If he had forced from the public and the critics respect and hearing for his eternal questioning of their best-loved "truths",' the text tells us, 'he must never allow them to feel that they were indulging the court jester. They should continue to take from him exactly the pill they did not like, and take it without any danger of whimsy.' Sands has his moral energy and point. But the moral scourge is also Wilson himself, who straightway moves beyond the moral sophistication of his agent to a point outside and beyond him: 'If on occasion he mistrusted his own powers, it was not a mistrust that he intended others to share.' Wilson establishes, as an aspect of his narratorial power, that Bernard Sands's humanism can arise from impure motives, psychological inconsistencies. This he does by establishing a critical perspective which contains equal parts of moral wisdom and toughness—of a kind that Jane Austen or George Eliot might have approved—and something very like malice. The moral toughness is concerned with eliciting self-awareness and responsibility; the malice is concerned with exposing such competences and establishing that there is, in the end, no such thing—all motives are impure, human action is puppet-like, absurd. This is, I think, one of the reasons why Wilson's six apparently substantial and stable novels, socially panoramic and dense, do not in fact hold steady when we read them, but dissolve into a distinctive kind of grotesque. And it is also one of the reasons why the narrator himself, moving between the creation of his characters and of a design and attitude which might contain them, tends to shift and increasingly to dissolve with the books, giving the writing an increasing flavour of mimicry or pastiche. This in fact becomes more or less the complete mode of *No Laughing Matter*, and hence a very explicit formal attribute. I link the pastiche and the odd moral stance because they lend, I fancy, a very distinctive texture to the writing and form a distinctive set of perceptions about our social and human nature. Above all, I think, they point towards or attempt to cope with an emptiness at the centre of all human action, manifest as a persisting theatricality which informs it. Human life is a role or performance, society is a theatre, the masks and disguises are irrevocable and they are total. The self we live with is counterfeit, and in that situation the trickery reaches back to the narrator himself, who acts too, as creators must, but in so doing does not so much make a meaningful society and meaningful agents in it as mimic them both.

This gives a very protean kind of comedy, one that makes Wilson's novels interesting, complex, and decidedly hard to assess. The fact is that it is all too easy to find in him the figure of the novelist he might have been, had his dedication to a kind of novel that he obviously values —the novel of great social substance, in which the fictional action illuminates through dense and serious individual lives the density and texture of the society as a whole—been that bit surer, more complete. But there surely also resides in his work a decided questioning—moral, intellectual, technical—of just that sort of novel; his comedy and creative energy partly depend exactly on this. In an early essay he claimed that the feel of the solidity of society is often gained fictionally at the cost of depth, especially depth in psychological perception and awareness. If the modern novel has become engrossed by anything, it is by the events in these realms, and it is clearly a substantial part of Wilson's own proceeding that an adequate compromise must be managed by any modern writer seriously concerned with the expanding possibilities of his form; as he puts it: 'We are on the threshold of a psychology for which the older novel forms do not provide.'[1] Any account of his interest and value as a novelist has to include the real attentiveness he has given to the moral uncertainty of the novelist once the idea of unconscious motive and Freudian drives is accepted, when neurotic or perverse experience of any kind becomes part of the central substance of fiction.

The difficulty in talking about Wilson's work, indeed, is that we can see very different species of novelistic activity and ambition proceeding at the same time. It is not surprising that various critics have sought to explain and explore his writings by stressing one or another. Some have recognized him as a direct inheritor of a central tradition in

[1] Angus Wilson, 'Diversity and Depth', *Times Literary Supplement*, LVII (15 August 1958), viii.

English fiction—the socio-moral tradition, concerned with the moral analysis of life in society; seen in this light, he carries on the habitual concerns of story-tellers from Jane Austen to Forster, and especially that vein of humanist concern with the moral conduct of persons, into the context of postwar uncertainty.[1] Of this tradition, a predominantly liberal and realist tradition, Wilson has written appreciatively; similarly he has praised the attempt of a number of postwar English novelists to restore 'the social framework in which human hopes and despairs must be viewed if duty and responsibility or defiance of duty and responsibility are to have full meaning.'[2] Wilson always creates his people, whatever his psychological concerns, as members of society; he creates society as a dense, historically specific web in which we are all involved; he expands his work contingently through social time and space. It is a selective society, characteristically upper- or middle-middle class (as is the community in which most English fictional characters live, though not most English people), vaguely intellectual, decidedly stylish—as is clear from the lists of dramatic *personae* that Wilson usually gives us; *No Laughing Matter* has an 'additional cast' of 'Husbands, wives, lovers of various kinds, university teachers, and undergraduates, Russians, members of Society, politicians, journalists, members of Lloyds' and of the Bloomsbury Group, Cockneys, German refugees, staffs of preparatory schools, English residents abroad, Egyptians, actors and actresses, Moroccans, financiers, Scandinavians, and representatives of the Younger Generation.' The camp and comic edge, as well as the metaphorical theatricality, of the list are all to the point; still, it *is* an extended world, and to see what a good reach it is we have to think back to the great Victorian novels, with their grasp of social and historical span. We also have to recall another feature of the liberal-realist novel, its controlling moral concern. Wilson is unmistakable in his tough-minded interest in moral responsibility, and the milieu of extreme strain and tension in which moral acts are conducted; at times he is unsparing in his capacity for satirical exposure. Even as he relishes

[1] For this view of him, see especially C. B. Cox, *The Free Spirit: A Study of Liberal Humanism in the Novels of George Eliot, Henry James, E. M. Forster, Virginia Woolf, Angus Wilson* (London, 1963). Also see the important stress of Valerie Shaw, '*The Middle Age of Mrs. Eliot* and *Late Call*: Angus Wilson's Traditionalism', *Critical Quarterly*, XII, No. 1 (Spring 1970), 9–27, which offers a valuable counterweight to the emphasis of my discussion.

[2] Wilson, 'Diversity and Depth', cited above.

his world for its style, its social flamboyance, he measures and judges according to a comic and ironic mode. And one of the functions of irony and comedy in his work is to be directed, as it is in Forster's novels, towards a centre, showing up moral and emotional atrophy, self-deceit and unrecognized failure in the realm of the personal. If, as Ian Scott-Kilvert tells us, the basic action of Wilson's work is satiric and its prime object of attack 'the façade of middle-class values and manners, the hollowness of the respectability, the decorum and the apparently "progressive" virtues which can mask hypocrisy, meanness, immaturity exhibited to a pathological degree, and above all cruelty,'[1] then that concern suggests a place in a liberal-radical line of writing that has spoken to the good for tolerance, personal sanity, and individual decency, a line of decided force and worth sustaining at a high level of credit. And any practised reader of Wilson's novels will indeed find his own instances of the way that delicate acerbity, that critical intelligence, that sane moral appreciation, has been exercised.

This is *one* of the ways in which the satirical thrust of Wilson's work has been employed; but it is not the only or the final way. There is something else, and again a tradition for it, reaching back to the Victorian period; what it is Wilson, in various essays and in *The World of Charles Dickens* (1970), has himself made very explicit. 'The intense haunting of my imagination by scenes and characters from Dickens's novels has continued and developed into my middle age,' he has told us; and gone on to say that he is aware not so much of the wholeness of Dickens's novels as of parts of them, of an 'atmosphere and scene which are always determinedly fragmentary'.[2] Dickens's vision of society is of course decidedly different from that of the novelists of more composed manners; society does different things to his characters and gives them different natures. Raymond Williams has helped to define this; as he puts it, Dickens's characters 'speak at or past each other, each intent above all on defining through his words his own identity and reality; in fixed self-descriptions, in voices raised emphatically to be heard through and past other similar voices.'[3] It might be

[1] Ian Scott-Kilvert, 'Angus Wilson', *Review of English Literature*, i, No. 2 (April 1960), 42–53.

[2] Angus Wilson, 'Charles Dickens: A Haunting', in *Dickens: Modern Judgements*, ed. A. E. Dyson (London, 1968), 30–9.

[3] Raymond Williams, *The English Novel from Dickens to Lawrence* (London, 1970), 32.

added that the expressing of identity is often a kind of flattening, a self-dramatization which is also a psychological simplification; and that we have the novelist there in his comic guise to encourage the process and elicit the individual nature as an aspect of social grotesquerie. This kind of comedy gives us a world both familiar and alien, lifelike and distorted, containing evil and nightmare as well as beneficence and community, a world where identity is easily lost, where the psychological and social interact strangely, that interaction being expressed by grotesquerie and surreality, by curious mimings and exaggerations which evoke stress and tension. Wilson has seen this in Dickens, noting his total 'unspoken atmosphere' made up of themes of wandering and imprisonment and flight, modes of make-believe and false seeming. This is social and panoramic, but not in George Eliot's or Tolstoy's way; the world is a strange and unreal city, the consequences of living in which are tension, psychological distortion, stress. And this atomization, this sense of personal fragility, awareness of society not as a solid substance but as a seeming, is in Wilson's writing too, and, as in Dickens, it poses strange problems of control. For the point of the writing is to release energy and invention, to generate fable, to draw deeply on autobiographical feeling and awareness, afterward shaping and designing what comes forth. The result is a novelist who is less a controlling artist capable of moral poise than one acting vigorously as an inventor and putting himself at risk by indulging the power of his own imaginings and obsessions.

To get at Wilson's work, one must note how strangely the two debts co-exist. The dimensions of the analytic moralist are there: so is the writer of running inventiveness, the mimer and player, the maker of grotesque. In places the rigour of moral analysis we know from Jane Austen is very evident, and ultimately, in *Hemlock and After* and *The Middle Age of Mrs. Eliot*, dominant. Even there it is strangely placed against the material, for the world on which Wilson works is not neat or contained, the characters judged and measured are tinctured with unreality, touched with absurdity, and so elusive. Often we are asked to apply the test of a moral realism to personages whose moral substance the method of creation throws into doubt. We think we discern a compelling flaw of character, the features of a social snobbery or exploitation or cruelty, which the writer excoriates, for these are the telling crimes of his universe; but the moral point here does not transcend the situation, for the creator depends too much on hypocrisies of this sort for his total vision of man. We see the bondage of the family, the harsh subtext of exploitation underlying conventional relationships, the endless war of parents and children, husbands and wives; the crimes are classic liberal violations, but then they become the very stuff of existence itself, for is not all love exploitation and are not all morals self-rationalizations of need? The same problem arises with social and political judgements. Wilson's politics are ostensibly liberal and progressive, and he seems to condemn false social institutions and values; there are hints of political exposé, and of higher historical promises, of better worlds that might be, greater equality, increased tolerance. His bourgeoisie is insecure and in some ways sunk in an illusion which the novelist exposes. But history, though an active force in all his writing, hardly looks, on closer inspection, regenerative. The world of the welfare state, of which he has offered many apt portraits—including the brilliant one of the new town in *Late Call*—does not transcend evil, but simply provides a new frame for its continuance; the revolutionary promise is never made real, but is another falsification or illusion. The point is that Wilson acts as if historical redemption might come; he writes the liberal-humanistic, or the radical, novel but qualifies it, taking its world often for his essential world but then touching in many insecurities.

These insecurities reach back into the narrator himself, as I have said. Wilson once commented that he had drawn from nineteenth-century fiction the form of omniscient telling he uses and needs: 'In *Hemlock and After* and *Anglo-Saxon Attitudes* I chose quite naturally the "God's eye view" in frequent use among the nineteenth-century novelists I admire. I was surprised to find how unfamiliar this had now become; indeed, in the United States it had to be explained as a revival (I am glad to say successful) of an archaic form.'[1] It is in fact a commonplace form of the times, and we find it in much modern realism, satire, and comedy. But the point about Wilson's way with it is that he uses it very freely and unpuristically, as a story-teller above all interested in his story might, moving in and out of his characters as the need arises, presenting his material through many eyes, committing himself to extended episodes of exposition, allowing himself to make acerbic moral points and judgements. This use is imprecise, which is to say that Wilson performs many transactions which writers for whom such things are prime ends, basic organizational instruments for eliciting the form of art, would

[1] Wilson, 'The Novelist and the Narrator', cited above.

eschew. His material has to grow of itself, by being freely mimed and acted, in a mock-theatre in which the author creates fixed terms within which the play may occur. What Wilson needs indeed is a mode of writing which allows him a high degree of social mimicry and involvement and then a means for the assertive control of it; this duplicates the narrative activity, and potently divides it. This, I think, he has seen and worried over, which is one reason why the mode has become itself a matter for study in some of his more recent books. He has spoken in a letter of his feeling 'that the traditional form has inhibited me from saying all that I wanted to say. I tried to move out of it. . . .'[1] The writer of secure management, the God-like writer with free entry everywhere yet the right to pause and judge, the author making a solid substance, has never been as secure as he might have been. And by *No Laughing Matter* he is very oddly placed indeed.

2

'But then the English novel is not an aesthetic novel, it is a social novel. *The Forsyte Saga* has great importance as the mirror of the British high bourgeoisie': so Herr Birnbaum, the Jewish-German children's novelist and refugee, who has a minor part to play in *No Laughing Matter*. The observation is clearly applicable to Wilson's own *œuvre*, and especially to some parts of it; Wilson does mirror the British bourgeoisie and its liberal intellectual associates, though with the extraordinary dimensions of mimicry, in the form both of self-identification and comic mockery, that I have mentioned, and with obvious aesthetic aspirations. The aspirations themselves have not remained steady, and they have taken him in many directions, through a pattern which seems less like a direct growth than a process of dissolution and recreation, a re-assimilation in new form of energies already employed, so that they break up the old frame. As a result of this Wilson's novels have been formally very various, and given to extraordinary surprises. As for *No Laughing Matter* itself, it is indeed a social novel, not an aesthetic one, and something of a *Forsyte Saga* or mirror of the British bourgeoisie done on a larger scale than Wilson has ever before tried. We could see it as Wilson's closest approximation to the 'condition of England' novel, a social and historical fiction of wide sweep and capacious ability both to reflect, and reflect on, the

[1] Quoted by Rubin Rabinovitz, *The Reaction Against Experiment in the English Novel* (New York and London, 1967).

culture. Its time span is broad, from 1912 to 1967; there are five books, and nine distinct time-sections, each chosen to illuminate some significant moment of interaction between the characters and modern times. Two World Wars are touched on, if indirectly and lightly; the apolitical bounce of the twenties, the darkening political and increasingly ideological picture in the 1930s, with the Bolshevik dream going sour and Fascism rising, the collapse of Empire and the crisis of Suez, the bleak emptinesses of the modern economic miracle—all these things are put with force at the centre, in a stylistic spectrum itself sufficiently variable to catch at the modes of the periods covered. There is much concern with money, and its general influence and specific usefulness; there is a good deal of concern with sexuality, especially in its more exploitative forms; there is much about class relationships, and the historical shifts and changes in social structure.

On all these matters the book is very knowledgeable, detailed, and eclectic; it is a book filled with styles, with the styles of life, self-expression, popular culture, and art which are the embodied and of course shifting historical life by which we feel the clock of things, the texture of things, changing. The novel's geography is socially broad; primarily English, but it takes in European and Northern African episodes, and the presence of Europe is very much felt. It is the geography of a modern politics. Politics and history are decided forces in the book, and administer, with usual Wilsonian severity, some salutary shocks and anguishes; in different ways the characters are forced into encounter with the outrages of Hitlerism, and a long episode about anti-Semitism and the pre-war climate, including two scenes of violence and more of weighty verbal assault, are there to drive home the point. There is a very large cast-list and a very ranging one. To it Wilson establishes a very fluid centre in his Matthews family, the six children of feckless parents who move, with some typological neatness, into various fields of modern experience and whose lives, given to us through a mode of multiple narration, separately followed out but brought on occasion back into significant conjunction, are given over a long span and involve stark experiences of change and dissolution. Through their lives, we see ways of living through a time of crisis, and the book moves from the hopes of a new world in the immediately postwar period through the political realities of the 1930s, into the post-Suez world of 'hire-purchased Hoovers and a sleeping-pill salvation' on which Quentin grimly comments.

We should add, though, that the historical background is presented only through these central characters, never really reported beyond them. Along with that, the family world and the historical one are held in interesting balance. So, for obviously calculated reasons, a number of significant events in modern history are dealt with very obliquely, as a glance at the basic time-slices (1912, 1919, 1925, 1935, 1937, (brief 1942), 1946, 1956, 1967) shows us. A number of significant years (for example, 1926, the General Strike) are avoided, and the two World Wars are shown only at a distance; only in the 1930s and in 1956 do we come close to compelling events and see the characters directly encountering, or evading, them. Wilson, then, does not seem interested in representing his characters facing some compelling historical event or threat head-on, learning history direct. This, you could say, has something to do with one of his recurrent concerns, which is the theme of evasion. Indeed evasion is a compelling matter for analysis. Thus Sukey's gentility, Marcus's narcissism, Rupert's and Margaret's artistry, Gladys's female evasion of full financial responsibility, and even Quentin's politics with their strange underlying sexuality, are figures for a certain sort of escape from history—which in turn *makes* a history. In this way their saga has 'great importance as a mirror of the British high bourgeoisie', and you might take it as a compelling condemnation of it. The bourgeois generational novel, the dynastic novel as we have it in *Buddenbrooks* or *Der Stechlin* or *The Forsyte Saga*, is a well-established realistic form, a very substantial and material species of fiction, able to give the sense of social substance, of historical motion, of familial rise and fall, of the interlocking of a family and a culture; but the telling point in *No Laughing Matter* is the subversion of this—the family is not a communion or a coherence, its financial roots are weak, and the substantive relationship between individual and culture is itself unreal.

The family, in fact, collapses in the opening chapter, as we see the Matthews group for a moment in 'a union of happy carefree intimacy that it had securely known before and was never to know again', sharing an interlocking or communal day-dream, and then walking out confidently together on the social stage with all the authority of their class until the scene collapses in squabbles, the financial dependence of the parents on their parents (and later on their own children) becomes apparent, and the farcical reverse of the images is made manifest. The Matthewses lose their identity and their familial com-

munion as the book starts; the effort, then, of the younger generation
is to try by various means to recreate and assert it again. In this they
may be said to fail; they make their peace with the older generation
and nearly all of them end outside England, in the Algarve or the
Moroccan desert of exile and dryness: 'There [Marcus] lay on his
stomach in the hot sand among the broom bushes and pressed himself
deeper and deeper into its dryness.... Didn't she ... know anything
of how he had let himself be measured and dried by life until he was at
peace with the hot sand?' The historical cycle moves, not with them,
but *beyond* them, so that they are superseded. They are dried, too, and
the novel seems to utter a moral and historical condemnation and
certainly creates larger horizons than any the characters have seen—
and hence a pre-eminent sense of failure. 'As we get older', says Rupert,
'we don't distinguish greatly between what might have been and what
is'; but the novelist seems to do that, to enforce the failure, and above
all to see it as a failure to connect with reality, the significance of the
relationship between modern politics and the characters' own situations
being evaded in narcissism and illusion. Quentin suggests as much in the
Game when he reveals his Marxism:

I thought when I retired that I should have to condemn you [the Matthews
parents] as a generation, or rather as two generations, indeed as all the older
generations, perhaps as the embodiment of accumulated history. You are, after
all, all we know of the past. It's you who've put us in the soup and you don't
seem prepared to help us out of it for fear of scalding your fingers. Not to put
any pretence on it, you are a guilty lot. But as in my moments of retirement I
reflected, I soon saw that this business of generations would not do. Here we
have a system and a class in decay ....

But the fact is that a directly political reading of the novel will not do.
For Wilson's satirical mode reaches beyond this into a much more
fluid position.

3

This largely arises because of Wilson's relationship with his central
family. The Matthewses are, from the start, one of the famous appalling
families of Wilson's fiction, camp, self-aware, high stylists, histrionic
performers. They thus show themselves to be founded on a shaky
emotional and fiscal economy; but this state of being is one which
Wilson is particularly fond of entering into, and a decided element of

identification occurs. Moreover the great gift of the Matthewses is for caricature, for self-caricature and the caricature of others. And they in their turn are caricatured by an author who proves, as I want to say in a moment, very active, very creative, and also decidedly protean, a figure notable for extraordinary disappearances, rhetorical disguises, mixed registers, and much pastiche and parody on his own account. The world of false-seeming is not an object for satire as such; indeed it is precisely the world which the book seeks not just to expose but also to enjoy. In this way *No Laughing Matter* is very much a laughing matter, or history as a certain kind of farce. It is shrill farce; the farce is itself conditioned, for one feels that the comedy and absurdity, the entire theatre, is a theatre derived from society. But theatre it is; the metaphor is very exact, and it is very total. The idea exists in all of Wilson's novels; in the earlier books we have the text presented as a kind of play, in which well-defined characters exist and well-defined scenes occur, the author then participating as actor and mime and standing back as dramatist to produce his distinctive scenario. But in this novel the metaphor is very obsessive and extensive.

It is, at one level, a figure for illusion, the social illusion, the false-seeming which allows the bourgeois family to feel that, whatever the facts of society and history, they stand at the centre of the stage. But to do that they cast off character and assume roles, roles with artificial social meanings; they are players in the sense of being people who take on other identities. The distinctive thing about the Matthews family, especially in the early pages of the novel, is that they are self-knowing actors, mocking as well as mocked people. They speak in an elaborate, self-parodying discourse drawn from stage, literature, music-hall, newspapers and general cliché ('His Nibs'); they play their part in life, so that they seem at once curiously over-full and over-empty, people with great self-awareness but no substance, people through whom society or cliché speaks. This is all part of a prevalent self-awareness, the knowledge each has of the self-deceptions practised by others; it has much to do with the insecure foundations in family, and money, and society, on which their lives are built. But the theatrical metaphor is also obviously a figure not alone for false illusions in society, the disjunctive images of a declining class, but for life. The novel does not simply reveal the false theatre of disconnection, which we could then measure against reality; it creates a more total theatre in which every human being is implicated, the theatre in which we are all products of many images and perspectives. It must be said that this total theatre, in which the author is highly involved, dissolves somewhat as the novel progresses; a more literal, realistic, and indeed traditional register emerges. But in the early part the theatrical metaphor takes in many modes of self-display and self-caricature, but also creativity and artistry, and it decidedly takes in the novelist himself.

It is to the point to say that we live now in a time when the analogy with theatre has itself become very compelling for us, in a time of extravagant event and extravagant self-display, coupled with an uncertainty about selfhood, in which the idea of life as a theatre has both a vigorous and a disturbing multi-significance. In sociology the 'dramaturgical analogy'—to take Erving Goffman's phrase from *The Presentation of Self in Everyday Life*—has become very telling and part of the essential basis of sociological imperialism; *homo sociologicus* is the role-player, his task ascribed to him by the total and already written social theatre in which he must take up parts, his degree of individual interpretation small, his nature made manifest in interaction with others. In psychology the theatre is social and mental; it arises in the play of early relationships and is re-manifest in all later ones. The analogy has significantly penetrated recent fiction, in, for example, Muriel Spark's *The Public Image* and John Fowles's *The Magus*, two novels stylistically not remote from what Wilson is doing here. But both postulate narrative means for the control of the theatre; Muriel Spark operates at long technical distance, and John Fowles has his surrogate impresario, the Magus himself. Angus Wilson is his own impresario, is a part of the theatre he manifests. The world within the novel is a histrionic world of acting, false-seeming, game-playing; the task of the novelist, too, is that of the mime, the *pasticheur* and parodist, for he must live inside his characters, mime the dialogue, create the scene and the style, play out the drama of inter-relationships. On this kind of activity there is considerable speculation in the text, which repeatedly realizes the metaphor in problems of appearance and reality. The characters begin by miming their parents, in order to mock them; they attempt to turn the Game into a trial, with Marxist Quentin performing the newly needed part of Mr. Justice Scales. But can a trial by mimicry be judged? On the matter the text has an answer, and it runs:

Was the man or the woman able to be another also the most suited to defend that other's interest? Yes, for simulation, whatever its motive, demands identification. But was he or she sufficiently detached to be able to offer a defence intelligible to others as a defending counsel should, without the confusions and blurs of subjective statement? Yes, for simulation and mimicry also demand observation: in them compassion is tinged with mockery or mockery by compassion, and identification is distanced by the demands of technique. But could this simple mixture of opposites which mimicry requires, of affection with distaste, of respect with contempt, of love with hatred—be justly defined as a sort of reasoned apology? Yes, if passed through the tempering fire of the scrutiny of Mr. Justice Scales. The rules established, the Game could now proceed.

As for the novel itself, it proceeds according to the answer, and is indeed very game-like, especially in the earlier part. Here society is a very unsubstantial theatre; it gets more solid and severe, in the form of a basis for conflict between individual lives and onerous changes and threats from outside, as the book goes on. Some critics have found the opening parts the more brilliant; they constitute some of Wilson's freest invention yet and some of his cleverest, offering a world curiously rich and curiously unsubstantial, a very rococo and elaborate world of images and perspectives with very curious narratorial logics and very great delights: much parody, much comedy, much high style and camp, much drawing on the collage of popular culture and theatre, much allusion. It is also true that the theatre in question is very openly conceived, so that we have parodic devices used for an enormous variety of divergent intents: for the establishing of a histrionic extravagance common to all of the characters, for the presentation of subconscious fantasy, for the establishing of social style and texture, for the ironic observation of one character by another, for narrative presentation, and finally for authorial ironies.

This enables an enormous amount of perspectivization to take place in the text; the opening pages are, for this reason, extremely difficult to read. For the book opens on a plethora of images: first the screened images, Gaumont Graphic or Pathé Pictorial, of the Wild West Exhibition at Kensington, itself a mishmash of borrowed cultural artefacts, and then to a close-up of the Exhibition itself and the Matthews family, who 'as they came that hot July afternoon through the crowds . . . might so easily have been frozen and stored away in the files of the National Film Institute,' there to catch the eye of 'the costume designer, the lover of moments of good cinema, or the searcher for social types'—in short, other image-collectors. But

Wilson dismisses his camera to try to define their happiness: 'no recording machine yet invented' could have preserved their happy carefree intimacy, he says. The content of that is more images, communally passing from head to head and taking the form of fantasies about life derived from the Exhibition. These are presented as 'free' or 'unconscious' but at the same time strangely interfused, so that our perspective on them is unclear and the positional source of the discourse perplexing. But from what Wilson calls the 'parapsychological' stage we pass back to the social one; the shared communion links the family's social being, their *public* image; we stand with the crowd and watch them walk singing through the Exhibition. 'Many in the large crowd turned with amusement or surprise to see these posh youngsters singing so loudly in public. Mr. Matthews, by now conscious of the public gaze, smiled and swung his walking stick a little at the attentions of the passers-by; his wife smiled, too, to see him smiling. "Billy loves public notice, don't you, darling?" . . .' In that he differs not at all from the rest of the family who, as the communion dissolves and the ongoing family quarrel reveals psychic and financial stress, retire on to their own stages. They act themselves and, in a sense, they act what others expect them to be. They are the central point of multiple perceptions, collations of images and products of long angles and distances; and throughout the novel they appear in counterpoint on stages, or alternatively through images themselves very plural and flamboyant. As Margaret reflects, returning to her novel: '. . . she had to hurry home to let Aunt Alice fall apart into all the various unrelated persons that she now knew bobbed up and sank down like corks in the ocean inside that old raddled body as inside all our bodies.'

The cultural and psychic confusion in question is itself the result of social being, social languages and styles. The characters project roles on each other, and the world too—thus Stoker, the comic cockney servant, and her 'Wild West' fantasy:

Needed indeed now and again by Miss Stoker who, a good-natured, true serving cockney, will do anything, does do anything, for her charges. Yet in Miss Stoker's mind is the clear realization that faced by buffalo, grisly or Indians it is she, the 'down at the Old Bull and Bush I shall shortly own er, walks among the cabbages and leaks' Hetty Stoker who (in her masters' version), for all her gallery roaring, heart-as-big-as-the-Elephant-and-Castle loyalty, will panic, take fright, pee her knickers or otherwise betray her lowly origins instead, as the legend should be, of dying by sucking the poisoned wound of her youngest charge (Master Marcus) when the Indian arrows are flying fast and furious. Sensing their hidden view of herself indeed, Miss Stoker needs all the force of Miss Rickard's (Sourpuss to her) communicated grim irony to restrain her wish to spit in their bloody faces. But as it is, and so fortified, her version takes in theirs and, Comic Western to the life, she falls over the prickly pear, mistakes the porcupine for a camp stool . . .

The language here is so difficult because it comes from everywhere. As discourse it arises from many corners of society and literature, from popular song and children's dirty joke, cockney and mock-cockney, story and stereotype. As a set of perspectives it arises from many of the characters, from Billy Pop to Miss Rickard's, a set of overlapping, played-off versions of self. As narrative rhetoric it arises from Stoker's own inner consciousness, the consciousness of those who see her as servant or protector or comic clown, and from the novelist's own pleasurable extravagances and repetitions. It is this gives all the characters the flexibility to appear in the various modes and manners of narration; but it also allows each of them to be at once very self-aware and very unreal, and be so because he or she exists in a play in some sense predetermined by others. All are types, and play themselves at the rococo edge of things where it verges on camp or self-parody; each takes the self-mimicry of others as real or valid, but then further mimics it to show its falsity. They guy their own parts dreadfully, as fat Gladys does, or camp them to stylistic excess, as Marcus does, or turn them into forms of art, as Rupert and Margaret do; society becomes social farce—'Giggling and imitating, it was some time before they fell asleep.' The Matthewses' capacity 'to be another' is part of their psychic salvation too; the theatricality used for moral blackmail is used for moral recovery and finally moral judgement, through the Game, itself 'born of their need to relieve their pent-up shame, distress and anger in histrionics, to heal their hurts with mimicry's homeopathic sting, and no doubt as well to indulge some sexual urges.'

The mode *starts* in the characters; it extends to the author. It gives us a very protean mode of narration, marked by enormous variety of means and point of view. There is straight narrative, sketches, interspersed playlets, extended mock-plays. At all levels, there is much direct pastiche, which is to say the use of borrowed stylistic modes and manners, rhetorical mimicry; and much outright parody of particular authors—the text contains an Ibsen parody, a Shaw parody, a Chekhov parody, a Beckett parody, and, in the episode in which the kittens are killed, some pastiche *Macbeth*. Elsewhere in other ways the register is playful and in that way less than authoritative. Much literary allusion occurs; a number of stories—Margaret's Carmichael stories—are included. Much of this is very funny, in the spirit of revue. But it is also functional, another logical aspect of the multi-functional perspectives in which all life on this human stage takes place. Similarly, there is a striking element of double presentation of characters, so that structures associated with them are subverted, as in the laughing mirrors at the Kensington Exhibition; Sukey is made 'soppy', Margaret 'sour', Quentin 'sneery', Rupert 'wobbly', Marcus 'beaky', and Gladys, upside-down, is ridiculous. These modes of ambiguity and distortion, and parody and pastiche, make it hard to discover the authentic register of the novel; there is a decided stabilization of the text in the latter half, but it is an evolution itself somewhat disturbing, since it involves a reduction of rhetorical energy. On these matters, too, there is speculation, especially through the character of Margaret, who has her problems in making words authentic. Her writing itself is a fearful activity, constantly at risk—'these imposed patterns falsify'—and also a psychic necessity, so that through it she evades relationships and quells anxiety, relaxing by means of 'the familiar stringing together of words'. Margaret advances far into irony and becomes something of a writer's writer; the danger is that of the human figures 'being petrified into figures and lettered proportions', the dangers of escaping life.

To Margaret's risk Angus Wilson himself offers an implicit compensation; she is ironic and anti-Dickensian, but he has a sense of thriving life as well as an asperity. At the same time, though, there is a great literariness, a great caricaturing, an indwelling problem about the depth of individual being and the degree to which we feel what we are reading is life known and understood. Indeed the novel is in some sense about the interplay: 'Never', says one critic, 'except perhaps in James Joyce's work, has the pull between the two opposing tendencies of the novel, between its desire for an accurate "realistic" rendering of life and its desire for an autonomous creation, been so clearly demonstrated as in this novel.'[1] The demonstration is clear: there are questions about the outcome, for the result can hardly be said to be a balance, a synthesis. This, it seems, is because Wilson would like to have the ebullient

[1] Herman Servotte, 'A Note on the Formal Characteristics of Angus Wilson's *No LaughingMatter*', *English Studies* (Amsterdam), L, No. 1 (January 1969,) 58–64.

creative energy that makes parody and the mimetic sympathy that makes the sense of life on the same side. And this they cannot quite be. These produce an equivocal form. Thus Wilson raises large questions about the density of social substance, and its absence, about the wholeness of a person, and his emptiness; but he does not find the form for an answer, in part because the questions themselves are simultaneously 'real' and highly fictional. My own sense of the novel—and it is a novel that delights me—is that the balance is not exact and cannot be, that the rich and rococo display of the early pages and the sense of emotional desert that haunts the last pages cannot be brought together.

As for Mr. Justice Scales, the final judge on the world at once there and mimicked, his judgements are themselves at risk. 'Let me convey your verdicts . . . ,' says Quentin at the end of the novel.

> Sukey clicked in disapproval. Marcus quickly snatched up Sukey's fox stole that lay across the sofa back and cast it stylishly round his shoulders.
> 'Billy,' he called, 'Billy, is that God prosing away there, impertinently forgiving us all? Turn Him out of the house at once. Just because He's always been out of all the fun and games is no reason why he should bring his great self-pitying feet in here, ruining my carpet. . . .'

As Quentin's world and Marcus's angrily co-exist, so do the two elements of the textural management of this realistic *and* game-like novel. It is a book which has great rigours of judgement, but they can apply only if we take the characters as having lived out a real life; it has great freedom of literary invention, but that exempts the characters from seriously living in that life. What comes out of the book is the problem of its formal wholeness, the problem of significantly interpreting the historical sequence of events, which is a problem in judging the degree of their substance, the intensity of their reality. We have had this imbalance locally in Wilson's earlier novels, but it has never come through at this level of risk. Of course there is something here that is very much of a piece with other current speculation about fiction, and about the illusion of reality, and the significant breaking-up of or intrusion into the substantive reality of a fiction. One could deduce that something that is happening to realism is happening in Wilson's fiction too. This, I think, would be true, especially if we discern in a number of contemporary writers not the attempt to transcend realism by fiction but the attempt to make realism and fictiveness co-exist. In this case neither the form nor the narrator balances things, except in the way that all great fictions are finally balanced. For *No Laughing Matter* takes its chance as a great release of creativity; a remarkable, buoyant, comic creation, loose, contingent, rich, playful, and as humanely and intelligently done as it can be.

'A House Fit for Free Characters':
Iris Murdoch and *Under the Net*

> We are not isolated free choosers, monarchs of all we survey,
> but benighted creatures sunk in a reality whose nature we
> are constantly and overwhelmingly tempted to deform by
> fantasy. Our current picture of freedom encourages a dream-
> like facility; whereas what we require is a renewed sense of
> the difficulty and complexity of the moral life and the
> opacity of persons . . . . Literature must always represent a
> battle between real people and images; and what it requires
> now is a much stronger and more complex conception of the
> former.
>
> Iris Murdoch, 'Against Dryness'

> Love had a thousand shapes. There might be lovers whose
> gift it was to choose out the elements of things and place
> them together and so give them a wholeness not theirs in
> life, make of some scene, or meeting of people (all now gone
> and separate) one of those globed compacted things over
> which thought lingers, and love plays.
>
> Virginia Woolf, *To the Lighthouse*

I

Iris Murdoch's first novel, *Under the Net*, appeared in 1954 and was
immediately recognized by the reviewers, who brought into attention
one of the most brilliant and certainly one of the most compellingly
intelligent of our present-day English novelists. The praise was deserved,
but it was curiously angled; and the writer we admire now is not quite
the writer who was being admired then. *Under the Net* was promptly
brought under the net of anger, and readily linked with the 'social'

novels of Kingsley Amis, John Wain, and other 'Angry Young Men'. The linkage helped to make the public aware of the existence of a new literary generation, and had its uses, but it depended on a decidedly mistaken attribution. Miss Murdoch was not angry, but decidedly speculative; she was not young, or not quite, being by that time a very well-established and distinguished philosopher of thirty-five; nor was she a man, even though *Under the Net* is, narratorially, a superb exercise in male impersonation, and it is rather in the *persona* of later books, which have different expectations and preoccupations, that her sex acquires, narratorially, a great importance. Certainly, though, there are in the book decided period qualities, so that it seems part of what was becoming a new convention. There is a picaresque structure which moves the story through bohemian and intellectual milieux, in London and Paris, and through a variety of urban locations and social classes; there is a social and mental drifting, and a problem about the acquisition of social roles and duties; there is a raffish, classless, intellectual 'outsider' hero, Jake Donaghue. There is also a very impressive, knowing account of London, necessary and contingent, and of its pubs, river, and people; along with this exciting geography goes a sharp, accurate sense of contemporary life. But that said, the book is still substantially unaccounted for. It stakes very little on its accuracy, or its power to depict the detailed stuff of the welfare-state world in which it is set; it is dominated by an imagination of a different, and much more fanciful, flavour from that of the other novelists of the so-called 'angry' mode; and the dimensions of Jake's separateness or disaffiliation, his discomfort about purpose and role, are pursued in a completely other—a decidedly more challenging and complex—way.

Today we have many, many more novels by Miss Murdoch to guide us; she is not only one of our most brilliant but also one of our most prolific writers—a fact which surely channels or conditions the expression of her brilliance. That expression has taken her into the production of a very distinctive version of the novel of sentiments, or the love romance—made so distinctive by the fact that the forces and powers displayed give rein to metaphysical and emotional speculation of a decidedly unusual kind. In particular the notion of compelling or transcendent power, a transmutation of the texture of the love emotion beyond selfishness or self-engrossedness into a mysterious apprehension of otherness, is obsessive; and this in turn is the distilling context for her rococo plots, with their extraordinary psychopomps, like

Mischa Fox, Honor Klein, Hannah Crean-Smith, and their bewildered followers and apprehenders, and for that general milieu of erotic quest merged with fantasy which is the forceful centre of her more recent writing. Latterly the society of her books has narrowed socially— usually into a world of the professional or leisured, and civilized, upper-middle classes; into a small number of households among these; and into a prototypical group of figures who have justly the air of having known each other for a very long time—and these societies have been angled strangely towards the ordinary world, so as only on occasion to appear part of it. It has also become a world of strange sexual and moral expectation, of curious fornications, strange sympathies and contacts, and curious unconnectedness, curious ignorances. In short, it has become a convention; there is a recognizable Murdoch-land, with whose geography, mores, and erotics we have grown most familiar. This leads us back towards the earlier books with fresh wisdom.

Today, then, the veins we are likely to find strongest in re-reading *Under the Net* are the curious ornateness of mind in it—the Murdoch baroque which loves objects rich and strange, characters involved and mysterious, inventions of rich figurative quality (Jake in his bearskin, Anna fleeing without her shoes)—and a highly speculative or philosophical texture which organizes things. Asked about the novel by Frank Kermode, in his 'House of Fiction' interview, Miss Murdoch replied: 'It plays with a philosophical idea. The problem which is mentioned in the title is the problem of how far conceptualization and theorizing, which from one point of view are absolutely essential, in fact divide you from the thing that is the object of theoretical attention.'[1] These of course are matters that stretch through into the more than a dozen of her later books, which make them the more patent. So, too, do Miss Murdoch's subsequent reflections on the state of the novel, especially in her pieces 'Against Dryness' and 'The Sublime and the Beautiful Revisited', which are very powerful distillations of her aesthetic thought, and have a high importance for the way we think of novels, as well as of *her* novels. And so does her by now somewhat

[1] Frank Kermode, 'The House of Fiction: Interviews with Seven English Novelists', *Partisan Review*, xxx (Spring 1963), 61–82. (For other interviews with Miss Murdoch, see Ann Culley with John Feaster, 'Criticism of Iris Murdoch: A Selected Checklist', *Modern Fiction Studies*, xv, No. 3 (Autumn 1969) (Iris Murdoch Special Number), 449–57.)

articulate moral philosophy.[1] But these are subsequent wisdoms; the
biases I am talking about were in fact, for those who cared to attend,
perfectly observable at the time *Under the Net* came out. The dedication to Raymond Queneau, for example, might have brought to more
notice the book's decidedly surrealist qualities, its elements of free-
running comic fantasy; Miss Murdoch's book on Sartre, a tight, sharp
little study published the year before,[2] might have stressed her preoccupation with the idea of the novelist as philosopher and the kind of
philosophy enabling to the act of fiction; the text of the novel itself,
with its pressing obsession with aesthetic speculation and above all
with the nature of language, and its relationship to experience and
knowledge, and to concept and form, might have shown us that here
was a writer with a degree of self-analytical pressure and procedure
unusual among her coevals, working in very much her own way. But
these were not the pressing matters then; the fact that they are now is
undoubtedly due in part to the extraordinary dominance today of the
aesthetic concerns she was aware of then.

   Still, there remains a difficulty; and it is one that, in this guise or
that, attends not only *Under the Net* but all her books. It has to do with
the prevailing idea of reality in Miss Murdoch—an idea which is
attached to a view or belief about character in fiction and a notion of
the moral and philosophical location of persons in the universe, these
matters being compellingly of a piece with her convictions about art
and man and thought. Interviewing Miss Murdoch, Frank Kermode
noted the very high level of actuality in *Under the Net* and asked her
about it: 'That was just self-indulgence,' was her answer. 'It hadn't any
particular significance.' In speaking of that realism of actuality as if it
were a dress easily cast off—as in part it is in later novels—Iris Murdoch
potentially confuses us, because reality is a matter on which she has, in
her philosophical comments on the novel, central things to say. So in
'Against Dryness' she talks of the state of the contemporary novel, and
speaks as if the substance of the social world were the basis of a humane
art: 'We no longer use a spread-out substantial picture of man and
society. We no longer see man against a background of values, of
realities which transcend him.' The essay is early, the views have

[1] 'Against Dryness', *Encounter*, XVI (January 1961), 16–20; 'The Sublime and the
Beautiful Revisited', *Yale Review*, XLIX (December 1959), 247–71; *The
Sovereignty of Good* (London, 1970).

[2] *Sartre: Romantic Rationalist* (London, 1953).

shifted slightly, the word 'reality' is not here entirely easy to attach; elsewhere she uses it to talk now of a sense of density and social texture, now of a sense of otherness or mystery. Still, there is a touch of ambiguity which is basic to her entire mental cast, to the stylish manner in which she represents to us her philosophical judgements and in which she presents and structures her fictions.

To try to put it simply: Miss Murdoch is a theoretical empiricist, and that is a strange thing to be. Her novels are in flight from concepts, and conceptualize the flight. Her drift is towards the grasping of the contingent, but this is done by way of a theory of very flexible necessity, or growth into form. She is a critic at odds with the crystalline fiction of symbol and myth, above all the hard, dry modernist symbol which 'has the uniqueness and separateness of the individual, but ... is a making sensible of the idea of individuality under the form of necessity, its contingency purged away' ('The Sublime and the Beautiful Revisited'); yet the elegant phrases, which are condemnatory, almost amount to the best possible account of her own disposition towards the symbolistic. The object her anti-symbolist, realist theory is primarily concerned to protect is the substance of individuality or character, both at the philosophical level, in terms of a definition, and at the imaginative level, in terms of a created human agent in a fiction. So she says (in the same essay): 'Contingency must be defended for it is the essence of personality. And here is where it becomes important to remember that a novel is written in words, to remember that "eloquence of suggestion and rhythm" of which James spoke. A novel must be a house fit for free characters to live in; and to combine form with respect for reality with all its contingent ways is the highest art of prose.' Yet the theory —which has a decidedly liberal complexion, points back towards the nineteenth-century novel, and has, at least for the present writer, a profound moral attractiveness—is qualified by Miss Murdoch, partly because *her* liberalism is given to some severe reservations about liberalism's capacity to encounter evil or otherness, and partly because she herself has a decided disposition as a writer to place or fix her characters, to scheme and design their business. And finally there is her attack on 'fantasy', which she says tends to limit the operation of the vigorously curious imagination; it is very much an attack on the mode in which she seems most to write. So it is the life-giving framework of knowable society, the substantial and naturalistic idea of character, the weakening of the urgent emphatics of plot or myth, that she appeals to as the virtues of a significant modern fiction; yet her own work typically veers back in the direction apparently condemned. One way of saying all this is that Miss Murdoch's theory of 'unutterable particularity', which is a moral theory and a theory or justification of the importance of the novel and the novel's way of knowing, is strangely transacted into writerly practice—partly, perhaps, because Miss Murdoch retains in her writing something of the dimension of the philosopher. But she is also very much the novelist, and she creates unexpected and strange resolutions to her contradictions. In fact she forces us into close accounts of the pleasure that she gives us, and perhaps it is for that reason that we would do well to consider, for a moment, the curious events that occurred on the road to Rathblane, two nights before the Easter Rising of 1916.

Rathblane, fifteen miles south of Dublin, not far from the river Dodder, is the house to which Millie Kinnard has retired on a kind of secular retreat. Millie is the central female character of *The Red and the Green* (1965), which is one of Iris Murdoch's later—but also, it is usually recognized, one of her more realistic—novels. But where *Under the Net* is clothed with a certain social realism, *The Red and the Green* has a very conditioning historical specificity—it deals with particular public and political events at a significant time (and with great knowledge, possibly even some inside historical information). It is therefore not entirely spun from within itself, and from that fact a certain contingency arises. Nonetheless, had you stood on the Rathblane road that night, you would have seen a sight surely strange to the average mind, which respects contingency, though tolerably probable to a normal habitué of Murdochland; four male figures, somewhat heated, would have passed by, quite separately, on their cycles, en route for Rathblane and Millie Kinnard. The four are in fact the four main male personages in the novel. One, Andrew, loses his virginity to Millie; another, Pat Dumay, hard and violent, comes for sexual satisfaction; a third, Christopher, to whom she is engaged, wishes, at the least, to see her; a fourth, Barney, who is a failed priest and an elderly withdrawn figure out of a not unfamiliar Murdoch stable, comes to spy on her out of a kind of love. Nearly all these persons are related. Now in the earlier pages of the book—which is, on the road to Rathblane, coming in more than one sense towards its consummation—Miss Murdoch has given us these characters in great social, moral, and psychological detail, separating their lives and exploring them in their distinctive separation, responding without overt coercion to their different moral natures and political sympathies, and rooting each of them for us in a dense contingent society and a milieu of his own, as well as in the specifics of a Dublin of a particular time vigorously re-envisioned. The reader may have sensed in the four men and the woman a certain symbolic aptness, recognizing that they are micro-cosmically related to the larger nature and struggles of Ireland.[1] Still, of these early pages, one might say that this strategy actually helps to relax the novelist's view of his agents, and that Miss Murdoch's claim that she is a 'novelist concerned with the creation of character' has a very understandable meaning.

But now these characters enter Rathblane, commonly impelled on the same night towards the novel's focusing character; and they pass in and out of the bedrooms, up and down the stairs, in and out of the front door, hither and thither on their various bicycles. Amid the chaos love is made, to no one's real satisfaction. This is stylish and funny, the coincidence having that much more force from the relatively un-distilling bias of the earlier telling; the separate life of persons yields to a symbolic eliciting of meanings and connections and that in turn affords a certain kind of classic farce. As Millie says, it is like a comic opera. It is one of those virtuoso moments that set the author's stamp on things; and I do not believe that as readers we are sorry to have it. It recalls the elegant pairings of *A Severed Head* (1961), a book of very fine compactness, where—with a limited cast of six, a superb gift for bringing together elements of surprise, rococo detail, and moral energy, and a comic mode—the novelist exploits from within the world of convention and expectation so established a development via the range of sexual relationship, making all the pairings you might think of and one you probably would not. The relationships of *The Red and the Green* push to the centre, and through this process some prime and essential Murdochian plot and tactic seems to distil. It does so because the work contains within itself the idea of distillation, partly as an attribute of plot (the Easter Rising itself is the culminating probability of that) and partly as an attribute of the moral universe of the book, which is clearly ripe for disruption.

The importance of Millie is that she herself, as a charismatic agent, contains the idea of culmination; she is a human figure with more than

[1] See Peter Kemp, 'The Fight Against Fantasy: Iris Murdoch's *The Red and the Green*', *Modern Fiction Studies*, xv, No. 3 (Autumn 1969), 403–15.

human purport who draws the other characters through a field of force. And she is tricked out appropriately with the special emotional density, and also with the exotica, that make her seem compelling. In this she resembles Honor Klein, in *A Severed Head*; Miss Klein's startling characteristics—her hairy upper lip, which Martin Lynch-Gibbon notes as he strikes her violently three times in his cellar, and her skill with the *Samurai* sword, for example—are somewhat more earthy than Millie's (and by way of being high points in Murdochian invention), but they are of the same general order. Millie, though, with her pistol, with which she undertakes target practice in her boudoir, and the altar-like dressing table at which she metaphorically celebrates decadent rites, is somewhat more ambiguous morally. But, by virtue of being at the centre of the sexual interplay of the novel, Millie becomes its emblematic centre as well—becomes, indeed, something like a symbol, a figure a little other than human, in that through her the narrative firms and distils. She serves partly to act as a human focus for the emotional powers and violences which have alternative expression in the subsequent political events; but patently she also serves to urge forth form or design in the book, an urging which is in turn a testament to otherness, to strange powers and mysteries that transcend the local self-images of the persons in it. The tactic comes over a little more uneasily than usual in *The Red and the Green*, because this is the one novel where the prevalent concern with the violent apprehension of otherness has an explicit political dimension, and the move from the ceremonial themes of sexuality and violence to the realm of social violence, in the Easter Rising, is, I believe, decidedly uneasily managed. But the problem for the reader is a more general one; in 'The Idea of Perfection', Miss Murdoch speaks of great art's having a 'selfless attention to nature', which is of a piece with moral virtue, and she comments that 'aesthetic situations are not so much analogies of morals but cases of morals.'[1] Do such culminations—not all her novels have them, be it said, but most offer variants of the problem—do these forms of formal and moral urging give us the design beyond contingency or do they destroy the sense of contingency, the moral substance of persons in their milieu of relationships and responsibilities to others?

One faces the question because there are very few novelists today who have the capacity or desire to represent a serious moral agent. What is

[1] 'The Idea of Perfection', in *The Sovereignty of Good*, 42.

so striking about Miss Murdoch's work is that her selfless attention to nature does let her do that, give her characters a great competence in moral matters. But then she patterns them. 'Wherein does the reality of a person reside and in what way can one, or should one, display that reality?' The question she asks in 'The Sublime and the Beautiful Revisited' is about the nature of human substantiality and about the nature of art; and it has always had a very active place in Miss Murdoch's working out of her writerly intentions. The answer to the question appears notionally to be that there exists a relationship between a certain kind of love and a certain kind of formal making. Of this it is hard to be sure, for what I think to be the odd reason that her essays on the novel give us, not a theory of contemporary form, but a contemporary theory of man and an historical-philosophical theory of form, encompassing the modern writer in a dilemma but leaving him many openings for escape. In short, Miss Murdoch gives herself a very dialectical aesthetics, where the writerly task is to pass elegantly between the rocks of realism and symbolism, the slackness of unmitigated contingency and the small, dry consolations of fantasy and myth. The passage is made by love; and love is a moral thrust towards the apprehension of reality or the good, or towards an abstraction outside the self, and hardly to be defined liberally, which starts to look like a symbol. This one can see in *A Severed Head* at the point of its highest elegance. The novelist starts as a comic realist of social relationships in a line that can be taken back to Forster and perhaps to Virginia Woolf, in that effective personal intercourse seems to offer a promise of ethical and aesthetic redemption, but we move (as in fact we do in the two earlier novelists) beyond this liberal theory of love as understanding, here to an account of it as morally imperative by virtue of its totemism, its violence, its irrationality. Martin Lynch-Gibbon drops his 'talent for a gentler world' and enters one of control and power which has 'nothing to do with happiness'. To get us that far Miss Murdoch gives her story an anthropological and mythological underpinning; that makes it both morally energetic and pleasingly fabulous. The real is outside us, and is love or the good: it is other than action and therefore elusive: 'If apprehension of good is apprehension of the individual and the real,' she observes in 'The Idea of Perfection', 'then good partakes of the infinitely elusive character of reality.' Or in fiction, of the dark gods of Honor Klein.

Miss Murdoch's novels contain a high aesthetic joy and self-awareness, a gift for fabulation;[1] they contain a very great moral pleasure, which is to say that they contain, in different degrees, the capacity to say something which is humane and true; and they achieve this by a high sceptical caution about consoling us too easily in either area, be it that of art or that of truth. As Miss Murdoch's range of persons and postures has narrowed and as her production has increased, all this has been increasingly hard to do; the devotee of her work senses, I think, a tightrope walk being undertaken over the dark pit of consolation waiting below. But consolation, the loss of the high particularity of persons and things, the unwillingness to be true, is still a little away; the novels stay severe, and they keep up a local compulsion which makes them forceful objects to us. That takes us back again to the area of difference among them, the presence of very plural modes in her work. I myself find that the power of creating intense individuality resides at its richest in the earlier works.

2

I want now to look at how the broader theme gets its local clothing in *Under the Net*, a book which still stands out with considerable force. It is a highly philosophical novel, done in comic-picaresque form. Its subject is the relation of words to actions, and also what makes for good and bad human intercourse; it is hence a good book about virtue though also a good book about contemporary life. Its shape derives from certain events which form a phase in the life of Jake Donaghue, and which are also events in his mind and emotions, involving a deep change in them. Jake is a *picaro* and the action is a quest, which takes the form partly of an illusory comic chase, constantly repeated, involving lockings in and out, cages and masks and disguises and theatres, and partly of a pursuit of home and money, love and wisdom, intellectual clarity and emotional release. The book begins with Jake homeless, jobless, and with only an accommodation-shop address; it ends with these things not greatly changed—after much talk of love Jake is still alone; after much exchange of money, he has still the same low bank balance—but vastly better understood by him. A process of

[1] Robert Scholes discusses Miss Murdoch's 'fabulation' in *The Fabulators* (New York and London, 1967) and sees her working in a modern allegorical mode. He takes *The Unicorn* as text and reminds us that at the end Effingham Cooper feels he has passed through 'a fantasy of the spiritual life'.

renewal has taken place in Jake: 'It was', he comments at the end, 'the first day of the world.' In particular two things have altered for the better. He has passed from being a translator and literary hack, who has to separate words from ideas, into genuine creativity; and he has developed from his original state of 'shattered nerves' a new capacity to apprehend others and hence to come to terms with the boundaries and measurements of his solitude.

The novel begins with a portrait of a recognizably contemporary 'uncommitment'. Jake is intellectually and by life-style the free-floater in a stable society. He early confesses to a traditional bohemian failing— 'There's nothing that irritates me so much as paying rent'—and, though generous, he makes it policy to appear penniless. He observes: 'It is not in my nature to make myself responsible for other people. I find it hard enough to pick my own way along.' Though he has strong literary interests, he lives by hack work and prefers this to original writing, which he does 'as little as possible'. He has

... shattered nerves. Never mind how I got them. That's another story, and I'm not telling you the whole story of my life. I have them; and one effect of this is that I can't bear being alone for long. ... I love to be protected. I am therefore a parasite, and live usually in my friends' houses.

To some extent Jake is the conventional hero of many fifties novels— the intelligent rebel, the sleeper on other people's couches, the honest man of art poor amid the world's riches—but he is also in a philosophical impasse, which is the theme of the book. His problem is a traditional one of the classless artist; it is there, for example, in the discussions of Ladislaw and Dorothea in *Middlemarch:* how much is owed to the aesthetic and the social, with their contesting claims? Jake's need is to find a mode of detachment that will not leave him dry and barren; and the book is about his half-accidental motion towards a *modus vivendi*. His creative urge has been silenced: 'Nothing is more paralyzing than a sense of historical perspective, especially in literary matters,' he says, telling us he is virtually convinced that he lives in an age in which novels cannot be written.

And in his acquaintance he confronts people who dramatize doubts about the artistic use of language; three of his friends afford different philosophies of silence that reflect his own state. One, Dave Gellman, is a linguistic philosopher committed to the spoken word only and to a spartan, very social philosophy of life. He lives in 'contingent' London;

his flat is next to, and dominated by, the cold walls of a modern hospital; he represents a spare, utilitarian view of the world. To him Jake is the 'incorrigible artist' and he wants him to get a job as a hospital orderly. In contrast there is Anna Quentin, who offers a more aesthetic world, of silks, toys, romantic passion, though again as a form of silence. A former singer, she is now devoted to mime, 'very simple', 'very pure'. The way in which what are clearly philosophical notions are conveyed through characters, objects, places, and lines of action is nowhere clearer than in the chapter—very dream-like and surrealistic, dominated by ideas of and images of silence—where Jake searches out Anna at the miming theatre in Hammersmith. It is significant that, in a book where the male mind and male characters are so accurately rendered, the female ones should be rich, romantic objects; this is partly Murdochian disposition, partly because they serve as objects of search for the mentally as well as emotionally inquisitive males. Anna is an ornate person done in ornate style; she is first shown in a vast toyshop of rich objects—'amid the enchanting chaos of silks and animals and improbable objects that seemed to arise almost to her waist she looked like a very wise mermaid rising out of a motley coloured sea' —and is 'like a great doll'. Her silence is artistic purification: the singer exploits charm to seduce, the mimer is more aesthetic, more honest. Likewise in love: Anna tells Jake that love is not a feeling or an emotional straining for possession, but is action and silence. Jake resists his temptation to shake the thundersheet, a hangover from the old theatre which Anna is going to sell, accepts the silence of the place, and spends the night there, sleeping in a bear's skin.

But the third man of silence is the one who dominates this stage of Jake's philosophy, Hugo Belfounder, whom Jake calls 'my destiny'. He proposes his acquaintance with this man as the theme of the book. We have a detailed history for Belfounder: of German stock, he inherited an armaments factory which, being pacifist, he turned into a fireworks factory, and the creation of firework set-pieces has become the ideal of impermanent and perishable art, akin to music, needing 'both manual dexterity and creative ingenuity'. If, as seems intended, the mythological story of Vulcan, Mars, and Venus is used to provide a loose framework for the novel, Belfounder certainly stands for Vulcan. Indeed the association is worked out with much surrealistic ingenuity— even down to the use of such locales as Hammersmith and such arts as fireworks, film, and finally watchmaking, to fit the myth into the new mythology of Miss Murdoch's fiction.[1] Alas for Hugo's theories about an impermanent, momentary art, his fireworks are classified into styles by the newspapers, and expressionist films—his next venture —turn into box-office successes, if only because he is, accidentally, a good businessman. But Hugo's impact on Jake is philosophical; when they are immured together in the typically Murdochian setting of a cold-cure research centre, he impresses Jake with a set of attitudes which lack 'both the practical interests and the self-conscious moral seriousness of those who are usually dubbed idealists.' Hugo needs a theory for everything, but there is no master theory: 'I never met a man more destitute than Hugo of anything which could be called a metaphysic or general *Weltanschauung*. It was rather perhaps that of each thing he met he wanted to know the *nature*. . . .' His theory is opposed to description, even to language itself, a machine for making falsehoods; but it goes the way of the fireworks and the films: Jake, impressed, starts making notes and produces a book called *The Silencer* in which their arguments appear—appropriately in touched-up form. Hugo's theme is the contradiction between theory and the warmth of life:

. . . the movement away from theory and generality is the movement towards truth. All theorizing is flight. We must be ruled by the situation itself and this is unutterably particular. Indeed it is something to which we can never get close enough, however hard we may try as it were to crawl under the net.

Hugo, like his author, argues too that art works against theory, but presses the logic towards silence. This leaves Jake with the problem of picking his way between the extremes of theory and silence, the un-utterable particularity of human experience and their social mediation as art. G. S. Fraser notes that this is part of a struggle between the

---

[1] This part of my essay is abbreviated from an article which appeared in *The Critical Quarterly* in 1962. I have left this point, which was picked up by A. S. Byatt in her *Degrees of Freedom: The Novels of Iris Murdoch* (London and New York, 1965), who comments: 'I was very impressed by the argument, and thought I had found a continuation of the use of this myth of Vulcan's net in *A Severed Head* . . . . But Miss Murdoch assures me that she had no intention, when writing *Under the Net*, of referring to the myth in this way. . . .' I am sure Mrs. Byatt is right in taking the prime allusion of the title as to Wittgenstein (*Tractatus Logico-Philosophicus*, 6.341); but the other allusion is also there, to embellish the philosophical with the mythological, and is so explicit as to be inescapable.

private will and the social spirit,[1] but the conclusions are comic and not straightforward, and Hugo's position is not entirely left standing.

Hugo has a dialectical opposite in the figure of 'Lefty' Todd, leader of the New Independent Socialist Party, and arguer for a practical and political unity of theory and practice. Lefty's world is shown as constantly in pursuit of Hugo's universe of silence and art. And it offers a different role for the artist and intellectual: Lefty glosses the Marxist theory that social being is the foundation of consciousness as meaning that political parties must think and then act; he urges Jake into political responses ('Nothing destroys abstraction so well as hatred') and into writing plays by uniting popular techniques for success with a political message. Jake doesn't accept these crude demands, but they tighten his dilemma. It is after the NISP take over the mime theatre that Jake finds he *can* shake the thundersheet—'my previous pattern of life was gone forever.' Soon after he is pushed for like reasons into stealing Mr. Mars, the film-star dog, and releasing him from his cage.

It is amid these options that Jake explores his intellectual role. It is unpleasantly isolated and solitary; none the less, by refusing an offer of an easy scriptwriting job, he commits himself to this. In Paris on the 14th of July, he finds himself both emotionally lost and artistically empty; like Polythemus on the fountain des Medicis, all he can do is overlook the lovers, and when he suddenly sees Anna and pursues her he is left simply with her shoes. When, back in London, he returns to Dave Gellman and a job as hospital orderly, this is clearly an alternative choice; it unites the aesthetic with the social, the expedient which is still his at the end of the book:

It occurred to me that to spend half the day doing manual work might be very calming to the nerves of one who was spending the other half doing intellectual work, and I could not imagine why I had not thought before of this way of living, which would ensure that no day could pass without *something* having been done, and so keep that sense of uselessness, which grows in prolonged periods of sterility, away from me forever.

This balance provokes the radical revaluation and rediscovery that changes Jake at the end; for Hugo appears in hospital as a patient— victim of a head wound sustained at an NISP meeting—and reveals to Jake the falsity of his account of the world and the relationships he had

[1] G. S. Fraser, 'Iris Murdoch: The Solidity of the Normal', *International Literary Annual*, No. 2 (London, 1959), 37–54.

understood to obtain between people. Now Jake begins to 'get the facts; theories could come later.' 'A pattern in my mind was suddenly scattered and the pieces of it went flying about me like birds,' he notes; this fragmentation is later reinforced by the image of the starlings which live in hundreds outside Hugo's flat and enter it finally through the open window in the concluding pages. It is now clear that it is Jake who has imposed his theories, about relationships, on everyone, acting as if his hastily formed deductions were always true. Hugo's revelations open up all the events and relationships in the book to new interpretation. It was Anna who felt unrequited love for Hugo (and not the reverse); it was Anna who initiated the mime theatre; in fact it may have been Anna who has led Hugo to his anti-theoretical theories, and she *in turn got it from Jake*. 'I knew everything,' says Jake. 'I got it all the wrong way round, that's all!' This wrench 'which had dislocated past, present and future' gives Jake a new response to people, and especially Anna:

It seemed as if, for the first time, Anna really existed now as a separate being and not as part of myself. To experience this was extremely painful. Yet as I tried to keep my eyes fixed upon where she was I felt towards her a sense of initiative which was perhaps after all one of the guises of love. Anna was something which had to be learnt afresh. When does one ever know a human being? Perhaps only after one has realized the impossibility of knowledge and renounced the desire for it. . . .

The result is a very moral celebration: a recognition of the individuality of persons and of things as they are. Jake has learned what he really needed from Hugo; he has balanced the demands of the intellectual and practical life; he has renewed his creative energy. As lonely and poor as at the beginning, he has accepted solitude and does have Mr. Mars, on whom what money he has gained in the course of the book has been spent. But especially he has found a way out of silence and abstraction; the aesthetic must answer to the moral, to reality, and he must respond to the individuality of others and to the demands of his own distinctive nature and his professional and social role. He accepts his intellectual solitude much as he accepts the separateness of other things and people; if he began the book with Vulcan, he ends it with a freed Mars.

The discovery of the ending is a traditional one, one we know from George Eliot or James; it belongs with the historic business of the novel. Still in her way of making the book and reaching the ending

Miss Murdoch strikes, or ought to strike, us as an inventor of a very unusual sort. For one thing it is an ending as much philosophic as moral; to encroach on the individuality of others is less a failure in sensitivity or moral competence, as in the tradition, than in knowing truth. Then there is the very playful, inventive aspect of the book; its neat, flexible style has to comprehend both the variousness and literalism of Jake's mind and the decidedly surrealistic fantasies of the novelist, that consort oddly with the philosophical and moral intensity. By *A Severed Head* the contrast between the weighty, scrupulous Jamesian style and the very unJamesian invention and subject-matter becomes a comic strategy. There as here, many of the scenes are contrived for their sheer ornateness, their capacity to turn surprise. This clearly has something to do with Miss Murdoch's fertility of mind and art, but it also has to do with the problems of eliciting a moral development in modern fiction. Where once the characteristic shape of a novel could be a pattern of the hero's sin, repentance, and absolution, in the modern novel there are other terms to assert: wrong thinking, reappraisal, true vision, arising from a sense of struggle with predictive form itself. In this book Jake comes to what we now know to be a Murdochian truth. There is a difficulty for the reader in the unsatisfactory rendering of the crisis itself; something of its point is dissipated, its terms left unclear. It takes later novels to clarify it. Thus, where in *Under the Net* there is a mythological and symbolic imagination at work, in a novel like *A Severed Head* this is turned to the service of a ceremonial initiation in which Martin Lynch-Gibbon does not so much acquire Jake's understanding as face the forces that compel it.

What *Under the Net* possesses is, despite its fantasy, a real density of cultural exploration. We have now learned to see how, in Miss Murdoch's novels, this is in some ways incidental; it is not what we *have* to discover when we discover 'the density of our lives'. Over-all, Iris Murdoch has two purposes; one is to lead her characters towards that density, and the other is, through energy and zest of creative working, to invoke it. This is an enterprise of great delicacy, dependent, in her case, on a very high moral scruple and insight coupled with a fertile buoyancy and extravagance. Beyond *Under the Net*, that mixture will prove to have many forms; but it *is* her mixture, and it is one that makes her of much importance for the present-day novel, whose nature and dimensions she has opened to us in a variety of thoughtful ways.

XV

Muriel Spark's Fingernails

The sense of a system saves the painter from the baseness of
the *arbitrary* stroke, the touch without its reason.

Henry James, preface to *The Tragic Muse*

I

Muriel Spark has always been an interesting, and a very amusing,
novelist; but observers of her recent work will have noticed that
something fresh has been happening with her—she is turning into a
very high stylist indeed. A new authority has come into her work, in
the form of great tactical precision and a growingly high-handed
manner both with her readers and her characters; and from *The Public
Image* (1968) on she has given herself over to works in the novella form,
very tight, very clear, works in which every compositional decision
and every compositional device is traded at the same high economy as
in Hemingway's better stories, though for very different reasons. The
result is in some ways a limiting of the pleasures—especially the comic
ones—of the earlier books; but Mrs. Spark has not ceased, in the process
of self-purification, to be a comic writer, a Catholic comic writer. She
remains as macabre as ever; the tactics of indifference which make her
aesthetic manner so poised are also part of an appalling *moral* manner, a
splendid impudence; as with a number of our Catholic writers (who
have contributed more than their proportionate share to aesthetic
speculation in the English novel), an ingrained casuistry has always
touched her dealings with the form, and these recent books have been
open celebrations of it. As to the kind of Catholic aesthetics, it is not
the tradition of humanism in the Catholic novel that lies behind her—
Mauriac's 'the heroes of our novels must be free in the sense that the

theologian says man is free. The novelist must not intervene arbitrarily in their destinies' is hardly for her a conviction but a matter of witty speculation.[1] She is much closer to the Catholic novelists of detachment, to Joyce's God-like writer, paring his fingernails, or to Waugh at the height of his comic powers—who, despairing of God's sensible presence in modern history, feels free to represent the contemporary world as chaos, and his characters as bereft of significant moral action. This makes for an absurd and macabre universe, but at the same time for a sense of what is absent, a knowledge of true things and last things. Like Waugh, in fact, Muriel Spark is very much a *memento mori* writer, and indeed her novel of that title is a central testament—a farce which shows the comic unreality of human and historical concerns in its senile cast, and also evokes for the human lot a cool, instructive pathos. Unlike Waugh, though, she is decidedly an asesthetician, not only because she is a poet and one of our most intelligent novelists, but also because she senses a necessity for wholeness and coherence. Indeed that seems at present her main preoccupation; and it is the relation between the chaotic or contingent and the teleological that seems now to direct both her artistic and her moral interests and to make her recent books into very exact, very formal, and very duplicitous objects.

To a point, they always were. Among the recurrent themes and modes of her work has long been a curiosity about the relation of an author to a fiction and its agents; another is an interest in extravagant, disturbed social milieux and camp or high-style figures, productive of comedy; a third is an interest in diabolic or charismatic figures with strange interventions to make in human affairs. In earlier books these often produced an extended social world and a large and varied cast of types, handled with a quirky moral and formal concern and a sense of foreknowledge and fate, putting the novelist in a flamboyantly strong position. She has always been disposed towards being Mauriac's novelist of intervention, whose plots are destinies. What seems to have happened in her more recent work is that the means of conveying such a view of life have come to interest her much more. The original extended world of her books has become pared down and partialized, and the basic structure very open and explicit. Indeed her *œuvre* between 1968 and 1972—the three novellas *The Public Image*,

[1] David Lodge comments excellently on this in 'The Uses and Abuses of Omniscience: Method and Meaning in Muriel Spark's *The Prime of Miss Jean Brodie*', in *The Novelist at the Crossroads* (London, 1971), 119–44.

The Driver's Seat, and *Not to Disturb*— appears to be a distinct aesthetic phase, not unlike those occurring in the careers of a number of modern painters who, by localizing certain aspects of an originally eclectic endeavour and working them in detail, have made their formal nature very articulate. Over these books certain common things occur: the length is reduced; the expository material is sharply diminished; a good part of the substance is conveyed through pointed, economical dialogue; the time-span of the narrative is shortened to one or two days; the extent of particular scenes—what James calls the 'discriminated occasion' in the telling—is increased; and a self-aware abstemiousness, coupled with a skilled, exact use of prime fictional variables like point-of-view and time-pointing, establishes a high authority with the reader. A psychological centre in a given character tantamount to sympathy is avoided as part of the general economy. There is exposition through small, contingent, material things, precisely stationed in this world. Metaphor is limited and, where it occurs, exactly managed.

But what is especially striking about these books is that they are all novels of ending. Indeed, they are all endings, as if all material prior to the resolution has either been eliminated or given a reduced status as exposition. The luminous scene begins on the edge of finality, avoiding any bulk of earlier attention, and completes it. Frank Kermode tells us that endings in fiction and apocalypse in history are analogues, that a problem of fictional art is to relate the time of a life and the time of the world, that endings attach significance to time.[1] The reading back of meanings from the end towards the beginning, a proceeding that Fielding recommends for our aesthetic and moral appreciation of *Tom Jones,* is an operative presumption. Hence perhaps the fact that death is very much Mrs. Spark's present subject. In *The Public Image* Frederick makes a plot of his own death; his suicide is an attempt to expose the public wealth and private squalor of his wife, the English tiger-lady actress Annabel Christopher—though the story is seen 'through' her and she manages to include the plot inside her life and to master it. In *The Driver's Seat*—to which, as the most economically perfect and

[1] Frank Kermode, *The Sense of an Ending: Studies in the Theory of Fiction* (New York and London, 1967). One might say that the closeness between an important novelist and an important critic one senses here has itself a cultural significance; certainly Kermode's reviews of Mrs. Spark's novels – see *Modern Essays* (London, 1971) for most of them – are sympathetically very inward comments upon her work, and represent the finest criticism she has received.

precise of the three books, I want to return—the action moves straight to the mortal terminus; how straight it takes us time to discover. In *Not to Disturb* the main events are told from an oblique angle, as with Frederick's suicide, and the book is a pastiche of the old situation in which the main story happens to the middle classes but is told (as in *Wuthering Heights*) by the servants, traditional fiction-makers and reporters of crimes of high passion. But Mrs. Spark's servants are modern and have learned the manners of their betters, acquiring press agents and aspirations to film-script writing, as well as sharing with their author a gift for forward plotting. So they have no small interest in discouraging callers and encouraging appropriate developments in order to make sure that the ending is indeed in accord with their prefigurative fictions; technically innocent, morally implicated, they aid death's business, as well as giving the novel the sense of dark necessity that is part of the *memento mori* disposition.

In all this, these books seem the antithesis of the concern for freedom which has been much at stake in the modern novel and the idea of plot that has grown in it. In *The Portrait of a Lady* James—like his analogue inside the novel, Ralph Touchett—tried to set Isobel Archer free, from onerous economics, tight determinants, inexorabilities of plot; this, his preface tells us, he did by taking her as the 'essence' and placing her in the centre of his creative imagination so that she might find her own 'end', a not uncruel one at that. In a more modern variant John Fowles, in *The French Lieutenant's Woman*, offers us two equal endings to choose from in the interest of the freedom of his characters. But where Fowles's book is beginning-directed, and James's novel an inquiry, Muriel Spark's are end-directed; no author could be surer about where things are going. From her novels the beginning, which creates expectation and freedom, and the middle, which substantiates and qualifies it, seem absent. Her people arise at the last, *from* the last; what has withered is a world of motive, purpose, aspiration. The curious inescapability of plot is her subject, in some real sense her satisfaction. Compared with James, she has nothing to offer about the significance of impressions, the taking in of experience, the value of the vaunted scene, and there is no substantial self to be made from apprehending the contingencies of experience. In that way her work conveys significant absences, a feeling of omission, and so has considerable resemblances to a good deal of contemporary art, including the *nouveau roman*. In the end, it seems finally to deny the notion of personal authenticity out of which humanists, gently, and existentialists, assertively, make character.

That may press the point too far; still, the essence of the art is its hardness. This is partly because the psychological centre virtually disappears from it. On the one hand, there is a substantive material world, contingent and solid and given in high specificity; so the detail of Lise's apartment, or the plastic horrors of the airplane meal, in *The Driver's Seat*. On the other, there are Mrs. Spark's people, who have will and style but no psychologically established motives, real history, or conditioning milieu. No pathetic fallacy links the two; things are inert in their quiddity and very present in their presentness; people move among objects, as if they themselves were object-like, in a present shading into a future (*The Driver's Seat* is a present-tense novel, the 'she was to . . .' tense is structural to *The Public Image*). This hard world is part of the high aesthetic clarity of the books, but it has also an historical—by which I mean a contemporary—reference; this is why Mrs. Spark's technics have, like some contemporary film technique, a pointed immediate importance. For her people, in their instantaneousness, their want of psychology and history, populate a random world. Socially, they inhabit the decidedly trendy milieux of a highly modernized Europe, expanding materially, intensifying its inner communications, sharing its institutions, throwing off the past. These are milieux which have become very much hers and which, since her move to Rome, she has had the better opportunity to observe. The film-star Rome of *The Public Image*, the northern and southern cities of *The Driver's Seat*, the *dolce vita* of the modern aristocracy in *Not to Disturb*, have common roots in a Euromart, trendy bohemian scene taking shape for her as a stylized society, rather like that of Antonioni's films. This modernized scenario—to use an analogy that clearly interests Mrs. Spark—consorts with her sense of the human stage of behaviour; her characters are a-historical figures exposedly playing their parts in that large group theatre of fashion, role, and publicity which is modern history and in which any practice that is stageable is apparently tolerable. It would be hard to say of Mrs. Spark that she loved any world, especially hard to say that she loves this one; the overtones of decadence are compelling, even if they are to her cool eyes no more than might be expected. But it is in this universe of moral psychic contingency that Mrs. Spark's sense of an ending is so decidedly telling; she forces us to read contingency for significance. Only at the simplest level is her strategy designed not to disturb, in short: we should take her preoccupations with plots, grids, and fictions not just as a part of the current rage for aesthetic order, but as a distinct urgency about truth—a desire to raise through the model of the writer's action the eschatological questions, a concern particularly clear in *The Driver's Seat*.

2

The Driver's Seat is the narrative of a few brief, continuous hours in the life of Lise, a middle-aged, inelegant, shrill woman with a 'final and judging mouth', a not untypical Muriel Spark heroine. She is on holiday from the normal run of her life; she leaves her job in an accountant's office somewhere in an unnamed northern city, buys new clothes, including a dress that will stain, makes arrangements to leave the key of her flat, and takes a plane flight to a southern city, where, it appears, she expects some kind of encounter to occur. Throughout the journey she seems about to meet someone; she behaves flamboyantly, drawing considerable attention to herself, and is attentive to all the people she encounters. Muriel Spark, who tells it all in a present tense with a future element, ominously promises significance in all this, and details about it in the forthcoming issues of the newspapers. On arrival, Lise shops in a modern department store, encounters a student demonstration, acquires a car, and in the last lines of the novella meets her death by murder. Of this ending Muriel Spark is in full foreknowledge, and she shares this slowly with the reader. What is more extraordinary is that she shares it with Lise too. Lise's flamboyance, her stainable dress, her selectivity among her acquaintances are all part of a pursuit of the ending, in which she is an active participant. This means complicity with her murderer, and hence an issue about moral responsibility; it also means complicity with her own author, and hence an issue about form. Lise takes over the driver's seat from the pathological agent she finds to kill her; but she also takes over from the novelist, becoming, in her search for the ending, an alternative plotmaker, and a giver of form to the contingent events of the book. Like Annabel in the earlier novel, Lise has a public image to consider; she knows she is ripe for a story in the newspapers, ripe for a fiction. It is Mrs. Spark who plants and plays with the plot, the economy of the telling, and displays and preens its elegant delight. But Lise has more to lay on the line than the novelist has, namely her own mortality, and you could say that, like Caroline in *The Comforters* ('I intend to stand aside and see if the novel has any real form apart from this artificial plot. I happen to be a Christian'), she defeats her author, not by standing aside from the plot but by assuming total mastery of it.

In this Lise overwhelms, outwits contingency; that is her victory. On first reading *The Driver's Seat* is a most contingent book, with some of the hardness and inconsequence of the *nouveau roman*. The fact that Lise is shown taking a journey to a new, unknown place, so that her impressions are apparently tourist's impressions, fresh, instant, unrelated, is one reason for this. Another is the relationship assumed between the material things of the world and its human occupants; Lise's flat is a very physical and quite impersonal milieu. Then there is the tight unified time-span, which means that the novelist appears to be doing little more for us than filling the slow-moving clock of hours. The present-tense telling also increases instantaneousness at the cost of connectedness. Finally, though Lise's will to movement is given, her motives are not; the omniscient narrator, the narrator above, retains her hard complexion. But the telling *is* future-directed, which means that expositionally it works like a detective story, implying motives that we will one day come to comprehend, coherences that we will grasp if only we can wait. We push towards hypotheses; it is Mrs. Spark's great gift for being appalling that makes for suspense, and only with the ending does it all come clear. But clear it comes: read from conclusion backward the book becomes a sequence in prime logic, complicated by a series of elegant aesthetic perspectives. Both character and novelist are awarded their own victories, which are victories having to do with the value both attach to plot and above all to the fact that plot is, indeed, destiny. The character's victory, Lise's victory, is that in the chaotic run of the present she has always known a future. The casual relationships with strangers, the hints of sexual complicity, the passing claims of politics, the truth or otherwise of revolutionary promise and of the substantial world of economic or material temptations: these are the things that make up the main substance of the story, diverse alternatives which are then put in their place by her own discounting of the contingent by the morally, philosophically, and theologically artful use of her own mortality. Lise has a soul to consider, and she makes the subtlest use of it she can, the most dangerous flirtation with suicide she might; she has all the casuistry of the higher Sparkian heroine, and in this partakes of her narrator to high degree. The novelist's victory—happily derived at lesser cost,

though the language, in its precision, shows that it is not at little cost—
is also casuistical, a kind of outwitting of the *nouveau roman* by showing
that if the world is all present and disconnected there is always the
claim of a future; plot can be won from a plotless world.

Not only is it far from being a humanist novel; its elegant and
macabre wit and its moral and theological sophistication make it
decidedly fancy as a religious one. Of course in the end Lise may not
outwit or excel her author, whose mastery is complete; smaller fictions
lie within bigger, the one who commands the language of the telling
commanding everything. Still, in establishing the power of plot both
Lise and Mrs. Spark establish what they want to show; by, so to speak,
natural deduction destiny or purpose does exist. This is a point, and in
many respects a comic point, located very close to the heart of the
fiction-making process; it is partly because it is so close that the sheer
purity of the novel delights so much. But the matter does not end there.
One elegant result of the book is that the reader witnesses how out of
contingency comes a fiction, in all its paradox; the practised devotee of
novels is granted an extraordinary professional joy, as the sequence
unfolds and his own tactics of hypothesizing and cohering fictional
matter are played with, as he watches the way in which a character who,
at the start, seems the subordinated victim of writerly manipulation in
a preordained world becoming, by virtue of the maximization of the
greatest risks she can take, the consort of the writer herself—hence an
ironically free agent, doing willingly what the lesser novelist would
compel.

But if this sounds like a book for critics only, then let me add that the
creative energy of it is dense, vigorous and in some ways most erotic,
and that there is an avid precision of rendering which makes Mrs.
Spark's consciously fictional world sit in illuminating relationship with
the real one. In fact it is precisely this capacity Muriel Spark reveals to
turn our familiar world into an exceptional, even a surreal, milieu that
makes the book work so well. In this universe of strangenesses—this
universe where the very act of shopping becomes a strange and terrifying human performance among things and choices—Lise's own
mania or oddity becomes itself a kind of sanity. She appears before us
first as a victim of this vivid but somewhat onerous milieu of obiects
and events; she concludes her time before us as an instigator of its
grim comedies and grotesqueries. Muriel Spark has got effects somewhat like this before, in *Memento Mori*, for example; but it is in this

case a very pure endeavour indeed. The phrase 'black humour' fits this side of things; but one then has to add that there is a very distinctive quality in her particular version of it whereby the follies of this world are threatened from the next, and that the sense of the deathly reminder, the skull beneath the skin, is very much part of the point. In this respect Mrs. Spark's aesthetics are a kind of religious or rather metaphysical wit—a very *modern* kind. There is a pure elegance here then; we read backwards and forwards, for *integritas, consonantia, claritas*. There is also a decided comic pleasure to be had. But given the extremities it reaches to, its movement not only to the aesthetic but also to the moral extreme of its own substance, its neatness is hardly designed not to disturb.

XVI

The Novelist as Impresario:
John Fowles and His Magus

There is about the clothes, in the lavishly embroidered
summer waistcoat, in the three rings on fingers, the pana-
tella in its amber holder, the malachite-headed cane, a distinct
touch of the flashy. He looks very much as if he had given up
preaching and gone in for grand opera; and done much better
at the latter than the former. There is, in short, more than a
touch of the successful impresario about him.

John Fowles, *The French Lieutenant's Woman*

I

Foppish, Frenchified, flashy and 'very minor', the lavish figure who
inserts himself into the final chapter of *The French Lieutenant's Woman*,
looking back at Mr. Rossetti's house in Chelsea 'as if it is some new
theatre he has just bought and is pretty confident he can fill' and turning
back time on his watch, is patently none other than a figure for the
novelist John Fowles himself. He has, in fact, popped into the novel
before, in several guises and voices, and we are used to his here
faintly worried and there grandly confident, here contemporaneously
nineteenth-century and there a-chronologically twentieth-century,
presence. However, his final appearance in the guise of a stout impresario is not entirely creditable either to himself or to the ongoing novel,
for it is as a confidence man he shows himself, a notably unresponsible
intrusion that he makes and the small mechanical task he performs—
setting the clock back a little in order utterly to transform the fortunes
and futures of his two central characters, Charles Smithson and the
French Lieutenant's Woman—he performs blandly, vainly, and trivi-

ally, out of an arrogant power and while en route for fresher pastures. He is the novelist in one of his less likeable guises.

Fortunately the writing continues in more reliable hands, for there is another John Fowles—a much more sober, sententious, and omniscient figure, capable of reporting and reflecting on events, and so of taking seriously the destiny of his characters and establishing with authority an ending which, however, may or may not have any authority whatsoever. The doubt arises because this narrator has already given us, in the previous chapter, one ending to his story. He has, for that matter, given us one two-thirds of the way through the novel, but that one he has rescinded in order to enforce deeper possibilities. But his two final endings have a different status. Both of them, we may say, are structured with all appropriate scruple out of the eventful plot; both of them are substantiations of the argumentative level of the book, or what used to be called its 'sentiments', closing in an aura of Arnoldian humanism, existentialist authenticity, and Marxist history, all of which textures of thought and feeling have been part of the work as a whole. Authorial authority is relativized not in order to lighten responsibility for the characters, thrusting it on the reader, but rather to take full responsibility for showing their freedom, their faculty of choice. The book closes and the reader can fall back only on recognitions themselves duplicitous; here is the writer's great power both to set his characters free to act and choose as they like, and his power to make them his victims, to set them free from his plot but by withdrawing his power himself exposing them more vigorously than if he had fulfilled it. The trickster and the voice of fact and authority; the manipulator and the humanist concerned in all good faith over the fate and the individual freedom of his characters; the plotter and the plot-escaper—these are co-existent presences in the novel and they produce an extraordinary resolution to it, a resolution in which the substantial action seems to end in one world and the substantiating *machinery*, the technical modes and means, in another.

Which is the real Fowles? Readers may disagree, and in disagreeing come up with extremely varied readings. We may take the book as a very Whig novel, a novel about emancipation through history, with Victorian hypocrisy and ignorance yielding up to modern truth and authenticity, to good faith and freedom, the whole enterprise aided by appropriately sympathetic techniques in which the characters are set free from the formal containments of traditional Victorian fiction.

More obliquely and cunningly, we may take the book as a great pastiche novel, a novel of ironic counterpointings in which the present may make no such triumph over the past, in which emancipation is also a terrible exposure, a loss as well as a gain, and in which the substance of freedom is seen as something potentially other than that substance which the modern theoreticians and rebellious theologians define it as, this whole enterprise being aided by the way in which a modernist novel can be balanced by contrast—so that the modes weigh equally in the scales. There is a third possibility, which is that the modernist fiction is what is questioned, being attenuated and modified by the substance and realism of Victorian fiction. Certainly the novel crosses some of the stranger boundaries of form and for that matter of criticism—above all that between the nineteenth-century realist and the modern novel, a perplexing barrier—which is precisely why it is baffling *to* criticism; it invokes expectations, hypotheses, and probabilities we may best describe in terms of one poetics while it engages us with the sophisticated discourses of another. We may find our way through the book as we might through a great realistic work, a work of liberal realism attentive to character and social experience and the moral expansions possible at their intersection; we may read it by modernist canons and find it appropriately a work of self-conscious irony. In other words, like some of the work of Nabokov or Barth or Borges, the book seems to embody itself in the purist world of art while delighting in the obligation to attend to reality; and like that kind of novel it tends to expose our present critical debates and confusions and their greatest point of uncertainty—the point where arises the question of whether realistic or symbolistic norms of the novel can be reconciled, whether criticism itself can find the same language for talking about a nineteenth-century realist and a twentieth-century modernist novel.

What, at any rate, is obvious is that John Fowles is—though we have been slow to notice it—a sophisticated novelist; and it is worth asking briefly how it is that this sort of sophistication can have emerged in postwar English fiction. John Barth has taught us, whether truly or not, that it is all-important for an artist to be technically up-to-date; on that measure we have not had a wealth of contemporary English novelists to turn to, though we have had some. We have, with Fowles, as with writers like Nabokov and Barth and Borges, our difficulties in deciding just how modern a novelist he is or wants to be, for there is, as with them, a decided element of protective withdrawal from authoritative commitment to those elements of existential and revolutionary lore which his work obviously copes with and comprehends—from, in fact, the establishment 'modern' thought of our day. Nonetheless Fowles's work is modern in the sense of Richard Poirier's definition, that it 'includes the interpretation that will be made of it', and moves in the direction of self-parody and solipsism.[1] But whatever his particular aesthetics, they have not been entirely commonplace in the English literary scene. It is universally acknowledged that criticism of contemporary writing is a difficult task and that its deceptions are many, that the literature of one's age needs sifting by the purging wisdom of time, that reviewing is one thing and criticism another; and in England one of the consequences of that truth has been that little accurate critical attention has been given to contemporary writing. But if criticism withdraws from creative discussion, or else treats contemporary writing as compelled into insignificance, there is likely to be a general diminution in critical discourse—which may help to explain the more or less low morale of the postwar English fictional scene, its lack of mythology and sociology about the nature of fiction and art. The enterprise of certain postwar English writers who, reacting against the Bloomsbury tradition of experimentalism, asserted an anti-experimental, socially documentary, very empirical purpose for the novel, did not receive much serious attention, even from critics whose responsiveness to earlier phases of realism was considerable; and when or where the emphasis was changed, and in different ways writers like Iris Murdoch, Muriel Spark, B. S. Johnson, and Christine Brooke-Rose attempted to distil a debate and an aesthetic speculativeness, they too got little close reading. The situation doubtless helped to encourage the disproportionately low impression of the quality of contemporary English fiction which has existed in international circles. The curious and surprising thing is that out of such an environment a novelist like John Fowles, whose emphases and concerns are very much of a piece with aesthetic speculation in the novel elsewhere, especially in the American novel, should emerge. The perfectly uncurious, unsurprising thing is that, when he did, he attracted almost no attention in England, and that most of his critical reputation, which has largely come with his last and most flamboyant book, has come in the United States,

[1] Richard Poirier, *The Performing Self: Compositions and Decompositions in the Languages of Contemporary Life* (London, 1971), 27–44.

along with a considerable popular, indeed a best-selling, status as well. *The Collector* appeared in 1963; *The Magus* in 1966; *The French Lieutenant's Woman* in 1969, and it is only with the paperback edition of the last that his reputation in England has really become noticeable.

Yet there was always that in Fowles's work which might have attracted attention: a large intellectual and imaginative aspiration. The very scale of the enterprises he has undertaken as a novelist might well have stood out in any critical climate alive to such things. *The Magus*, for example, runs to 617 pages, and among other things it fairly clearly attempts a kind of history of the consciousness of the West in our present century, an act of recreation and invention carried out with remarkable range and deployment of intellect. *The French Lieutenant's Woman*, though somewhat shorter, is fairly clearly both a formal imitation of a Victorian novel and a very elegant endeavour at assessing the mental distance that must lie between a modern reader and a fiction of that sort—the result being a complex contrast between the psycho-social set of consciousness in the England of a hundred years ago, threaded through all the major areas of social, commercial, intellectual, and sexual life, and that of the present time in which the novelist consciously and articulately stands along with his reader. In one sense, the theme of Fowles's work is precisely cultural distillation, the task of rendering the way in which consciousness or structural coherence underlies all the parts of a society and produces a cultural unity between inner and outer worlds. That is why his novels are so broadly accumulative, so wide-ranging, so socially mobile or picaresque, so substantially populated and explored. Their task involves the interpenetration of many different levels of awareness or perception—requires, that is, social, emotional, and psychological exploration.

For a novelist who is sometimes described as 'existential', this is perhaps a curiously roundabout way of going at the writerly task; but then the reality with which Fowles is concerned is surely not exclusively a personal one, and when one looks to his aspiration, to the basis on which he has built his sophistication, it is not perhaps firstly or even primarily aesthetic. Or rather he presumes, and in this he resembles predecessors rather than contemporaries, that the aesthetic exists inside the problem rather than at the abstract level where the writer performs his arabesques of complication and coherence and resolution. Thus Fowles's last two books each have heroes for whom voyage, journey, evolving movement is a matter of social, emotional, and psychological exploration, carrying an obligation to discern a basis of personal authenticity. For each of them, the world is a theatre in which his role must be finally substantiated; the image or metaphor is precisely used, very much in the sense in which it has become a central metaphor for sociologists concerned with the hinterland where sociology and psychology meet. In that difficult world where modern man, seeking to validate some sense of authenticity, meets *homo psychologicus*, programmed via the unconscious, and *homo sociologicus*, programmed by society, man as role-player, what Erving Goffman calls the 'dramaturgical analogy', becomes a pervasive metaphor, touching not only on the question of whether the theatre of society, in which we act our parts, is substance or shadow, but whether the stage is one we can ever leave.[1] The metaphor challenges authorship; it throws back at the playwright or the novelist or the fiction-maker or the impresario a question about the substantive reality of what he is creating: is it a copy of reality or a competing fiction to set against a fiction? 'Perhaps what he was doing sprang from some theory about the theatre—he had said it himself: *The masque is only a metaphor*. A strange and incomprehensible new philosophy? Metaphorism? Perhaps he saw himself as a philosopher in an impossible faculty of ambiguity, a sort of Empson of the event.' Nicholas Urfe's reflections on Conchis—the 'Magus' of the book of that title—and his 'godgame' are therefore centralizing questions, which touch on the relation of fictions to reality. And it seems clear enough that part of the purpose of that novel is to create a world vigorously dramatic, a world in which no part is ever inert, in which every street is a theatre and every object a prop—or, as Robert Scholes has said, the book seeks to give us back reality by passing beyond the inert banality we have come to associate with that very term, reality, in the deadening pages of the *nouveau roman*.[2]

It is in fact the achieved metaphorical energy of Fowles's novels that gives them power over us; the novels live within themselves, are highly inventive and linguistically vivid. Fowles puts right at the centre of his work a superb generative energy, a history-making gift, a power of what, until the word 'story' weakened in critical credit, was called

[1] Erving Goffman, *The Presentation of Self in Everyday Life* (New York, 1959; London, 1969).

[2] Robert Scholes, 'The Orgiastic Fiction of John Fowles', *The Hollins Critic*, VI, No. 5 (December 1969), 1–12.

story-telling, of such an order that the philosophical and aesthetic articulation of his works seems modified by its presence. The aesthetic problem, the problem of fictions, is in fact created very deep inside *The Magus*, made less an aspect of its construction and management than of its theme. It remains, of course, a book about art; it is the sort of book a novelist might write in order to assert, for himself and others, a sense of the possibilities open to fiction in a time when our ideas and notions of freedom, of selfhood, and of significant order are in ferment, and complex problems of modern history, modern psychic life or consciousness, modern notions of selfhood and of reality, and modern aesthetics of form have to be synthesized. These, we may propose, though the reviewers did not, are the inner themes of *The Magus*; and the hypothesis has a fair confirmation in *The French Lieutenant's Woman*, where a number of these themes rise explicitly to the presentational surface, implicating the novelist himself and becoming part of his technical self-questioning and self-development. In both books the hero is led towards a state of exposure or self-discovery, led out of one state of consciousness into another, in a world in which the historical determinants of consciousness are extremely significant and in which the capacity to learn through fictions is central.

If it is the case that we live in a time when it is difficult for a writer to establish the literal reality of plot and character as coherent meanings, and to express a fiction as a coherent linear development of knowledge; if language and structure have become quizzical properties for many of our writers, then Fowles is clearly an author who has come to know and explore such suspicions. The novelist who intrudes so carefully yet so flashily into the last pages of *The French Lieutenant's Woman* in the guise of impresario has earlier made it clear that he has, like any good student in a new university, duly read and digested his Roland Barthes and his Alain Robbe-Grillet, and knows what a novel 'in the modern sense of the word' is, which is not an omniscient narrative. Fowles understands and expresses an awareness of the status fictions and myths have with us; and he not only embodies the resulting technicalities but explores the version of history by which such a thing might be asserted. As his fictional world moves from superego to id, from stability to exposure, so does his sense of the commanding novelist move through a similar trajectory:

The novelist is still a god, since he creates (and not even the most aleatory *avant-garde* modern novel has managed to extirpate its author completely); what has changed is that we are no longer the gods of the Victorian image, omniscient and decreeing; but in the new theological image, with freedom our first principle, not authority.

It is perhaps worth noting, though, that Fowles does not dissolve the tradition of realism completely, and that in many respects his aim, like Iris Murdoch's, seems to be to preserve as much humanism for the novel as can be got. If the traditional novel may, by the linearity and rigour of its plot and by authorial omniscience, seem to control and limit, the modernist one may, by the placing of character in long formal perspectives, tend to dehumanize, to ironize. Fowles has reason to claim his contemporaneity, but also some to question it; and both these things I think he does. He knows his modernity, systematically, as a deep structure in consciousness; and his essential theme, the encounter of his heroes with the dreadful freedom pushed upon us out of history, supports his more flamboyant aesthetic pretensions. But his work has something of the air of forcing itself towards a formal self-consciousness of surface, rather than inherently needing it. So in *The French Lieutenant's Woman* one feels left, as I have said, with a sense of mystification. The realistic Victorian mode of the novel, in which Fowles seems capable of working at high intensity, is also represented as authoritarian and containing; the modern mode, which comports with Sarah's modernizing consciousness and also opens the door of formal opportunity, allows for unpredictability and contingency. Yet Fowles's real intensity of achievement lies above all in what he does in the former mode, and what he does there is only to be explained in terms of a realistic aesthetic that responds to the intensities created by living with the object or person the writer invents and develops. The larger framing apparatus has the air of being functional and enabling, and in some ways doesn't so much free the material as reify and distance it. The book actually succeeds, I suspect, on the level of its sheer impurity. Fowles is, in the end, an ethical novelist with a predilection for disguise; and he requires, clearly, many 'liberal' constituents in his novel which are not present in the formal wholeness of a novel by, say, Robbe-Grillet. His typical novel is perhaps a bridging enterprise, an aesthetic marriage of phrases of style. This may explain something of the oddity of *The Magus*, a rather more mysterious and I think commanding novel than *The French Lieutenant's Woman*, and therefore an excellent place to look at Fowles's tactics—and his distinction—in more detail.

2

The novelist today may feel himself under a growing need to present his fictions as fictive—because the problems of presenting the structure of a novel as authoritative or somehow co-equal with life are intensified and obscured where there are no communal myths or ethics; because in an age of prolix contingencies the novelist is hard put to it to give them in any necessary order. This self-consciousness he may represent by manifesting the unreality or the oddity of his own role as narrator; or he may delegate the function by creating the figure of a substitute artist who raises the problem. A number of modern fictions have therefore turned to the strategy of ambiguous revelation; there is within them a substitute author-figure who is both powerful and deceptive, the bearer of some supra-rational wisdom which he holds in quizzical status. The psychopomp figures of Iris Murdoch's early novels—Hugo Belfounder, Mischa Fox, Honor Klein—with their ambiguous philosophical or anthropological charisma, are much of this kind: voices of forces beyond and outside the familiar orders of society and its states of mind, possessors of ambiguous myths that yet contain both truth and falsehood. And this, it seems to me, is a primary premise of *The Magus*, a book in which a myth, a myth about consciousness and history, is offered to us, shown in its psychic power, yet questioned in its status—and the question touches the status of all fictions, including that of the novel we are reading. Fictions are not existence; hence an element of the charlatan exists in the novelist's own role. To some extent, then, *The Magus* is concerned with the familiar obsessions of modernism—with the hope that beyond the ordinary, contingent, and disillusioned world of real life there lies a meaning of fullness, balance, and regard for mystery, and the suspicion that this transcendent hope is one beyond life and time and therefore can only be a translucent, literary image. But it is also very much aware of the unsatisfactoriness of asserting simply a formal salvation, hope of redemption through an aesthetic unity. And Fowles does indeed manage to create the sense that his structures and obsessions are not borrowed properties but fulfil a logical need to consider how the imagination now may design, shape, and give meaning to the world.

The Magus begins in a world of familiar day-to-day reality; it shifts into a universe of theatrical mysteries; and it finally returns us to the day-to-day world conscious that the mysteries are not simply a theatrical extravaganza but a species of vision about our own needs and desires. Fowles does this by creating around his central character and first-person narrator, Nicholas Urfe, a vast and complicated psychodrama enacted, at great and improbable expense, for his benefit. Urfe is a young man recently down from Oxford; a rationalist, an agnostic, and a hedonist, he also possesses poetic ambitions and a strong feeling of 'inauthenticity'. In London, unsure what to do with his future, he meets and begins living with an Australian girl named Alison. Nicholas, through the British Council, gets a post as schoolmaster on a Greek island, Phraxos, and sees this in a familiar philhellenic way as a possible route to a fuller life. It becomes clear that Alison has fallen in love with him, but Nicholas really doesn't want the entanglement and is indeed incapable of adjusting to it; he goes off to Greece with vague feelings of having won an emotional victory over her. But once he gets there and begins his job, sensations of isolated despair, deeper convictions of inauthenticity, and an increased knowledge of the deathly element within him bring him to the brink of suicide. But he stops short, insufficiently 'authentic' even for self-murder, and resigns himself to a condition of *mauvaise foi*.

Up to this point, the story, though well-presented, is a 'conventional' modern tale. But the mood of the book now changes, and another kind of action starts to develop. Nicholas comes across a villa in another part of the island and meets his Prospero figure—Maurice Conchis, its owner, reputed to have been a collaborator with the Germans and to have some strange influence over the school. At his villa, Conchis is surrounded by magnificent, if sometimes obscene, *objets d'art*; he has the air of possessing a pleasured and privileged view of the world; and his life seems vaguely to contain meanings somehow related to Nicholas's fortunes. On invitation, Urfe starts to spend most of his weekends at the villa. Gradually the mysteries he encounters there take on a sequential form; they become a vast and continuing drama. First Conchis introduces Urfe to pamphlets on science and witchcraft; he also begins telling stories about his own life which move through some of the basic historical events of the century—its changes in style and thought, its two world wars. At the same time these events suddenly start to be mysteriously recreated, first at a distance from Nicholas, then, more and more, around him, involving him and threatening him. A girl called Lily, a figure from Conchis's past life supposedly dead during the First World War, appears on the scene. Nicholas, trying to penetrate rationalistically to the truth about these fantasies, starts to provide himself with an explanation—'Lily' is actually, as she reveals, an actress named Julie. But now that the masques begin to interlock with real life, what to begin with was a spectacle becomes a web around him.

Nicholas tries to break away from his involvement by going off to Athens, where he meets Alison again. But this is no solution; he rejects Alison for Lily-Julie, and does so basically because of the latter's role as an Edwardian girl, for she lies somewhere beyond the sexual directness of the 'androgynous twentieth-century mind'. (The same sort of trans-historical encounter appears, in reverse, as the main theme of *The French Lieutenant's Woman*, in the person of the 'modernized' Sarah Woodruff.) When Nicholas gets back to the island again, he is much more involved in the power of the mysteries and begins to see a line through them; they are a kind of fable of the action of the godless twentieth-century mind, and also provide a field of symbols and insights that might indeed give it meaning. Shortly after this, Conchis reaches the culmination of his own story—his experiences with the Germans on the island during the Second World War. The Germans order him to kill three resistance fighters; if he does not, he and eighty hostages from the island will be killed. Conchis refuses, in a vision of freedom— a modern freedom which is 'beyond morality' but which 'sprang out of the very essence of things—that comprehended all, the freedom to do all, and stood against only one thing—the prohibition not to do all.' This idea of freedom is ambiguously left, as a force of transcendence and a power of destruction; it is placed in the modern world and the history of Europe; it is the theme of the fables that have gone before.

This seems to mark the end of the mysteries. The masques cease; the party appears to conclude. And Urfe claims Julie, whom he believes loves him. But the final movement of the story is concerned with the complete penetration of all that has gone before into Nicholas's own life and his 'real' world. Urfe is carried off as a prisoner to the Greek mainland and undergoes a mock-trial. The masque-makers have now emerged with disguises from myth and classical legend and cease to be figures from Conchis's personal history. Then in the course of the trial they take on new roles—they reveal themselves as social psychologists, conducting a vast experiment on Urfe, whose life they know in full detail and document in the language of neo-science. In a magnificent set-piece scene, Urfe is taunted with all his psychic weaknesses and portrayed by his tormentors as a characteristic and typically distorted personality type of the modern world—autoerotic, autopsychotic, repetitiously hostile, dependent on aggressive sexual relationships. A parodied withdrawal-therapy follows. Urfe is made to watch as Julie is shown to him in a pornographic film; then she makes love to a Negro in his presence. After all this, he is told by Conchis that he is now 'elect'—he is an initiate into the cruelty of freedom.

But Urfe, though released, is hardly set free of the web that has been built up around him. After being dismissed from his job, he goes to Athens and there sees Alison, who is also mysteriously assimilated into the Conchis world. So are most of his friends and acquaintances, most of his life; no individual is reliably out in the world of unmanipulated reality, and no past event in his life is free from intrusion. In the final scene of the book, Urfe is led back to Alison, who has been escaping him. The question remains, is she still within the world of the plot, or is she free of it? And has it been a plot against him, or a plot *for* him— a plot to lead him to wisdom? The final pages are ambiguous; we do not know whether Urfe has been saved or damned by his experiences, whether the mysterious powers have withdrawn or remain in his life, whether he accepts Alison or ends the novel in renewed isolation. Above all we are left doubtful about whether the masques and mysteries, which have been given such fictional density as an experience, are a diabolic trap or a species of recovery and revelation.

3

The Magus is generically a mythic novel or perhaps rather a romance, and this kind of fiction of the mysterious web has a long and honourable ancestry. Indeed, Fowles himself draws on a number of significant literary allusions. Conchis is Prospero, magician, psychopomp—the mysterious creator of mysteries, the symbolist of the world of the unseen, the agent of the supernatural, the psychic force that can lead us through to a new version of reality. He is a splendid impresario, rather like the figure of the author who appears, in his lavishly embroidered summer waistcoat, to spy on the agents of *The French Lieutenant's Woman*. But Fowles deals with him in an ambiguous way, though in a way not unfamiliar in much modern fiction. An obvious comparison can be made to Iris Murdoch, some of whose novels—*A Severed Head*, *The Unicorn*, and others—involve a mythic universe in which mystery suggests the problems of a lost order or structure not available in liberal-conventional notions of reality. Like Iris Murdoch, Fowles is clearly concerned not simply with mystery for its own sake, or the vague evocation of powers undreamt of in our philosophy, but with forces and structures that underlie our rational being, socio-psychic forces that are not readily registered in the fiction of documentary modes. In Iris Murdoch it is, I think, fairly evident that we are invited 'out' of society in order to see the powers which under-pin it, powers which presume new relationships and new risks with selfhood that must by necessity be explored. The problem of the mode is that it characteristically involves a high degree of fictional faking, and there is a strong temptation for the novelist to create a sense of mystery and special insight which is no more than a numinously dramatic satisfaction, a building up of myth for its own splendid sake. Fowles obviously piles on the suspense by making Urfe at times less aware of what has to be going on than he should be, and the elaborate forgeries and ruses employed by Conchis require a kind of good luck to sustain the illusion which Fowles as novelist always grants.

Fowles's way of working the story is to make his reader identify with Urfe and so, to a considerable extent, to sustain his desire for a rational explanation, an unmasking of what Conchis calls his 'god-game'. Urfe belongs to the world of the real and ordinary, and he is a natural violator of myths; because he is cautious of being drawn into illusion the reader moves in with him when he does yield. In Urfe, then, Fowles catches many instincts, tones, obsessions and above all ambi-guities in our culture—its distrust of myth, its sense of the validity of the real and familiar world, its suspicion of revelation and authority, yet also its desire for metaphor, its wish to transcend the environment which gives only a literal meaning, its search for density of being. All these things in Urfe—together with his appreciation of the more spacious relationships of the past, his sense of the possibility of being a limited psychic type—make him available as a neophyte for the world for which Conchis stands. But that world itself is caught equally well and with a like density and ambiguity. Conchis is on the one hand the higher rationalist, who comprehends all that Urfe knows and is one jump ahead—he unmasks the desire to unmask, he historic-ally or psychologically locates the sentiments and fears amid which Urfe lives and finally does so in a language he understands. His 'god-game' is not only an exercise in timeless and traditional hermetic symbolism; it is also a masque and myth about contemporary history. He thus provides a structure for the comprehension of Urfe's world, though it is uncertain whether Urfe does or can accept it. His dark but ultimate wisdom—the wisdom of serene endurance, the wisdom of the archaic smile that holds experience complete and stands above it, and which is vouchsafed to Alison in the final scene—is enacted within the terms of modern experience. It has the prophetic pull of Honor Klein's dark wisdom in *A Severed Head*, and the same sense that it is a knowledge beyond the novel's capacity to register; only an image will do. The primary action is conducted in relation to a hero less far along life's path; and, as with *A Severed Head*, the rationalistic underpinning of day-to-day life, with its casual sexual relationships and its vague codes of personal relations, is left behind, yet without our knowing clearly what is put in its place.

But Conchis is of course not only the wise magician but also the faker, the sleight-of-hand artist enabled by his wealth, his gift of persuasion, and his mysterious authority to dominate and transform his environment. As Fowles's epigraph to the book suggests, the Magus is both the mountebank and, in the world of Tarot symbolism, the magician who operates the cards. The duplicity of role is structural to the book, though of course it also leaves it in an insoluble ambiguity: can a trick which reveals so much and costs so much in goods and spirit really be only a trick? And what, apart from fictive purposes, would be its point? Fowles leaves the interpretation open. If Conchis could be destroyed by Urfe's rational search, he would be nothing; in fact, he always dominates Urfe's world of 'reality' as well as the fantasy world which at first is all Urfe credits him with creating. But if he were the total mystic, his wisdom would have to be rare indeed; he would have to provide a total version of the modern world. What in fact he serves to do is to draw us towards transcendental images which lead us outside the world, yet create a sense that there is a density missing from the rational view of experience. It is evident, at the end—when it seems the watching eyes are withdrawn, the theatre in which Urfe has so long conducted his actions has disappeared, when he feels at once escape and loss of 'their' interest—that Urfe is the man in the Platonic myth of the cave in a modern variant: the man who has seen the real and then returned to life. The powers that he has seen are not, however, only those of art in its sense of an observed theatrical drama; they are those of art seen as psychic revelation. The dilemma it concludes with—that of how the orders and symbols which transcend life but also reveal and order it can really be mingled with it—is the dilemma of the artist himself, and it is in this sense that the book is a self-conscious inquiry into its own structure.

4

So of course the real Magus in the novel is the novelist himself. The creation of myth in our modern employment of language is itself a precarious exercise. We use language to explore contingent reality and not to create systematic and numinous orders. But the rationalistic use of language (here roughly associated with Urfe) implies no logic, no structural unity. For realism and rationalism, our basic ways of making discourse, are a-mythic species of description; it is in this sense that we live in an age of No-Style. Fowles's purpose in the novel is therefore to create a context of illusion and a language of illusion which has the capacity to go beyond theatrical play and display and actually create structural myths. This, by confronting and connecting the world of rationalism and the world of illusion, feeding the former into the latter and then withdrawing it in its incompleteness, he does. Urfe's dilemma is at the beginning of the book that of loss of structure, and this he knows; that part of him which is the poet, the lover, and the man seeking a meaningful history of his age, in order that he might have an identity and an authenticity, seeks and values the Magus. And the Magus, whatever his deceptions, provides precisely that—a structure for feeling art, and history, which makes possible not only a fantastic world beyond 'reality' but art itself. In order to create this awareness, Fowles has in the book effectively to create another language or at least another order of notation. To do that, a large part of the action of the book has to develop in a world of feigning, convention, stylization, which we historically associate with high art, art as play and display. At one point in the action, Conchis makes a comment about novels: they are, he says, artefacts that make inferior orders. Fowles feeds the literal events of his novel into the hands of the myth-makers he has created within it, and so is able to create a sense of a higher artefact. But this of course leads him into a consciousness of the fictiveness of the enterprise; and if on the one hand he is able to make the shift from illusory theatricals to a suggestion of a more binding structure for modern experience, he must also sustain the fictiveness of that structure. It is in accomplishing this delicate balance, I think, that the success of the book lies—whatever its local failures. In an age of No-Style, this sort of painstaking yet finally questioned mythography is about as far as the novel can go; and this, I think, is the artistic encounter that must finally interest us in the book. It involves, that is, a real encounter between modern man and art, and does justice to the dilemmas of both. Fowles, then, not only registers the fictiveness of fiction, the spuriousness of structure, but also its inevitable claim and its psychic urgency, and he does this against modern history. In doing that, he shifts the resources of the current English novel in a significant way, and so manages to suggest the power fiction may still retain, to create fresh and inquisitive new alignments of experience.

TOWARDS A POETICS OF THE NOVEL

PART FIVE

TOWARDS A POETICS OF
THE NOVEL

XVII

The Novel and Its Poetics

something happened yes
Samuel Beckett, *How It is*

The study of the novel has become one of the great growth industries of modern criticism. Fiction has taken on enormous importance in literary study; in recent years many of the major reputations in the modern novel have been secured, a clearer consensus has emerged about the novelists of the past, and an implicit—increasingly an explicit—contemporary aesthetics has developed for discussion of the form. The debate began slowly and, though among practitioners of fiction a rich and powerful discourse had been elaborated by the turn of the century, it took a long time—much longer than for the equivalent reappraisal in poetry—for this to penetrate into general criticism. The delay has had significant consequences for that criticism, and has something to do with a certain disarray in it. For the modern aesthetics based on poetry made literary language, its symbol-making and tension-making power, the great object of attention; and it characteristically saw works of art as total symbolic objects, 'spatial' forms, single concrete wholes which could not be changed in any detail without changing total meaning. It was a view best ascertained if the object of critical attention was the short or lyric poem; and indeed (as I have shown earlier in this book) many of the most familiar contemporary critical assumptions are founded on the working of that exemplary object. New Criticism in particular went in this direction; the New Critical disposition has been easiest with intensely concentrated works, lacking directly represented characters or anything resembling a narrative line, and has tended to see works of literature as closed systems. Its disposition is anti-causal or solipsistic, concerned primarily with a single unit of art—the poem—seen independently of its creator or reader in its only ascertainable form: words on the page. This primary unit it has usually studied in terms of the methods by which it secures verbal coherence—processes of repetition and contrast in the use of language (hence 'imagery', 'theme', 'tone', 'tension', 'paradox'), these being usually taken as parts of a whole whose nature is a maximum realization of that language. A work does not imitate types in general nature; the theory is not neo-classic. It does not spring from the creative power's intense awarenesses of and responses to the vital springs in things: it is not romantic. The view is rather neo-symbolist and eminently a notion of language: it holds that language itself can, by generating tensions and energies, transform specified instances into a free-standing form, a concrete universal. My concern here is with the way in which this now generalized aesthetics affects, enlarges, and limits the possibility of an adequate poetics—by which I mean a generalized but not finalized account—of the novel form; I also want to make some proposals for a broader view.[1]

I

Certain main assumptions of this generalized aesthetic, which has been powerful with us, are these: (1) works of art are autotelic discourse, concrete representations in heightened, literary, non-discursive language of an experience which criticism can do no more than abstract, clumsily, from the complete work; (2) because works of art exist in this way, and contain tightly all the matter necessary for their appreciation and elucidation, we should be less interested in their structure than in the over-all texture and the modes of linguistic unity; (3) literary language being the distinctive aspect of a work, procedures which distinguish that language from other forms of language are a crucial part of the critical accounting; (4) criticism is hence not conceived as a means of reference to objects imitated by literature, and will find no inherent universals in the external world, only in the metaphoric or symbolizing action of language itself; hence 'content'

[1] This essay was originally written to initiate a new series called 'Towards a Poetics of Fiction', and begin an extended debate, in the magazine *Novel: A Forum of Fiction*. It appeared there in the first issue, for Fall 1967. In revising the text for this volume I have tried not to change it too greatly, since it now appears to have a place in controversy: see, for example, David Lodge's comments on it, originally the subsequent article in the same series, as collected in his *The Novelist at the Crossroads* (1971).

must be subsumed into 'form' and seen as a species of verbal or thematic recurrence. The deduction from this is that, on grounds of direct critical logic, criticism must concern itself with devices of presentation rather than representation. The logic has rightly been applied to criticism of fiction, as to longer poems, and in many respects and with regard to many novelists proved highly fruitful. The New Critics sometimes distinguished poetic from prose language categorically, proposing a lower mode for the novel; but this was always an uneasy distinction, and in his book *Language of Fiction* (1966) David Lodge argues clearly and firmly that the attributes applied by New Criticism to poetic language must apply to prose language in fiction as well, since novels, whatever their differences in dimension, must be regarded as autotelic discourses. The fact is that, though Lodge vastly sharpens and clarifies the argument, many such assumptions about the unitary nature of the work of art, the relation of form to content, have been long adapted to the study of some fiction; Lodge shows that they should be adapted to all, including highly realistic fiction. But the two main consequences of this fact have seemed until recently to be that (1) much criticism of fiction has a submerged symbolist aesthetic behind it, and (2) a large amount of fictional criticism has devoted itself, often in vulgarized form, to finding stylistic or verbal unities, symbols or motifs, in literary matter more discursive than most poetry and harder to account for in this way.

A further consequence of the latter point is that, since novels do have an enhanced referential dimension, which such criticism risks leaving unsubsumed, it has tended to see a subtext of representation beneath the process of presentation. The compositional scale of fiction must be one appropriate to the complexity of life; hence, for example, the effort of essays like Mark Schorer's 'Technique as Discovery' (1948) to capture as much for rhetoric and composition as can be got without entirely sacrificing the mimetic or representational dimension. But the presence of an unreconciled element—that of fiction's empiricism, its attention to workaday reality—is apt to leave the case incomplete, to produce division within the poetics. An important compensatory element has, however, been given by those critics who have stressed the referential quality of fiction, its closeness to life. Ian Watt in *The Rise of the Novel* (1957) advances an argument of this kind, finding the distinctive nature of the novel in, precisely, its empirical disregard of traditional conventions, structures, completenesses of form. Other critics have carried that approach further by stressing that what most typifies fiction is what Henry James would call its 'illustrative' nature— its singular attentiveness to life, its empirical curiosity, its instinct for the luminous rendering of the particular, its realism. An important endeavour which attempts to draw together realism and form is Barbara Hardy's *The Appropriate Form* (1964), which holds that the ideal design of the novel is a work like *Anna Karenina*, which is 'an assertion of dogma in an undogmatic form, the last pulse of a slow and irregular rhythm which is a faithful record of the abrupt, the difficult, the inconclusive.' Another is F. R. Leavis's *The Great Tradition* (1948), which holds that 'an unusually developed interest in life', a humane and moral concern, is central to fictional seriousness. But the problem with such weights and stresses is that they emphasize a particular kind and phase of fiction and perhaps even particular features in that; and also that where there are technically oblique modes of representation these are apt to be discounted.

These two views of fiction, the two most familiar views, diverge in a variety of respects, and perhaps are most effective when dealing with particular traditions in fiction which are most consistent with their own general account. What they share is an unwillingness to give an eclectic account of the novel species as a type. The neo-symbolist view, which stresses the verbal proceeding, has difficulty in suggesting features which make novels recognizably novels; the realistic view, which stresses fiction's special degree of interest in life, tends to see novels as an a-generic genre. Yet full description of the novel is impossible if we do concentrate only on those characteristics which make for verbal unity, or alternatively on those which make for specificity and solidity of specification. Both views do have an implicit poetics—one symbolist, one realist—which can only lead to radically different critical emphases and preferences; and that of itself must create the desire for a more inclusive typology.

2

What seems needed is an approach to fiction concerning itself with the special complexities of novels, and the distinctive kinds of artifice and imitation employed in their creation. This we can only achieve by recognizing that the novel is not a traditional literary genre, like tragedy or comedy, but a general, varied, categorically distinctive form like poetry and drama, yet a form which, though recognizable to the writer when he writes one and to readers when they read one, is far less definable than poetry and drama. Hence no generic theory can let us define closely the kind of matter it is likely to imitate, or the kind of formal mode it will use, nor the kind of effect it is likely to produce; we cannot even clearly define its diction or mode of presentation, as we can poetry and drama. Novels are usually presented to us in prose as bound books for private reading; they are fictive and autotelic; but there is no one kind of matter they contain or effect they produce. Any attempt at generic classification is hence likely to end up with some splendid monstrosity of definition, like Henry Fielding's 'comic epic poem in prose'. Yet, though a progressive and cumulative scepticism seems very characteristic of fiction, to regard each new novel as utterly novel, and to conclude from this that an empirical rendering of experience is the characteristic feature of the species, is no more satisfactory. From the point of view of a poetics, then, a more profitable approach is surely to propose that novels are distinguishable and have much in common with each other, even over an extended chronological period; that while they have no *typical* action (as does tragedy), there are typical compositional problems, recurrent practices, definable options; and that these characteristics are particular derivatives of their fictive nature, their character as prose, and their lenght, or epic dimension.

A novel is a fictional prose discourse which is, in Aristotle's terms, 'necessarily of a certain magnitude'. The problems of magnitude, and hence of the necessary range of the novel, the difficulties and potentials arising from what E. K. Brown noted, the reader's 'inability to possess a novel as a picture or a lyric can be possessed',[1] are surely fundamental; they determine the essential conditions of engagement with fiction, whether we are writers or readers. They require larger terms than many critics possess for talking about the temporal and spatial extension of novels, their likeness to history, the range and fullness of the composed worlds they explore. As for the writer, they commit him to a certain scale of attention, an epical dimension in writing; as Henry Fielding notes, the novel is a form whose action is 'much more extended and comprehensive' than that of tragedy, contains 'a much larger circle of incidents', and introduces 'a great variety of characters'. The prose medium also, of course, significantly determines the matter. Prose,

[1] E. K. Brown, *Rhythm in the Novel* (Toronto, 1950), 33.

compared with poetry, has an accentuated referential dimension; it is the normal instrument of discursive communication, and the primary mode of narration and verification. In compositional terms, an extended piece of prose will use forms of discursiveness and persuasion impossible in poetry, have a different tonal, structural, and cultural address to its reader, and will persuade at a different pace in a different mode and with very different registers, formal and cultural. The result is difficulty of another species from that of poetry: so that, for example, novels often involve extremely varied uses of language, various potentially intersecting structures of it (from reportage to extreme fabulation, looseness to wholeness), and very mixed and very complex large-scale or over-all rhetorical strategies, of the kind so well explored in Wayne Booth's *The Rhetoric of Fiction* (1961). As for the fictive nature of novels, this is the feature it shares with all other invented discourse, but a finer definition would need to distinguish how fiction is conditioned by an extremely verificatious verbal form, prose, and what sort of fictions are appropriate to this form on this scale. In other words, there are distinguishable matters for invention *appropriate* to this scale and mode of discourse, such as to make a writer feel that he will develop his insight, germ, or matter in this medium and not in another, or condition the decision once perhaps more abstractly made. The matter is typically events and characters, presented of course by verbal means, shown in extended interaction. In sum, the novel is a complex structure by virtue of its scale, prose character, and matter: it is more extended than most poems, deals with a larger range of life (this being a definitional statement, not a moral judgement), appeals to the reader through a broader variety of approaches, has a different relationship to working language, and above all states its character and intentions and conventions with less immediate clarity and a greater degree of gradual, worked, and in this sense empirical persuasion. Hence novels will tend to be more discursive, and more contingent, than poetry; and their stronger referential dimension will be shown not only by attentiveness to people as they talk, think, and act, places as they look, institutions as they work, but also to large processes of human interaction as they occur over a long chronological span, a large area of space, a large sector of society.

The structural principles deriving from these features are various; and they cannot be clearly and closely defined in terms of a subject-matter. Although there is no necessary kind of action, either in substance or shape, as in tragedy or comedy, there are often structures comparable to those of comedy according to neo-classical definition— a plot where fortune intersects with misfortune, a character range wide in classes and social types, the social and moral worlds discordant, though moving perhaps towards resolution. Hence there is no necessary kind of hero, though there usually is a central experiencer, hero or heroine. But if there is not a necessary structure, there are things of which a fictional structure must almost necessarily consist—basically a chain of interlinked events unified by persuasive discourse and by coherencies arising both from materials in life and features of language, which take on for the author a character of interconnectedness and thus synthesize those elements sometimes distinguished as a 'material', a 'style', and a 'vision'. We cannot provide an outright typology for such a structure, but we can suggest related typologies, as in the writing of history, or science, or in other forms of modal address to experience and the culture. And we can, and need to, seek empirical means for describing what is predictably present in any novel. It seems that any effective account of such structures—structures thought of not as prior typologies but as compositional constructs arising from mimetic and rhetorical sources—must be concerned both with discourse, as it occurs in the given case, and that which in life determines and organizes an author's interest in such discoursing. If we say that the character of a work of fiction is primarily verbal, a linguistic effect, we will tend to be committed to questions about the role of language, and find the unity and order of the work in it; if we say that the nature of the novel is primarily to render, make vivid, give a sense of life as lived, we may be primarily involved in judgements about life and society, and find order and unity lying in a typology of the world. But if we say that the novel is determined by conditions both within the medium itself and outside it in life, we ought to be able to move freely between language and life, and find order in the kind of working a novel must have, that a given novel *has* had, in achieving its persuasive ends. And thus we may be able to allow for the book's referential dimension as an account of life, its rhetorical dimension as a species of language, its sociological dimension as an exploration and crystallization of a cultural situation, its philosophical dimension as a mode of thought, its stylistic dimension as a species of formed cultural gesture, and its psychological or mythic dimension as an exploration of individual or broadly social psychic experience.

3

I should make it clear that I do not wish to disparage, reject, or underplay stylistic concerns, especially those analyses of verbal and rhetorical procedures that have done so much to enlarge our comprehension of the workings of fiction and to dissipate many illogicalities. My appreciation is tempered only by the way this has made us suspicious of considering at all the referential dimension of literature. A quiver of unease comes to us when we sit down to talk about a novel and use terms like 'plot', 'character', or 'incident'—mimetic terms imposed on what we know as a block of words, apparently arising from some historically distant and more innocent terminology. Hence we tend to suppose that, if we can show how an imagery of cash and legality runs through a Jane Austen novel, a whiteness–blackness opposition through *Moby-Dick*, we have rendered more of the book's real being than by showing how it deals with a society, with dispositions of character and relationship, and so creates a unified social and moral world and an attitude to it which is steadily worked from page to page to produce certain sympathes, responses, emotions, and feelings of coherence, logic, and probability. If we are interested in such things, we may regard them as more diffuse versions of the essentially linguistic relationship words create between writer and reader. But it is worth considering that most writers appear to presume that they communicate not words alone, but *through* words: 'I have never heard of a novelist so Platonic', says George P. Elliott, 'that for him there was for *this* novel a preordained and perfect arrangement of words which it was his art to discover.'[1] A writer is, I suppose, always conscious that he is mediating verbally a devised succession of events; and that the organization of those events, their relations one to another, their selection and disposition, are primary to his task as a writer, and utterly crucial to the success and effect of the work. And most writers would, I think, consider that they are making verbal approaches to a reader which would engage him with a devised reality they both might know, and that the working out of the relationships with that reader, so that he might have expectations and values, sympathies and

[1] George P. Elliott, 'The Person of the Maker', in *Experience in the Novel*, ed. Roy Harvey Pearce (New York and London, 1968).

repulsions, appropriate to that reality, is an essential part of creation.[1] We may then take the writer's language as an enabling feature in composition, one of a variety of elements he can dispose of in making a work (so that, for example, he may employ rhetorical modes, tones, and devices quite differently from book to book). We ourselves have nothing but the language; still, if we assume this as a possible status for it, we are likely to find the author's signature not simply in stylistics, but also in his urging on us, through verbal means, a particular complex matter verbally achieved in this way.

To provide an adequate account of the structure of fiction, then, I propose that we must honour the fundamental recognition of modern criticism, that all things in a fiction are mediated through words, and yet allow ourselves to consider that certain things can be held logically and temporally antecedent to those words, as a matter which the words mediate.[2] We cannot isolate these as a species of prior content seeking an appropriate form—though this is often the posture adopted by the novelist in telling the story, in organizing the sense of antece-dence *within* his own narration. The important fact for critical purposes is that the sense of a thing 'told' can only be given meaning in terms of all sorts of ideas, insights, prior obligations, and compositional commit-ments that are quite other than simple 'content', or what a novelist, negotiating his own narrative position within a work, might call 'my story'. What we might look at are those processes of inventing or making a world, with the dynamics by which that world is shown and evaluated by forms of rendering and distancing, ordering and urging, which are involved in the act of fictional creation and constitute some of the largest negotiations performed in it. The problem with inquiry into such matters is that, though we accept such things as necessary conditions of fictional creation, there is no satisfactory method of

[1] On this relationship between writer and reader, and the complex variables involved in it, see Walker Gibson, 'Authors, Speakers, Readers, and Mock Readers', in *College English*, XI (1950), and Wayne Booth, *The Rhetoric of Fiction* (Chicago, 1961). Clearly these spread beyond the compositional to the socio-logical, and as such affect not only the tone of the presentation but the entire matter presented, the social and linguistic world as one negotiable whole.

[2] This is the point David Lodge particularly disputes; see *The Novelist at the Crossroads*, 55–68. I have slightly moderated my terminology here; but my emphasis stays. I might add that another interesting essay in Lodge's book, 'Choice and Chance in Literary Composition: A Self-Analysis', offers a very good instance of the sort of understanding I am commending.

ascertaining what they are save *through* the words which finally express them. Yet our successful reading of those words, our capacity to organize them, involves our hypothesizing the sort of decisions of relevance, judgements, and insights that have been taken to create a material so made and organized. Thus a just object of attention—assuming that the task of criticism is an adequate and full response to a text, not the creation of an outward typology which is then applied to it, an activity therefore of the middle ground—is, not the projection of some matter or action prior to the writing, which the writing either copies or fleshes out, but a steady appreciation of the way in which a writer has shaped and been shaped *by* his undertaking. If we project the situation back in Aristotelian terms, proposing a prior working out of the action in the writer's mind, which the compositional process then sets down, we surely must say that the action imitated exists for the writer simultaneously with that which has to be written (that which motivates and directs the compositional process) and that which is worked, achieved, realized in the writing. Any novelist will admit that the novel prefigured is not the same as the novel achieved, but that nonetheless the interaction between what is prefigured and the obligations of the achievement 'create' the novel. That is to say, a novel is inevitably determined by prior intentions and choices (the most crucial one being the choice of the novel as the right form), but the crucial selection, and rejection, lies in finding means of persuasion, articulable forms, compatible with those prior interests and with the conditions of the novel form itself as a particular species of working.

Thus we must avoid defining the structure of the novel as a prior typology; equally, though, we must avoid supposing that it is formed only by the aesthetic logic of literary form and structure, the neo-symbolist tendency. This means that we are wise to avoid looking for a prior action, a story to be told, but ought still to derive from the novel some sort of causative hypothesis, a unifying purposefulness which sets the aesthetic logic into action and perpetually keeps shaping it. Thus we may discover how the novelist limits, by formalizing, the total environment offered by life—creates a conditioned world with its own laws and probabilities, a world in which experience can only assume certain shapes, characters only assume certain dimensions, in order that 'structure' may exist. By this view, structure would be that devised chain of events and aesthetic purposes which, presented by narration, condition the successive choices, the weights and emphases, tones and angles, made not only sentence by sentence but paragraph by paragraph and chapter by chapter, and which constitute not only the narrated matter but the formative attitudes towards it. In other words, structure is the substantive myth of a novel which we can contemplate without regarding it as an utterly separable entity, for it is a compositional achievement, *this* action existing in *that* social and moral environment and *that* context of rhetorical effects. 'Structure' is, then, a plot-like compositional achievement: composition meaning the making of an action in a social-moral environment itself invented, as well as the rhetorical effects of point of view, tone, technique, which make it possible for the reader to position himself in relation to the gradually revealed events of that world, and so win gradual citizenship of it. Hence the arts of making should be seen not in the realm of style or rhetoric alone, but rather in the realm of persuasion, where the novelist undertakes so to shape and use the fictional transaction as to elicit, from himself and the reader, the highest sense of meaning, relevance, significance, of variation and richness, but also of concord and elegance, he can in a work of such magnitude.

Novelists tell, or narrate, a something; that something they invent; this is the procedural paradox of novels. It is one novelists manipulate, so that in the working of their text they will often articulately distinguish between the telling and the told, the exposition and the action, the means and the matter. The ideal of closing the gap has often been important in fiction, especially modern fiction, as in James's ideal of the 'self-expository thing'; even so James proposed, in his own thinking about fiction and his writing of it, a definite action and a telling of it, though one which he sought to bring to the maximum point of realization—all matter ought to emerge, he held, through 'the unfolding of the action itself—the action of which my story essentially consists and which of itself involves and achieves all presentation and explanation.'[1] In late years we have heard much of the disappearance of the narrator; but we still have narrative, and the manipulated use of the act of telling is one of the basic constituents of form and perspectivization in novels. One of the most familiar ways in which this manipulation occurs is the exploitation of the relation between antecedent and present, between the time-span of what is told and the time it takes to tell, between narrated time and narrational time, between

[1] *The Notebooks of Henry James*, ed. F. O. Matthiessen and K. B. Murdock (New York, 1961), 375.

matter attended to scenically and in detail and matter scanted or sketched. Thus a novelist will himself often propose a material temporally antecedent to his 'real' story, or what James would call his 'discriminated occasion' (as when Jane Austen makes logically antecedent to the narrative present of *Persuasion* the original act of persuasion from which the story arises). But there are other forms of antecedence than the temporal; a writer may propose that he has a 'true' story he knows and is now telling; he may propose that he has invented something and is now telling it; he may propose that he is discovering something which the act of writing is reporting; he may propose that the act of writing *is* the discovery.[1] Much modern fiction has attempted to close both the temporal and the mimetic gap by putting the material in the narrative present at the time of discovery; James, Proust, Virginia Woolf, and the *nouveaux romanciers* have all tried forms of this. The effect is to weaken in our eyes a belief in a preconceived sequence, which is what was often meant by 'plot' in literature. Yet it is precisely some such term that we need to restore to cope with the patent fact that in fiction we normally encounter a sequence of events made whole and significant by reference to the actions of persons in a knowable, temporally extended, internally coherent world, a world or set of events that is purposefully persuaded to us. It is in this sense I use the word 'structure': to mean not alone that sequence of events but the coherence elicited, that ordering and selecting process which confers on them significance and meaning.

Here it is best to have an example: I take Bernard Malamud's novel *The Fixer* (1966), since it is a clear case of a book, part realist, part modernist, which has a distinct and discernible story, more or less chronologically sequential, placed in historical time, yet is clearly not accounted for simply by defining that story. It is the story of Yakov

---

[1] The important notion that a novelist does have a prior *mythos* which, if not creatively antecedent, is at least strategically so, has always been central in fictional practice and in novel criticism. The Aristotelian word for 'plot' contains, in the original exposition, precisely these associations; it has been devalued in subsequent use, though critics like R. S. Crane have tried to recover it. Perhaps a fresher form of the point is to be found in Russian formalist criticism, which distinguishes between *fabula* and *sujet*: the former refers to a coherence of a causal-chronological kind which can be abstracted or hypothesized from the work; the latter to the particular arrangement of the finished working. These terms, alas, become 'plot' and 'story' in the translations in *Russian Formalist Criticism: Four Essays*, ed. Lee T. Lemon and Marion J. Reis (Lincoln, Nebr., 1965).

Bok, the fixer, who leaves his village in the Pale of Settlement in Nicholas II's Russia and journeys to the city of Kiev to find fortune. Befriended by a Gentile whom he helps, he obtains a job in a brick-yard, but in a part of the city forbidden to Jews. When a Gentile child is found stabbed to death in a cave, he is accused of ritual murder. Though the Investigating Magistrate becomes convinced of Bok's innocence, he is kept in prison by officials concerned to exploit anti-Semitic feeling for political ends. At last, when the pressure on his behalf mounts, he is committed for trial. Attempts are made to kill him; but the novel ends as he rides towards the court, his conscious-ness crowded with strange visions of vengeance and convictions of his political and racial identity. This is a perfectly coherent story, with indeed a factual source, and it contains, as good stories are supposed to, a development or act of inner growth, for Bok himself is shown as changing in awareness and so making a sense of his experiences, and on this, rather than an 'event', the book ends. Yet at the same time we recognize that the conditions which for Bok are essential are for the author optional; the life Bok makes sense of is the life that the author invents; when we see Bok regarding himself at the end of the novel not as a private man seeking to fulfil in the best way under adverse conditions his own personal hopes and destinies, but rather discovering himself as a symbolic figure in the world of history and politics, as in fact the Tsar's emblematic adversary and assassin, we see him learning a truth patent in the world Malamud, with whatever reference to historical, sociological, and political facts, has *made*. It is a world historically coherent, but it is also emotionally and intellectually coherent; we can show not only how Bok makes sense of it, but how Malamud does. In short, we can look at the events, their selection, their mode of presentation, their order, to consider not the status of Bok's view of himself and the world, but the means by which these events have been so organized that Bok's view of things can, perhaps *must*, arise. If we do this it is evident that the events and the organizing means are not neutral but chosen, and chosen as part of a total making in which creation of a very different kind—the creation of a sense of history, the creation of a moral discourse, the creation of a feeling about the way man lives and assesses himself in the universe—is an ongoing part of the artistic task.

It is not necessary to prove that Malamud thought of his 'story' first in order to suggest that his task was of this kind; the critic's concern is with the fulfilled creative process, not with its direct recreation. But what is clear is that Malamud has to invent, if Bok's development is to have any meaning, the eventful social and moral conditions of it; he must make a society, a moral life, a human lot. The society, that of Tsarist Russia, contains villages and cities, religious, legal, and political institutions, conflicts of value and life-style, these given in a significant order aligned by Bok's voyage from Jewish *shtetl* to Gentile city. The novelist has to create a probable moral and psychological universe; this he does by making Bok an intelligent man by virtue of his faith and reading, a man morally alive, concerned to assess, explore, test the human state. It is clearly part of his purpose to relate the two, and in some sense to force an encounter between the second and the first: between Bok's early belief that it is the task of a man to realize his worth and history, that 'web of events outside the personal' from which, Bok comes to believe, life is determined. The significant relation between these two things becomes for Bok the problem his own mind must face—and for Malamud the basic area within which his material must be significantly created, ordered, realized, and out of which many of his technical problems will arise. And though some of his work in this area will emerge close to the level of germination, other parts of it are likely to emerge as *ad hoc* decisions once the book is well under way. All of these matters—the line of events, the society in which they occur, the related psychology and intellect of the hero, the moral milieu in which they are possible, the thematic or motif-like elements or symbols of the novel—thus are likely to develop together as parts of a whole world which has to be made probable, kept in development, and effectively persuaded to us. And it is only in the light of such awarenesses, such considerations, that we can make much sense of certain decisions that, when isolated, we are likely to call Malamud's technique: his use, for example, of an opening scene in fact derived from the middle of the action; his decision to leave us in no doubt as to Bok's innocence; his variations on the third-person presentational mode (there are first-person and second-person passages which serve to intensify our identification with Bok at particular points and give him greater inwardness); his use of dream, memory, fantasy.

In short, to pass beyond Malamud's book to the more general question, many of the features criticism frequently tries to isolate— the novel's language, symbols, techniques, themes, plots—are only comprehensible in terms of the total compositional enterprise, and do not of themselves constitute it or serve as the one best basis for revealing its 'significance'. We need to think in terms of a synthesizing action, which frequently will emerge as a dynamic evolution of persons in society and reveal itself through a sequence of events which are not neutrally events but are conditioned by their organizational and tonal place. And since each novel is, for reasons already given, a unique conjunction of variables, not having a definable generic nature, we must be particularly attentive and responsive if we are to project our hypothesis about what the determining principles and concerns embodied in the structure might be.

4

Still, I think, our business is to do that, and that means we must try to comprehend the complex integration of matter and means, the importance of the created life of the novel as well as of its tactical existence as 'form'. I am arguing for a fuller sense of what has been composed—a sense that restores the importance of the evolving tale. In speaking of the hypothetical structure we must understand, therefore, I do not mean to say that we must remember that novels are stories told. There are writers who do begin with a clearly defined story in their heads, and then creatively try to discover the best means for eliciting it from themselves and passing it to others, by dramatization and selection, by finding apt causalities inside the tale and apt tones and modes outside it. But there are others who begin without such a clear notion of a tellable matter; the creative act for them may start much more intuitively, and arise from notions about the forms they want to shape, the impressions they want to convey (so Alain Robbe-Grillet's: 'No true creator starts off with an idea of his "meaning"; the writer's project is always more or less a project of form. A novel must *be* something, before it can begin to *mean* anything'). Any structural hypothesis must take account of the apparent form in which the creative intent arises; but of course the critic's business is to understand the nature of composition and to contemplate, as finished, the finished work, where the compositional means cease to be provisional or enabling and have become definitive, where the novelist's presence may be a rhetorical or strategic feature, where the narrator intervenes but the real novelist, a man perhaps somewhat less certain of the success of his book, has passed from sight. Then the critic's task is to move through the parts until he comprehends how, over the passage of a long text, they come to be whole. That means recreating, as books ask us to, the arduous energy which, through a long series of choices about matter and manner, about wholeness in life and in words, sentences and grammar, developing action and ordering of events, turning of angles and points of view, has made it so. Some of that energy is concealed; but we live with much of it, precisely because the act of reading a novel to make sense of it depends on seeking out, by conscious effort or intuition, its presence.

In most novels, the cohering or synthesizing process I call 'structure' will come out as a gradually discernible spine; the provisional orders and groupings we make as new readers will start to create it. We usually enter a fictional world as a foreign visitor, taking its life as if it were contingent but likely to have laws, conventions, manners, probabilities eventually graspable, responding to its people, who are apparently capable of dynamic action here, somewhat similarly. In this milieu, with these figures, we will move through an unfolding of fresh happenings or sensations whose order we presume significant; towards all we will acquire, from the discourse, an attitude, which will arise compositionally. For by virtue of the fact that such things must be unfolded in some sequence, this being a condition of literary art and especially of a form of 'magnitude', the writer must decide what matters to explore and what defer; and it is likely that he will proceed by first revealing matter significant enough to let the reader take up tenure in the novel's universe and comprehend its operational laws without disposing of matter which—perhaps because of its value in creating expectation or suspense, perhaps because of its intrinsic depth, perhaps because it is by nature consequential or eschatological— is capable of intensifying, distilling, or completing the action. There are novels, especially modern ones, where a partial divergence from these ways of proceeding occur. An obscuring of the sense of causality and probability may be part of the novelist's vision, as in some of Beckett. Any feeling of the significance of human action in a social community may be deliberately dissipated. In an attempt to violate predeterminate structure—prior story, sequential logic—systems of designed contin- gency, from a lyrical impressionism to a 'cut-up' or 'fold-in' method, may be explored. There are works, by Marc Saporta and B. S. Johnson, which attempt to take the Sternean ideal of divergence from necessary structure to its logical conclusion by breaking the book's spine and putting its sheets in a box for random shuffling. These are all disposable options within the fictional logic; they do not, of course, finally deny that logic, but in fact sharply elicit for us some of the primary conditions of all narrative; they remind us of the extent of the novel's typological range, of the extendability of the hypothesis-making faculty. In this sense our awareness of a novel's structure must arise *ad hoc*, as we presume it arises for the writer. Still, we can determine some of the matter open to variation; and we can, even in the most modernly speculative works, find patent instruction in the field of significant choices the novelist has at his disposal. But what is clear is that such choices once made do constitute decisive commitments; they form the compulsive milieu of the book. My wish is to stress their range: the breadth of the option which, so to speak, the writer by starting writing starts to close.

In any satisfying novel, then, we find ourselves moving with a language that shapes a world, with its own defined conditions and conventions, which may seem life-like and probable or remote and hypothetical, and which we will judge, estimate, and co-ordinate. In a complex way we will dispose and relate elements and parts to form a growing hypothesis about the total action or evolution of the work, grouping blocks of experience according to aesthetic and evaluative postures we are guided to by the text, which both reveals and conceals, commits itself but promises evolution. We make our way here by providing ourselves with provisional assessments and classifications, arising largely from our own relation to the author's compositional sense; for example, we assemble characters in relationships, groups, classes, estimate the status of certain values in relation to others, acquire a conditioned sense of relevance. In doing this, we are not engaged by 'life' as such, not committed only to realizing the vivacity of the familiar—though there are novels where reading like that is essential. But neither are we solely engaged with something that can be called strategic discourse, or form, or language, analyzable only as an image-system, a rhetoric, a semiological enterprise—though there are, again, novels where reading like that is essential. My point is that, while there is no single dynamic generically characteristic of novels, its main structural characteristics arise from its scale, narrative character, and compositional obligations; that this must be seen as a structure or action, one which involves persons and events in a closed, authorially conditioned world, in which inhere the principles, values, and attitudes by which they may be ordered, judged. To talk of this structural dimension, we need to be able to open up that closed world by asking questions about causation and effect, a procedure unfallacious if our questions are raised, and answered, from the cruces of the work. To do that is to elevate to prominence those choices, conscious or intuitive, every writer must constantly make, and to regard not only the discourse but the imitation as part of the matter to be persuaded. Thus, while we must regard novels as verbal constructs, which they inescapably are, we must see what is constructed not alone as a self-sustaining entity but a species of persuasion—the writer handling material for the reader to engage him properly in the world of this once-and-for-all work. And one point needs firm restatement: only if we have some such theory of structure, however empirical, are we likely to move near to a meaningful descriptive poetics of the novel.

INDEX

Aiken, Conrad, 184
Allen, Walter, 92 n.
Alvarez, A., 176
Amis, Kingsley, 143, 232; *I Like It Here*, 171; *Lucky Jim*, 177
Arlen, Michael, 89
Auerbach, Erich: *Mimesis*, 121-2, 124
Austen, Jane, 32, 35, 39, 55-78, 95, 143-4, 212-13, 215, 217, 282; *Emma*, 59-66, 68, 77; *Persuasion*, 67-78, 286

Balzac, Honoré de, 16
Barstow, Stan, 177
Barth, John, 21, 258
Barthes, Roland, 11, 262
Barzun, Jacques, 183
Bayley, John, 14, 17, 169 n.
Beach, Joseph Warren, 162 n.
Beckett, Samuel, 86, 170, 177, 181, 183, 228, 290; *Malone Dies*, 178; *Molloy*, 178 ; *Murphy*, 36; *The Unnamable*, 178
Beja, Morris, 124 n.
Bell, Clive, 125
Bennett, Arnold, 170
Bergonzi, Bernard: *The Situation of the Novel*, 3, 13, 14, 19, 26-7, 172-3
Bergson, Henri, 85, 123, 147-8, 158; *Le Rire*, 148
Bloomfield, Morton W., 9 n.
Booth, Wayne: *The Rhetoric of Fiction*, 9, 10, 280, 283 n.
Borges, Jorge Luis, 258
Braine, John, 192; *Room at the Top*, 177
Brecht, Bertolt: *Baal*, 84
Brontë, Charlotte, 16

Brontë, Emily, 16, 178; *Wuthering Heights*, 250
Brooke-Rose, Christine, 259
Brophy, Brigid, 43
Brown, E. K., 96 n., 279
Burgess, Anthony, 179
Burns, Alan, 179
Burroughs, William, 41, 173
Butler, Samuel, 92, 95
Butor, Michel, 22-4, 27
Byatt, A. S., 243 n.

Cape, Jonathan, 187, 189
Carens, James F., 156 n.
Cecil, Lord David, 96-7
Cervantes, Miguel de, 31, 143
Cleland, John: *Fanny Hill*, 41-54
Coleridge, S. T., 94
Connolly, Cyril, 176
Conrad, Joseph, 5, 7, 84-6, 92, 133-4, 141, 176; *Lord Jim*, 120; *The Secret Agent*, 162
Cooper, William, 133, 171; *Scenes from Provincial Life*, 177, 192-200.
Cox, C. B., 179 n., 215 n.
Crane, Hart, 183
Crane, R. S., 34 n., 67 n., 74-5, 286 n.
Crane, Stephen, 85, 133
Culley, Ann, 233 n.

Darwin, Charles, 85
Defoe, Daniel, 42-5; *Moll Flanders*, 43-5
Dennis, Nigel: *Cards of Identity*, 178
Dickens, Charles, 16, 35, 143, 169 n., 216-17, 228
Disraeli, Benjamin, 16
Donne, John, 53

Dostoevsky, Fyodor, 85, 121, 123, 209, 212
Durrell, Lawrence, 86, 177, 181–3; *The Alexandria Quartet*, 178
Dyson, A. E., 154, 179 n., 216 n.

Edel, Leon, 124 n.
Eliot, George, 14, 17, 81, 213, 217, 245; *Middlemarch*, 241
Eliot, T. S., 5, 89, 150 ; *The Waste Land*, 84
Elliott, George P., 282

Faulkner, William, 7, 121, 126, 176
Feaster, John, 233 n.
Fielding, Henry, 31–40, 43, 45, 58, 155, 170, 279; *Joseph Andrews*, 31; *Tom Jones*, 33, 39, 45, 65, 159, 249
Firbank, Ronald, 89, 155
Fitzgerald, F. Scott, 89, 120, 185, 206; *Tender Is the Night*, 184
Flaubert, Gustave, 7, 85, 138
Fontane, Theodor: *Der Stechlin*, 221
Ford, Ford Madox, 5–6, 85–6, 133–9; *The Good Soldier*, 134; *Parade's End*, 85, 134–8
Forster, E. M., 5–6, 33, 91–120, 130, 142–4, 215–16, 239; *Aspects of the Novel*, 8, 86, 93, 96, 109–10, 119; *Howards End*, 74, 91–109, 110–12, 134; *Marianne Thornton*, 93; *Maurice*, 92, 98; *A Passage to India*, 84–5, 89, 90, 91–8, 110–20, 122; *Two Cheers for Democracy*, 96
Fowler, Roger, 10 n.
Fowles, John, 256–71; *The Collector*, 260; *The French Lieutenant's Woman*, 10, 141, 180, 250, 256–8, 260, 262–3, 266–7; *The Magus*, 180, 224, 260–71
Frank, Joseph, 84 n., 142–3
Fraser, G. S., 243–4
Freud, Sigmund, 85–6, 123
Friedman, Alan: *The Turn of the Novel*, 14, 83, 119, 127 n., 141 n.
Friedman, Norman, 162 n.
Fry, Roger, 125, 127
Frye, Northrop, 143

Galsworthy, John: *The Forsyte Saga*, 219, 221
Garnett, Edward, 142
Genet, Jean, 41, 173
Gibson, Walker, 283 n.
Gide, André: *Les Faux-Monnayeurs*, 7
Gindin, James, 171 n.
Goffman, Erving, 224, 261
Gogol, Nikolai, 143, 155
Golding, William, 177; *Lord of the Flies*, 178
Gomme, Andor, 67 n.
Goncourt, Edmond and Jules, 21
Goode, John, 17 n.
Greenblatt, Stephen Jay, 156 n.
Greene, Graham, 86, 211
Grieg, Nordahl, 184

Hardy, Barbara, 17 n.; *The Appropriate Form*, 9, 278
Hardy, Thomas, 81
Harvey, W. J., 14; *Character and the Novel*, 9
Hawthorne, Nathaniel, 11–12, 56; *The House of the Seven Gables*, 12
Heller, Joseph, 173
Hemingway, Ernest, 134, 247
Hinde, Thomas, 177
Hoff, H, S. *see* Cooper, William
Howe, Irving, 176
Hoy, Cyrus, 99 n.
Hulme, T. E., 5
Huxley, Aldous, 89, 145, 151–3; *Antic Hay*, 90, 151; *Chrome Yellow*, 151–2; *Point Counter Point*, 151–3; *Those Barren Leaves*, 89, 151

Isherwood, Christopher, 86

James, Henry, 5–10, 12, 18, 55–6, 81–2, 84–6, 88, 92, 111, 121–3, 127, 133, 135, 141–2, 176, 235, 245, 249, 278, 285–6; *The Ambassadors*, 126; 'The Future of Fiction', 82; 'The New Novel', 5, 17; *The Portrait of a Lady*, 141, 250; *Roderick Hudson*, 82; *Washington Square*, 55
James, William, 85, 122–3

Jebb, Julian, 154
Johnson, B. S., 179, 259, 290; *Travelling People*, 178; *The Unfortunates*, 179
Joyce, James, 5, 7, 10, 84–6, 92, 119, 126–7, 130, 136, 149, 167, 169–70, 184, 228, 248; *Finnegans Wake*, 86, 126, 141; *A Portrait of the Artist as a Young Man*, 7, 124; *Ulysses*, 84–5, 89–90, 120–1, 141

Kafka, Franz, 15, 176
Karl, Frederick R., 171
Kellogg, Robert, 9
Kemp, Peter, 237 n.
Kermode, Frank, 11, 21, 89 n., 111, 233–4, 249; *The Sense of an Ending*, 9, 249 n.
Kettle, Arnold, 17 n.
Knight, Everett, 15–18

Laing, R. D., 178
Lawrence, D. H., 5, 7, 81–2, 85–9, 92, 106, 122, 126–7, 133, 153, 161, 176, 184; *Aaron's Rod*, 84; *Lady Chatterley's Lover*, 87, 89–90, 106, 163; *The Rainbow*, 123, 142; *Women in Love*, 120, 142
Leavis, F. R., 97–8, 278
Lemon, Lee T., 286 n.
Lessing, Doris: *The Habit of Loving*, 178; *The Golden Notebook*, 179
Levin, Harry, 14, 84
Lewis, Wyndham, 133, 144–50; *The Apes of God*, 85, 149; *The Childermass*, 85, 149; *Tarr*, 85, 146, 148–9; *The Wild Body*, 147
Lodge, David, 157, 179; *The British Museum Is Falling Down*, 179; *Language of Fiction*, 9, 277; *The Novelist at the Crossroads*, 174–5, 248 n., 276 n., 283 n.
Lowry, Malcolm, 177, 181–90; *Hear Us O Lord...*, 183–5, 188; *In Ballast to the White Sea*, 187, 189–90; *Lunar Caustic*, 187–8; *October Ferry to Gabriola*, 183, 188; *Selected Letters*, 182, 187, 189; *Ultramarine*, 186–7, 190; *Under the Volcano*, 178, 183–4, 186, 188, 190–1
Lubbock, Percy, 10, 86

MacCarthy, Desmond, 102
McConkey, James, 111 n.
Mailer, Norman, 20, 24, 173–4; *The Armies of the Night*, 20
Malamud, Bernard: *The Fixer*, 286–9
Mann, Thomas, 6, 96, 120–1, 127, 167, 176; *Buddenbrooks*, 221; *The Magic Mountain*, 84, 120
Mansfield, Katherine: *The Garden Party*, 84
Marinetti, F. T., 146
Markson, David, 189
Martin, Graham, 17 n.
Marx, Karl, 85, 184
Mauriac, François, 247–8
Melville, Herman, 35, 184; *Moby-Dick*, 282
Mercer, Peter, 10 n.
Meredith, George, 92
Miller, J. Hillis, 9 n., 17 n.
Mitchell, Julian, 174
Mizener, Arthur, 134 n.
Moore, G. E.: *Principia Ethica*, 102, 125
Moore, George, 85
Murdoch, Iris, 11, 14, 20, 172, 177–80, 193, 231–46, 259, 263, 264, 268; 'Against Dryness', 233–5; *The Red and the Green*, 236–8; *Sartre: Romantic Rationalist*, 234; *A Severed Head*, 237–9, 243, 246, 267, 269; *The Sovereignty of Good*, 234, 238–9; 'The Sublime and the Beautiful Revisited', 233–5, 239; *Under the Net*, 177, 231–4, 236, 240–46; *The Unicorn*, 240, 267

Nabokov, Vladimir, 258; *Ada*, 20
Nietzsche, Friedrich: *The Birth of Tragedy*, 147

O'Brien, Conor Cruise, 154 n.

O'Donnell, Donat, *see* O'Brien, Conor Cruise

O'Faolain, Sean, 154

Ortega y Gasset, José, 140, 142–3, 173, 189

Orwell, George, 86–7, 133

Pater, Walter, 128

Peacock, Thomas Love, 151

Pethick, Derek, 187

Poirier, Richard, 68, 76, 259; *A World Elsewhere*, 9, 56 n.

Popper, Karl, 93

Pound, Ezra, 5, 86, 146, 150; *Hugh Selwyn Mauberly*, 150

Powell, Anthony, 172, 211

Proust, Marcel, 7, 84, 95–6, 110, 121, 133, 136, 167, 176, 202, 286; *À la recherche du temps perdu*, 84, 123

Pynchon, Thomas, 173

Queneau, Raymond, 234

Quennell, Peter, 45 n.

Raban, Jonathan, 168 n.

Rabinovitz, Rubin, 171 n., 219 n.

Reis, Marion J., 286 n.

Richardson, Dorothy, 85; *Pilgrimage*, 123

Richardson, Samuel: *Clarissa*, 45; *Pamela*, 45

Rickword, C. H., 7, 86 n., 142 n.

Rilke, Rainer Maria, 84

Robbe-Grillet, Alain, 23, 173, 262–3, 289

Sade, Marquis de, 41, 51 n.

Salinger, J. D.: *Catcher in the Rye*, 189

Saporta, Marc, 290

Sartre, Jean-Paul, 11, 234

Scholes, Robert, 9, 174, 261; *The Fabulators*, 20, 240 n.

Schorer, Mark, 7, 134 n., 277

Scott-Kilvert, Ian, 216

Servotte, Herman, 228 n.

Shaw, Valerie, 215 n.

Sillitoe, Alan: *Saturday Night and Sunday Morning*, 177

Snow, C. P., 133, 201–10; *George Passant*, 208; *Last Things*, 203–5, 207–9; *The Search*, 206; *The Sleep of Reason*, 207–8; *Strangers and Brothers*, 202, 206, 208; *The Time of Hope*, 207–8

Spark, Muriel, 177–80, 247–55, 259; *The Comforters*, 252; *The Driver's Seat*, 249, 251–4; *Memento Mori*, 178, 255; *Not to Disturb*, 249–51; *The Public Image*, 224, 247–9, 251

Spender, Stephen, 171, 184

Spengler, Oswald, 85

Stein, Gertrude, 134, 149

Steiner, George, 22 n., 169 n.

Stern, J. P., 19

Sterne, Laurence, 31–2, 35–40, 43, 143–4; *Tristram Shandy*, 35–9, 143

Stone, Wilfred, 111 n.

Storey, David: *Radcliffe*, 178; *This Sporting Life*, 177

Sturrock, John, 124–5

Surtees, R. S., 169 n.

Swift, Jonathan, 39, 41, 51 n., 143–4

Tanner, Tony, 26

Thackeray, W. M., 16

Thomas, Dylan, 182

Tolstoy, Leo, 14, 16, 96, 217; *Anna Karenina*, 278

Towry, Peter, 177

Toynbee, Philip: *Tea with Mrs. Goodman*, 178; *The Garden to the Sea*, 178

Trilling, Lionel, 68–9, 111, 113, 168 n.

Turgenev, Ivan, 193

Twain, Mark, 56 n.

Valéry, Paul, 5

Van Ghent, Dorothy, 42 n.

Vico, Giambattista, 85

Voltaire, 41

Wain, John, 232; *Hurry On Down*, 177

Waterhouse, Keith, 177

Watt, Ian: *The Rise of the Novel*, 13, 277

Waugh, Evelyn, 86, 89, 145–6, 153–62, 172, 211, 248; *Black Mischief*, 158, 161; *Brideshead Revisited*, 156–7; *Decline and Fall*, 154–60; *A Handful of Dust*, 158, 161; *Men at Arms*, 156; *Sword of Honour*, 138; *Vile Bodies*, 90, 157–8, 160–1.

Wells, H. G., 170, 193, 206

West, Nathanael, 41

Williams, Raymond, 15–16, 216

Wilson, Angus, 172, 177–8, 211–30; *Anglo-Saxon Attitudes*, 211, 218; 'Diversity and Depth', 214–15; *Hemlock and After*, 177, 213, 217–18; *Late Call*, 211, 218; *The Middle Age of Mrs. Eliot*, 217; *No Laughing Matter*, 179, 211–13, 215, 219–30; 'The Novelist and the Narrator', 212, 218; *The Wild Garden*, 212;

The World of Charles Dickens, 216

Wittgenstein, Ludwig, 243

Wolfe, Thomas, 184

Woolf, Leonard, 6

Woolf, Virginia, 5–6, 82, 85–6, 92, 97, 119, 121–36, 169–70, 176, 193, 211, 239, 286; *The Death of the Moth*, 97 n.; 'How It Strikes a Contemporary', 83; *Jacob's Room*, 84; 'Modern Fiction', 8, 125–6, 129, 162; 'Mr. Bennett and Mrs. Brown', 125; *Mrs. Dalloway*, 125, 128–9; *The Voyage Out*, 123; *The Waves*, 125, 128–9; *A Writer's Diary*, 121, 132; *The Years*, 129, 135

Wordsworth, William, 94

Wright, Andrew, 37, 70

Yeats, W. B., 5, 84

Zola, Émile, 21